The Political Economy of Trade Reform in Emerging Markets

The Political Economy of Trade Reform in Emerging Markets

Crisis or Opportunity?

Edited by

Peter Draper

Research Fellow and Project Head, Development through Trade, South African Institute of International Affairs, South Africa

Philip Alves

Formerly Economist, Development through Trade Programme, South African Institute of International Affairs; now with the South African Competition Commission, South Africa

Razeen Sally

Director, European Centre for International Political Economy, Brussels, and Senior Lecturer, London School of Economics and Political Science, UK

Edward Elgar

Cheltenham, UK • Northampton, MA, USA

Published by
Edward Elgar Publishing Limited
The Lypiatts
15 Lansdown Road
Cheltenham
Glos GL50 2JA
UK

Edward Elgar Publishing, Inc.
William Pratt House
9 Dewey Court
Northampton
Massachusetts 01060
USA

A catalogue record for this book
is available from the British Library

Library of Congress Control Number: 2009922764

PEFC
PEFC/16-33-111
CATG-PEFC-052
www.pefc.org

ISBN 978 1 84844 050 0

Printed and bound by MPG Books Group, UK

Contents

Figures

Tables and box

TABLES

BOX

Contributors

Philip Alves

Philip joined the Development through Trade programme of the South African Institute of International Affairs (SAIIA) in 2005 after completing an M.Phil. (*cum laude*) in economics and philosophy at the University of Cape Town (UCT). He has researched for the World Bank Southern Africa office while at UCT, and for various international organizations while at SAIIA. He has been published in the *South African Journal of Economics*, the *South African Journal of International Affairs*, various books and reports, and in the print media.

Mohamed Ariff

Emeritus Professor Dr Mohamed Ariff, a specialist in international economics, is currently the Executive Director of the Malaysian Institute of Economic Research (MIER). Previously he held the Chair of Analytical Economics at the University of Malaya where he had also served as the Dean of the Faculty of Economics and Administration. He was conferred emeritus professorship by the University of Malaya in August 2004.

Professor Ariff obtained his BA First Class Honours and M.Ec. from the University of Malaya. He completed his Ph.D. programme at the University of Lancaster, England, in 1970, as Commonwealth Scholar. He had a brief stint in the private sector as the Chief Economist at the United Asian Bank in 1976.

He has authored, co-authored and edited many books and monographs, in addition to publishing numerous articles in academic journals and mass media. Most of his works deal with international trade, foreign direct investments and regional economic integration. His book The *Malaysian Economy: Pacific Connections*, published by Oxford University Press, won the prestigious Tun Razak Award in 1993. In addition, he has also made some pioneering contributions to the theoretical and empirical literature in the field of Islamic Economics. Prof. Ariff is currently Vice President of East Asian Economic Association and Vice President of the International Association for Islamic Economics.

Bill Bowen

Bill Bowen joined ITS Global in 2005 as Principal Consultant. He is a former senior Australian diplomat with expertise in international environmental and economic issues.

In his most recent government position he was adviser on domestic and international environment policy in the Department of the Prime Minister and Cabinet (2002–2005). He was the Director of the Climate Change Section in the Department of Foreign Affairs and Trade (DFAT) from 1999–2001. His most recent posting with DFAT was as Counsellor Economic in Australia's High Commission in New Zealand (1996–1999). In addition to his international trade and environment policy experience (including leading Australia's delegation to a range of OECD trade and environment negotiations) he was the assistant to Australia's Executive Director at the World Bank from 1984–1987.

As well as postings in Africa and Central Europe with DFAT, he was seconded to AusAID, the Export Finance and Insurance Corporation (for the development and negotiation of a cofinancing agreement between the Berne Union of Export Credit Agencies and the World Bank and Inter American Development Bank) and to the Senate Standing Committee on Finance and Government Operations (where his report on the economics and financing of Commonwealth statutory authorities informed subsequent corporatisation and privatisaiton policies).

He has as a B.Comm. (Hons) majoring in economics from the University of Melbourne and a Master of Science (Economics) from the London School of Economics.

Peter Draper

Peter Draper joined SAIIA as a Trade Research Fellow and Project Head of the Department through Trade Programme in 2003. He previously headed the Department of Economics and Economics History at the University of Durban-Westirlle; the Asia and Mercosur deghs at the Department of Trade and Industry; and Economic Analysis and Research at the DTI's International Trade and Economic Development Division. He is a member of Business Unity South Africa's trade committee and lecturers International Business at Wits Business School. He is a board member and non-resistant senior fellow of the Brussels-based European Centre for International Political Economy; a member of the IMD-Lausanne's Evian group including its 'Brains Trust'; and a board member of the Botswana Institute for Development Policy Analysis. He holds a Masters in Economic from the University of Kwazulu-Natal. He is based in Pretoria.

Lawrence Edwards

Lawrence Edwards is an Associate Professor in the School of Economics, University of Cape Town. Lawrence graduated with an M.Sc. in Economics from the London School of Economics in 1998. He completed his Ph.D. in Economics at the University of Cape Town in 2003.

Lawrence's research falls within the field of international trade with a specific focus on international trade and labour, the determinants of trade flows and economic adjustments to trade liberalization. He has published in a number of international and local journals including *World Development*, *Journal of International Development*, *South African Journal of Economics* and *Journal of Studies in Economics and Econometrics*. He has also consulted widely with the World Bank, the National Treasury, the Department of Trade and Industry and is currently a member of the South African Growth Project managed by the Centre of International Development at Harvard University.

Sebastián Herreros

Sebastián Herreros has served since 1996 at the Economic Directorate of the Chilean Ministry of Foreign Affairs, where he is currently Head of the Latin America Department. From October 2002 to December 2007 he was posted as a Counsellor at the Chilean Mission to the WTO in Geneva, with responsibility, among other areas, for the negotiations on agriculture and market access for non-agricultural products. He holds a Bachelor of Arts in Business Administration from the Catholic University of Chile (1994) and a Master of Science in Politics of the World Economy from the London School of Economics (1999). He has lectured in International Political Economy at the University of Chile's Institute of International Studies. He is the author of 'The Chile–Canada Free Trade Agreement', in Steve Woolcock and Gary Sampson (eds), *Regionalism, Multilateralism, and Economic Integration: The Recent Experience* (United Nations University Press, 2003).

Gregore Pio Lopez

Greg Lopez is a Senior Research Officer at the Malaysian Institute of Economic Research (MIER). Prior to joining MIER he worked in various research positions both in the private and non-governmental sector. His areas of research are development in Malaysia and institutional economics. Greg is a member of the Federation of Manufacturers Malaysia Private Sector Task Force on FTAs. He has a Bachelors and Masters in Economics from the University of Malaya. He is currently completing a Ph.D. at the Crawford School of Economics and Government at the Australian National University in Canberra. His research concentrates on trade protection in Malaysia's services sectors.

Mario Marconini

Mario Marconini is the President of ManattJones Marconini Global Strategies, an international strategic consultancy firm based in São Paulo, Brazil, a branch of Washington-based ManattJones Global Strategies. He is also the President of the Council of International Relations at Fecomercio, Brazil's most prominent federation of its kind in Brazil (half a million firms represented) and of the 'Dialogo Serviços', a Brazilian coalition of service institutions. He was Counselor at the GATT/WTO, Geneva, for eight years, from 1988 to 1996, during the Uruguay Round of Multilateral Trade Negotiations. In 1996, benefiting from a leave of absence from the WTO, he took on the post of Deputy Secretary for International Affairs at Brazil's Ministry of Finance where he would stay until 1998. After some time in the private sector, he came back to Brasilia as Foreign Trade Secretary in 1999, where he led much of the government's work on trade policy, operations, negotiations and remedies. As recognition for his government service, he was awarded the Order of Rio Branco, Brazil's highest honorary award, in the rank of Commendator.

In the 2001–2004 period, during Minister Luiz Felipe Lampreia's mandate as Chairman of the Board of Trustees, Marconini was the Executive Director of the Brazilian Center for International Relations (CEBRI). He publishes extensively and has been a consultant to private and public interests around the world. He sits in the advisory boards of the International Air and Space Law Institute in Leiden (the Netherlands), of the European Centre for International Political Economy (ECIPE) (Brussels) and of the Center for Hemispheric Policy of the University of Miami. He is also a member of the Executive Committee of the US–Brazil Business Council and a Senior Associate at the Washington-based Center for Strategic and International Studies (CSIS). He holds an MA in economics from the Graduate Institute of International Affairs (Geneva), an M.A.L.D. in international law and diplomacy from the Fletcher School of Law and Diplomacy (Harvard and Tufts, Boston) and an MA in political science from Illinois State University.

S. Narayan

Dr Narayan completed an M.Phil. in economics at Cambridge University and a Ph.D. from IIT Delhi. He spent nearly four decades (1965 to 2004) in India's public service, in the State and Central Governments, and in the Development administration. Most recently (2003–2004), he was Economic Adviser to the Prime Minister of India, and was responsible for implementation of economic policies over several economic Ministries including Finance, Trade & Commerce, Energy and Infrastructure.

Prior to this, in the Ministry of Finance, responsibilities included the formulation of macroeconomic policy for the Government, including tariff and taxation policies, as well as initiatives for modernizing the capital markets. He was a member of the group of officers responsible for trade policy making in the context of WTO-related issues, including TRIPS.

Dr Narayan is currently a Visiting Senior Research Fellow at the Institute of South Asian Studies, NUS, Singapore, and an adviser to various think tanks in India, importantly the Observer Research Foundation, Delhi. He has two recent publications: *Growth Opportunities in Indian States*, Marshall Cavendish, Singapore (2005); *Documenting Reforms: Case Studies from India* (ed.), Macmillan India (2006).

Razeen Sally

Razeen Sally is a Director of the European Centre for International Political Economy (ECIPE), which he co-founded in 2006 together with Fredrik Erixon. He is also Senior Lecturer in International Political Economy at the London School of Economics and Political Science, where he has taught since 1993. He received his Ph.D. from the LSE in 1992, and did post-doctoral research at INSEAD in France. He is Visiting Professor at the Institut D'Etudes Politiques (Sciences Po) in Paris, and Associate Senior Fellow at the Institute of Southeast Asian Studies, Singapore. He was also Director, Trade Policy, at the Commonwealth Business Council in London in 2003. He is on the Academic Advisory Council of the Institute of Economic Affairs in London, and on the advisory board of the Cato Centre for Trade Policy Studies in Washington DC.

Razeen Sally's research focuses on trade policy in Asia, the WTO and preferential trade agreements. He also writes on the intellectual history of political economy, especially the theory of commercial policy. He lectures and consults on trade policy for governments, business and international organizations, and comments regularly on international economic policy issues in the media.

Ron Sandrey

Ron is a former Specialist Economist for the New Zealand Ministry of Foreign Affairs and Trade (MFAT). His work there involved the production of trade statistics for the Ministry and researching a wide range of policy-related trade and international economic issues, mostly with a strong quantitative emphasis and often focusing on trade data consistencies and related issues. Over the last few years these have included an assessment of the GATT/WTO outcomes and the APEC process, analysis of New Zealand's negotiating positions in numerous Free Trade Agreements (FTAs) including a lot of work with China during 2004, analysis of New Zealand's services, manufacturing, forestry and fisheries exports, studies of 'new generation' trade issues, quantitative analysis of New Zealand's trade with Australia and Asia, continued research on the competitiveness of New Zealand and the agricultural sector, and research into greenhouse emission policy and other environmental issues.

More recently Ron was appointed Senior Research Fellow of the Trade Law Center in Stellenbosch, South Africa, as well as Professor Extraordinary in Stellenbosch University's Agricultural Economics department. He has worked extensively on South and Southern African trade-related topics in this time.

Foreword

The evidence of liberalization of trade in goods, services and investment is quite clear. Since the late 1940s, countries have moved mostly in the direction of greater openness, particularly in the non-agricultural sectors, as well as services and investment. In most developing countries liberalization began in the decade of the 1980s.

The economics is straightforward: under most scenarios trade liberalization is of benefit to the economy undertaking it. It is therefore not surprising that most of the liberalization, particularly in developing countries, has been unilateral and not a product of negotiations, whether bilateral or multilateral. Ultimately, liberalization through negotiations, bilateral or multilateral, is achieved because the parties see benefits and not because it is an imposition; any such arrangements are based on mutual consent.

However, the process of liberalization becomes more difficult as it gets closer to free trade, and as behind-the-border barriers are tackled. In most cases, this is due to the resistance of individuals who don't want to lose their protection rents and who perceive that it is cost-effective to spend time and money to oppose liberalization. 'Strategic industries', 'multifunctionality', 'policy space', 'level playing field', 'fair trade', 'infant industry', are some labels used by protectionists to mask their interests. While it is true that some of these concepts have some sound foundations in the economic literature, it is more often the case that their use is reflective of special interests who seek to appropriate them for uses far removed from the underlying economic rationale. A sector that has been sheltered from competition for 40 years under the infant industry argument should raise some questions to say the least. In the absence of forces that promote liberalization in a politically effective manner, it is often the case that beyond a certain point, it is more feasible to overcome resistance through multilateral, plurilateral or bilateral agreements. The fact that these are reciprocal and that they are packages, with both 'offensive' and 'defensive' interests, undoubtedly is part of the explanation.

But, in addition, such arrangements, besides making a reversal of policies unlikely, contain legal obligations with rules and disciplines that make the administration of trade policy more transparent, accountable and predictable, as well as protecting parties against breaches through dispute settlement mechanisms. Trade agreements indeed protect governments from falling captive to their own special interests.

Trade liberalization is but one of several economic policies. Probably the perfect trade policy by itself will not be successful if, for example, there is macroeconomic instability, the exchange rate is grossly misaligned, labour markets are too rigid, safety nets for the poor are non-existent, corruption is rampant, tax evasion is pervasive, infrastructure is very poor, and so on. Thus there is need to ensure coherence and consistency among the several policies. In turn this also requires strong and stable institutions, with skilled human resources.

There is abundant literature and research on these and other aspects concerning trade liberalization. The reality of liberalization is of course very rich with mixed results. The relevant question is to examine different cases to attempt to determine why some countries have been more successful than others.

This book is about the political economy of trade and investment policy reform in emerging markets. It adopts a case study approach, analysing seven different countries spanning four continents (Australia, Brazil, Chile, India, Malaysia, New Zealand, South Africa), eventually pulling out the strands common across all countries in a concluding chapter.

The book introduces the subject with Razeen Sally's sweeping review of these reforms in developing countries since the 1980s. In this chapter Sally sets out the most common political economy drivers of reform processes; then discusses the three principal ways in which trade policy reform is brought about (unilaterally; through trade negotiations of any form; or through donor requirements); then sets out the agenda for the remaining reforms most developing countries and some developed countries need to tackle. These concern the so-called behind-the-border regulatory reforms, in services, procurement, labour markets, investment rules, and so on. They are technically and politically more difficult than 'at the border' reforms, take longer to formulate and implement, and are more difficult to 'see'. Of course the traditional trade agenda remains relevant since many countries continue to retain high border barriers to trade, in the form of tariffs, QRs, and so on, as well as trade-distorting measures such as subsidies.

Sally's central arguments/lessons are mostly uncontroversial. First, he reviews the evidence suggesting that those countries that opened decisively and comprehensively to international trade and investment have grown faster than those that did not, and have reduced poverty more quickly. Second, all meaningful reform episodes have been unilateral in nature. All seven countries studied in this book bear witness to this, despite widely varying historical circumstances.

Third, most trade reform during the 1980s and 1990s formed part of a broader stabilization and liberalization package. That is, the global 'climate of ideas' strongly favoured and encouraged trade liberalization as an important part of strategies to achieve macroeconomic stabilization and higher economic growth. In some countries these ideas still enjoy widespread political support, but in other cases they have given way to resurgent belief in the ability of governments to direct economic activity through industrial policy interventions, which has in turn encouraged governments to be more sceptical and wary of economic liberalization.

Fourth, the pressure for liberalization in the form of negotiations (multilateral and regional/bilateral) has risen in importance. However, the multilateral agenda (Doha Development Round), while maintaining high levels of ambition, has not been able to conclude as it tries to overcome the resistance to improve market access, particularly on agriculture and to eliminate agriculture export subsidies and restrict trade-distorting domestic support. Bilateral/regional arrangements, on the other hand, cannot respond to the challenges of agricultural support, fisheries subsidies or antidumping rules, to name some issues that can only be dealt with in the WTO. In addition, many such arrangements are far from optimal from the point of view of the coverage of goods, services or investments possibly generating distortions in terms of the allocation of resources.

Having set the scene, the book then examines the seven aforementioned cases of trade reform and their associated wider economic reforms. The emphasis is always on the trade policy reforms themselves, and the political economy of the reform processes. In addressing the political economy issues historical context becomes very important, and all seven papers present plenty of relevant detail. Three cases – Australia, Chile and New Zealand – are more 'clear-cut' than others, and are presented first. Despite this important similarity, however, all three are very different. In Chile and New Zealand crisis was an important driver, whereas in Australia only the spectre of a looming crisis was enough. Chile implemented reforms under a military dictatorship while New Zealand and Australia did so in democratic circumstances. But even then, in New Zealand the nature of the reform process led to important electoral reforms, to ensure that in future greater checks and balances would be in place.

The second set, comprising the reform experiences of Malaysia, Brazil, India and South Africa, present a mixed picture. The circumstances in each differ widely, but the nature of the reforms undertaken was largely similar. However, success, measured in increased productivity, output, income growth, lower poverty and inequality, and so on, also differs widely. Malaysia has advanced the most and in a steady manner. Brazil, India and South Africa all have done much to achieve sustained and widespread poverty elimination and substantially improved living standards for the majority of their populations, but much remains to be done. This should be seen against the fact that their reform efforts are young (all beginning in the 1990s) and are works-in-progress undertaken in democratic regimes.

In the conclusion Razeen Sally and Philip Alves review what these seven countries have achieved and what they have left to do. They restate the argument that actually doing the remaining hard work is very important. The stakes are vastly improved living standards for millions of people. All these countries are, to varying degrees, 'first division reformers', having done much of the at-the-border reform work already. Some, notably Australia, Chile, Malaysia and New Zealand, have also made significant inroads into the much harder second generation reforms (regulatory and relating to trade in services). The authors conclude that Brazil, India and South Africa have before them a substantial agenda both in terms of border and behind-the-border reform. They also discuss the different ways in which these reforms could be brought about, arguing again that the unilateral route offers by far the greatest advantages.

Overall, this book provides an in-depth analysis of different experiences in trade reform and identifies the pending agenda in each case. Though there is no recipe or one-size-fits-all model, each country study provides valuable insights that should be taken into consideration by policy makers and analysts worldwide. The book is an important contribution at a time of huge challenges like food security and prices, inflation, financial instability and climate change. It also underscores the need to conclude the Doha Development Round quickly, which should provide the basis for further reform and liberalization.

Alejandro Jara
Deputy Director General, World Trade Organization.

NOTE

1. The opinions in this foreword are personal and they do not represent those of the WTO Secretariat.

Preface

This book has been two years in the making. The project behind it was made possible by a generous grant from the Regional Trade Facilitation Programme (RTFP), with supplementary funding from Australian Aid. The latter is a core funder of the Development through Trade Programme at the South African Institute of International Affairs (SAIIA), whose team members ran the project.

We would like to thank all involved in making this a success, beginning with Mark Pearson, Joan Pilcher and Stella Mushiri at the RTFP. The SAIIA events team, headed by Sarasa Ananmalay, worked tirelessly on two workshops and a major international conference in Johannesburg, and therefore also deserve special mention. Many others deserve thanks for their contributions to the body of work presented in this book, through comments and insights provided at review workshops, the final conference, and in informal discussions.

We have enjoyed editing and contributing to this book, primarily because we have learned so much interesting detail. Thus our most heartfelt thanks go to the authors of the individual chapters, who worked diligently to meet deadlines, tolerating all manner of administrative and other frustrations along the way.

Peter Draper
Philip Alves
and Razeen Sally

1. Introduction: trade liberalization in the twenty-first century

Razeen Sally

What are the prospects for further economic liberalization in the twenty-first century? The 'Washington Consensus' attracts greater scepticism now than it did in the 1980s and 1990s, and the momentum of liberalization, globally, has slowed down. An ever greater number of countries seem increasingly reliant on trade negotiations to deliver change, but none seem to want that change to apply to themselves. Besides, historically trade negotiations have delivered little real liberalization; the vast bulk has been driven unilaterally, and the benefits have flowed to the reformers.

How necessary is further liberalization of trade and foreign direct investment? What obstacles lie in its path? What are its political requisites? What are the links with domestic economic reforms? What is the balance between unilateral liberalization and reciprocity (liberalization through trade negotiations and agreements with donors)? How have countries managed these kinds of reforms in the past, and what are the challenges to that process today?

These questions inform the chapters in this excellent collection of country case studies. The seven countries studied – Australia, Brazil, Chile, India, Malaysia, New Zealand and South Africa – present an eclectic mix of histories and circumstances, but are unified by the thrust, if not the finer details, of their trade and broader economic policy choices.

Australia, Chile and New Zealand are the 'strong' reformers in the group. They have more or less eliminated all border barriers to trade and investment, and are well into the much more difficult domestic regulatory reforms that trade opening induces. Malaysia and South Africa have reformed strongly only in parts – both are relatively open at the border (Malaysia much more so than South Africa), with important exceptions, but neither has undertaken any substantive domestic regulatory reforms, or opened sensitive services sectors. Brazil and India are the 'weak' reformers, having each undergone a brief but deep bout of opening within a few years, but very little since. These countries, although transformed by their own standards, still have plenty of border and 'behind-the-border' liberalization to do.

Why are these countries' stories important now? The lesser reasons are that a) most of these countries remain understudied, and b) most of their experiences to date have been subject to widely varying interpretations. But the more important reason is that the reform agenda for the twenty-first century remains large and complicated, and the potential benefits from responding to it substantial. By understanding these countries' experiences better, we may draw lessons both for their own remaining reforms, and for those countries further behind in these processes. Many of the countries provide lessons both in what works and what should be avoided. Generally speaking, inward-looking protectionist policies have led to stagnation and ultimately crisis, opening the way for a more sustainable set of policies – outward-oriented liberal policies – to take hold.

This introductory chapter reviews the recent history of trade and broader economic liberalization. Much of this has taken place in the developing world (Australia, Ireland and New Zealand are the exceptions), and that is where this chapter is focused. It sets the scene by first assessing the current global climate for external liberalization, which includes debates over the efficacy and usefulness of the Washington Consensus. It then reviews the record of trade and FDI liberalization across the developing world, before probing the political economy of these processes. The framework introduced in that section is replicated in the book's concluding chapter, where lessons are drawn directly from the case studies. It then weighs the effectiveness of the different vehicles for liberalization. What have been the respective roles for unilaterally-driven liberalization as opposed to bilateral, regional and multilateral negotiations, and what will be their respective roles moving forward?

THE GLOBAL CLIMATE FOR EXTERNAL LIBERALIZATION

> To expect, indeed, that the freedom of trade should ever be entirely restored ... is as absurd as to expect that an Oceana or Utopia should ever be established ... Not only the prejudices of the publick, but what is much more unconquerable, the private interests of many individuals, irresistibly oppose it. (Adam Smith, *Wealth of Nations*)

There is less appetite for further liberalization and associated structural reforms now compared with the heyday of the Washington Consensus in the 1980s and 1990s. Reforms have not been reversed, but their forward momentum has slowed. Governments are more sceptical and defensive about further liberalization; and there has been relatively little in the way of 'second-generation' reforms (in domestic trade-related regulations and institutions) to underpin external liberalization and boost competition.

This applies to the West, and to most developing-country regions. In the developed world, pervasive agricultural protectionism continues, with an admixture of new protectionism directed against China. The new 'green' lobby concerned with carbon footprints and 'food miles' coupled with the rise of private standards further threatens the openness of the world trading system. The West has no grand project for liberalization in the early twenty-first century to compare with the Reagan and Thatcher reforms in the 1980s, or the EU's Single Market programme in the late 1980s and early 1990s. Eastern European countries are suffering from 'reform fatigue' after their accession to the EU. This is also the state of play in much of Latin America, Africa, south Asia and southeast Asia. It is true of leading developing countries, notably Brazil, Mexico, South Africa and India. All have their real bursts of trade-and-FDI liberalization behind them. In Russia, liberalization has been put into reverse gear. This has also happened in other resource-rich countries enjoying a revenue windfall, for example Venezuela and Bolivia. Overall, protectionist flare-ups and lack of reform momentum in the West have reinforced liberalization-slowdown in the rest.

China is the conspicuous exception: liberalization proceeded apace before and after WTO accession, in what has been the biggest opening of an economy the world has ever seen. However, domestic political conditions for further liberalization are now more difficult. Vietnam has followed in China's tracks, with internal and external liberalization accelerating in the run up to its WTO accession in 2006.

A variety of factors accounts for liberalization-scepticism today. There is much anxiety about globalisation, despite record growth across the world in the last five years. Macroeconomic crises provided windows of opportunity for fast-and-furious liberalization in the 1980s and 1990s, but that has not happened since the Asian and other financial crises of the late 1990s. Indeed, the latter may have brought about a popular backlash, and certainly induced more caution regarding further liberalization. Also, further liberalization entails tackling border and, increasingly, domestic regulatory barriers in politically sensitive areas such as agriculture and services. Inevitably, this runs up against more powerful interest-group opposition than was the case with previous waves of (mainly industrial-goods) liberalization. Individuals matter too: the new century has not yet brought forth a Cobden, Gladstone, Erhard, Thatcher or Reagan to champion free markets or free trade.

Not least, the climate of ideas has changed, for prevailing weather conditions have become more inclement since the Washington Consensus reached its zenith only a decade ago. There is, now as before, an extreme anti-globalization critique, a root-and-branch rejection of capitalism. But this is street theatre on the fringe. Of greater political importance is a more mainstream critique that accepts the reality of the market economy and globalization, but rejects the comprehensive liberalization associated (perhaps unfairly) with the Washington Consensus.

Critics point to tenuous links between liberalization, openness, growth and poverty reduction; wider inequalities within and between countries that result from globalization; the damaging effects of large and sudden trade liberalization in developing countries; the renewed emphasis on aid to poorer developing countries, without which trade liberalization will not work; the need for developed-country liberalization while retaining developing-country protectionism; and the need for more flexible international rules to allow developing-country governments to pursue selective industrial policies, especially to promote infant industries (Stiglitz, 2002; Rodrik, 1998, 2001; Oxfam, 2002; Chang, 2002; Grunberg, Kaul and Stern, 1999; Sachs, 2005). Lastly, there is the pervasive fear – in the South as much as in the North – of being run over by an unstoppable Chinese export juggernaut.

It is important to confront the liberalization sceptics and industrial interventionists head on; to defend liberalization to date, while accepting that its record is mixed; to make the case for further liberalization; and to identify the political conditions that might make it succeed. Protectionism and industrial-policy intervention has mostly failed across the developing world: history, not just theory, should be a warning not to go down this route again.

First, in-depth country studies by the OECD, NBER and World Bank, going back to the 1970s and 1980s, suggest strongly that countries with more liberal trade policies have more open economies and grow faster than those with more protectionist policies. These are much more reliable than superficial cross-country regression analyses (Bhagwati and Srinivasan, 1999; Lal and Myint, 1996). That said, even most of the latter point to large gains from trade liberalization (for example Sachs and Warner, 1995; Winters, 2004; Winters et al., 2004).

Putting together calculations done by the World Bank and Angus Maddison, a snapshot of the developing world in the year 2000 reveals the following. There are about 25 'new-globalizing' developing countries (the World Bank's term) with a total population of about 3 billion. Since 1980, this group registered massive increases in their trade-to-GDP ratios and real per-capita incomes, alongside big cuts in levels of tariff protection. In the same period, over 50 'less-globalized' developing countries, with a combined population of about 1.5 billion, saw stagnant trade-to-GDP ratios, a modest increase in real per-capita incomes, alongside relatively modest cuts in average import tariffs. The – overwhelmingly Asian – new globalizers have also seen dramatic reductions in poverty and improvements in human-welfare indicators (such as adult literacy, infant mortality, life expectancy and nutritional intake) (World Bank, 2002a: 34, Table 1.1; Maddison, 2003).

Secondly, it is not true that globalization 'excludes' certain developing countries. Rather globalization provides an enabling environment that some countries have taken advantage of and others have not. New globalizers in east Asia, south Asia (first Sri Lanka, and now India), central and eastern Europe, Latin America (notably Chile) and elsewhere have reaped the benefits through more market-oriented policies and institutions. They are narrowing the wealth gap with the West. This is why global poverty has been massively reduced (especially as a percentage of world population, and even in absolute numbers, despite a growing world population). Political disorder, macroeconomic instability, insecure property rights, rampant government intervention and high external protection have kept other countries 'non-globalized' and thereby retarded growth and development. Most of these countries are cursed with dysfunctional or failed states run by venal, thuggish, even murderous elites. None of this is 'caused' by globalization (Henderson, 2004: 52–58; Wolf, 2004: ch. 9).

Thirdly, NGOs and developing-country governments have been clamouring for one-sided liberalization in the Doha Round. Their interpretation of 'development' in the Doha Development Agenda is that it behoves developed countries to liberalize in areas that are protected against labour-intensive developing-country exports. But developing countries should not reciprocate with their own liberalization (Oxfam, 2002). What Oxfam and others fail to say is that developing countries' own protectionist policies harm them even more than developed-country barriers. The World Bank estimates that 80 per cent of the developing-country gain from worldwide agricultural liberalization would come from developing countries' liberalization of their highly protected agricultural markets. It is unskilled rural labour – the poorest of the poor – who would gain most, as such liberalization would reduce the anti-agricultural bias in domestic economies (Ingco and Nash, 2004).

Fourthly, the historical record is not kind to 'hard' industrial policies of the infant-industry variety. Infant-industry success in nineteenth-century USA and Germany is contested. In east Asia, its record is mixed at best in Japan, South Korea and Taiwan; non-existent in free-trade Hong Kong and Singapore; and failed in southeast Asia (for example national-car policies in Malaysia and Indonesia). In northeast Asia, there is scant evidence to show that protection of infants actually led to higher social rates of return and higher overall productivity growth (Little, 1999; World Bank, 1993). Southeast Asia's conspicuous success is in FDI-led electronics

Table 1.1 Bound and applied tariff rates

	Bound		Applied	
	Developed economies	Developing economies	Developed economies	Developing economies
All goods	17.8	43.6	5.5	11.8
Agriculture	24.3	60.6	9.5	16.3
Manufactures	16.7	32.5	4.8	11

Note: Developed and developing economies by World Bank definitions. Developed economies: category 3–4 (2002–2004) and developing economies: category 1–2 (1998–2004).

Source: World Bank Trade Databases: http://siteresources.worldbank.org/INTRES/Resources/469232-1107449512766/tar2005a.xls

exports – a result of drastically lower tariffs and an open door to inward investment. China, like southeast Asia, has grown fast through FDI-led exports, not infant-industry protection. Arguably, other factors – political and macroeconomic stability, competitive exchange rates, private property rights, openness to the world economy, education and infrastructure – were much more important to east-Asian success than 'picking winners'.

Finally, infant-industry protection in Latin America, south Asia and Africa has been a disaster not dissimilar to industrial planning in ex-command economies. Protected infants sooner or later ran into severe problems; and governments continued to subsidise and protect perpetual children. Such incestuous government–business links provided a fertile breeding ground for corruption. Besides, most developing-country markets are too small to support infant-industry promotion; and their states are too weak, incompetent and corrupt to efficiently administer the complex instruments required.

Protectionism in the World: Unfinished Business

Protectionism remains high around the world, even after six decades of liberalization, first in developed countries and then in developing countries. There are pockets of developed-country protection – agricultural subsidies, peak tariffs and tariff escalation in agriculture and manufactures, anti-dumping duties, assorted regulatory barriers such as onerous product standards, and high restrictions on the cross-border movement of workers – that continue to damage developing-country growth prospects.

But developing countries' own protection on almost all these counts is much higher and more damaging. Average applied tariffs in developing countries are more than double those in developed countries, with much

Table 1.2 Tariff rates in different regions and income groups

Country group or region	Applied	Bound	Agriculture (applied)	Manufactures (applied)
High income economies	5.5	17.8	10.6	3.3
Latin America and the Caribbean	9.9	41.2	14.9	9
East Asia and Pacific	10.5	29.5	16.8	10.5
South Asia	17.8	66.5	19.1	17.2
Europe and Central Asia	7.8	13.2	14	6.7
Middle East and North Africa	18	34.6	22.5	16.9
Sub-Saharan Africa	13.4	61.5	17.2	12.9

Note: The numbers are unweighted averages in percentages from 1998–2004. Regional definitions by the World Bank.

Source: World Bank trade databases: http://siteresources.worldbank.org/INTRES/Resources/469232-1107449512766/tar2005a.xls

higher bound rates in the WTO (Table 1.1). south Asia, sub-Saharan Africa, the Middle East and north Africa have higher average tariffs than east Asia, Latin America and east Europe (Table 1.2).

Bound and applied tariffs in agriculture are significantly higher than they are in manufactures. Developing countries have become bigger users of anti-dumping actions than developed countries (Figure 1.1). A few developing countries – notably India – have become much more frequent users of anti-dumping actions (Figure 1.2). Developing countries, with the exception of countries in transition and those that have recently acceded to the WTO, have far fewer multilateral commitments than developed countries in services (Figure 1.3).

There has been a general increase in the use of technical, food-safety and other standards that affect trade, as indicated by the number of measures notified under the WTO's Technical Barriers to Trade (TBT) and Sanitary and Phyto-Sanitary (SPS) agreements. This is one – admittedly very rough – indication of regulatory barriers to trade. Developed countries account for over half of TBT and SPS measures notified, but what is also striking is the increasing number of measures notified by developing countries (Figures 1.4 and 1.5).

Thus there is much unfinished business in terms of liberalizing trade, capital flows and the cross-border movement of labour in the developing world. That said, external liberalization is no panacea. In the short run, trade liberalization reduces the anti-import, anti-export bias of trade taxes. That is the prelude to dynamic gains – including those from trade-related

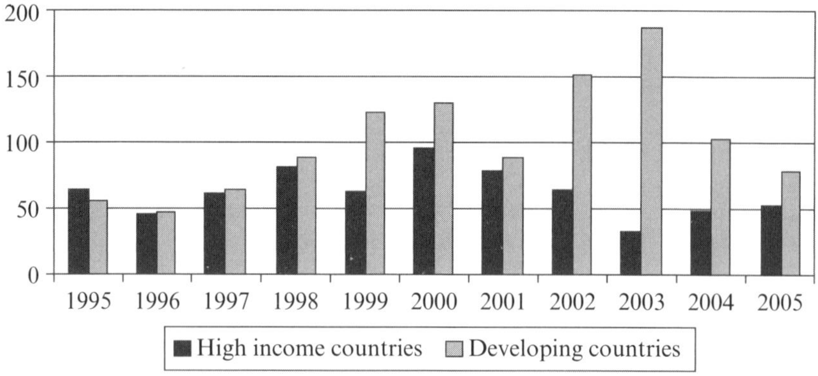

Note: Anti-dumping measures: by reporting Member. Classification of countries by World Bank Definitions.

Source: WTO, http://www.wto.org/english/tratop_e/adp_e/adp_stattab7_e.xls

Figure 1.1 Anti-dumping measures instigated annually, 1995–2005

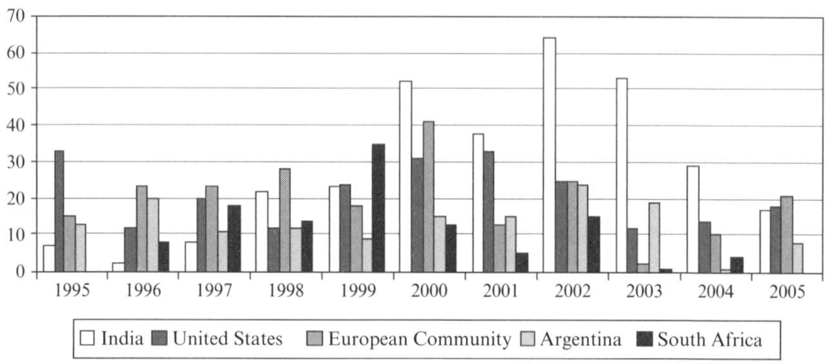

Note: Anti-dumping measures: by reporting Member.

Source: WTO, http://www.wto.org/english/tratop_e/adp_e/adp_stattab7_e.xls

Figure 1.2 Most frequent users of anti-dumping measures, 1995–2005

inward investment – that result in productivity improvements and growth. Capturing these gains, however, depends on additional factors: initial conditions for reform, including a country's factor endowments and historical legacy; complementary domestic market-based reforms; and the state of and improvement in domestic institutions. The connection between opening to the world economy and domestic economic and institutional

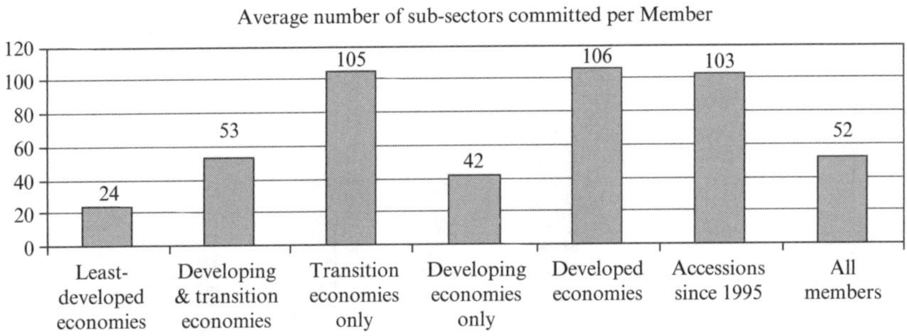

Source: WTO Staff Working Paper ERSD-2005-01, http://www.wto.org/english/res_e/reser_e/ersd200501_e.doc

Figure 1.3 GATS commitments by country group, 2005

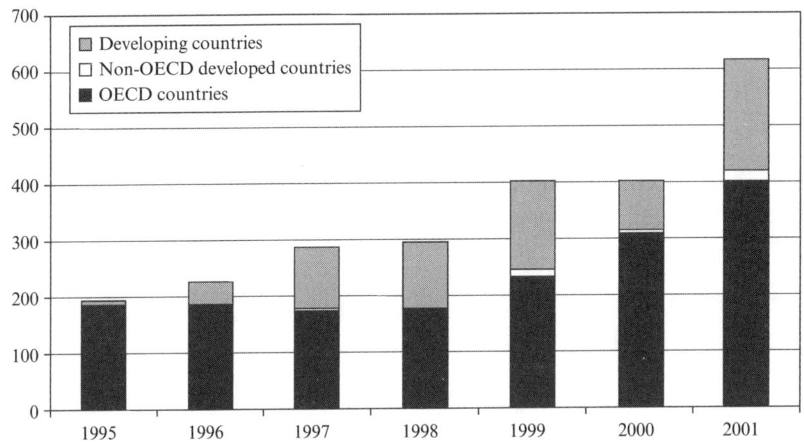

Source: OECD: COM/TD/AGR/WP(2002)21/FINAL, http://www.olis.oecd.org/olis/2002doc.nsf/43bb6130e5e86e5fc12569fa005d004c/7b8815fac33fe88ec1256bed002e5cb7/$FILE/JT00129244.PDF

Figure 1.4 Notified SPS measures, 1995–2001

reform is particularly important: it is this that explains much of the variation in economic performance in the developing world.

This is not a new insight: David Hume and Adam Smith strongly linked free trade (broadly defined to include cross-border flows of capital and people) to domestic institutions and growth, all on the canvas of the long-run progress of commercial society (Sally, 1998: ch. 3). But this also raises difficult political questions. In essence, successful external opening depends

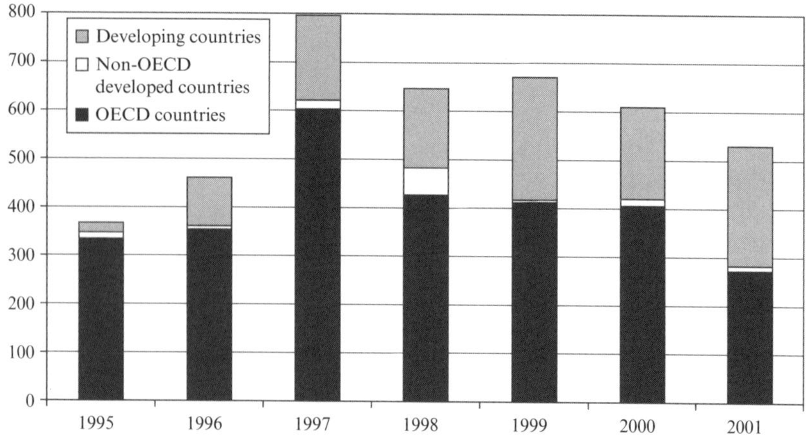

Source: OECD: COM/TD/AGR/WP(2002)70/FINAL, http://www.olis.oecd.org/olis/2002doc.nsf/43bb6130e5e86e5fc12569fa005d004c/baacb7d0229000f9c1256cdf00418c0f/$FILE/JT00140246.PDF

Figure 1.5 Notified TBT measures, 1995–2001

crucially on domestic politics and institutional capacity. Here there are very large and arguably increasing differences within the developing world.

TRADE-POLICY REFORM: THE RECENT EXPERIENCE

Trade liberalization has several definitions. Trade economists speak of moving to 'neutrality' of government intervention as between tradable and non-tradable sectors of the economy. They also speak of 'getting prices right' by aligning domestic prices with world prices of tradable goods. More broadly conceived, free (or free-ish) trade means the freedom to engage in international transactions, without discrimination (Henderson, 1992: 635). This exists nowhere – not even in Hong Kong, which maintains tight restrictions on immigration, though it is fully open to trade in goods and capital flows, and largely open to trade in services. If non-discrimination is the relevant criterion, all countries are still far from free trade, indeed more so than was the case in the late nineteenth century.

Nevertheless, there has been a distinct liberalization trend in developing countries in recent decades.[1] Cross-border trade and capital flows – though not of people – have become freer, and have boomed. There is less discrimination between domestic and international transactions. Domestic prices of tradable goods and services are closer to world prices (though less the case in services than in goods). In terms of measures undertaken: import and export quotas, licences, state trading monopolies and other non-tariff barriers have been drastically reduced. Tariffs have been simplified and reduced. So have foreign-exchange controls, with unified exchange rates and much greater currency convertibility, especially on current-account transactions. Foreign direct investment has been liberalized, with fewer restrictions on entry, ownership, establishment and operation in the domestic economy. And services sectors have been opened to international competition through FDI liberalization, privatization and domestic deregulation. Overall, trade and FDI in manufactured goods has been liberalized most; trade and FDI in services was liberalized later, and to a much lesser extent; and trade liberalization in agriculture has lagged behind. Lastly, trade and FDI liberalization has taken place in the context of wide-ranging macro and microeconomic market-based reforms – roughly the 'stabilization and liberalization' package of the Washington Consensus, as described by John Williamson (Williamson, 1994).

Cumulatively, this has been a veritable policy revolution in developing countries and countries in transition. Before the 1980s, the 80 per cent of the world's population who live outside the West lived overwhelmingly in countries with high levels of external protection, in addition to pervasive government intervention at home. By the mid-1990s, most of these people lived in much more open economies, in terms of both domestic and international commerce (Sachs and Warner, 1995).

Average applied tariffs in developing countries declined from 30 per cent in 1985 to 11 per cent in 2005. Core non-tariff barriers declined correspondingly in all developing-country regions. The bulk of regulatory changes on inward investment have been more favourable to FDI. There has even been a trend in favour of capital-account liberalization: 70 per cent of the developing countries in the IMF maintain capital-account restrictions today, compared with 85 per cent in the early 1990s.

This liberalization trend started in Japan, and then South Korea and Taiwan, in the 1950s, at a time when most developing countries were tightening regimes of import-substitution and other forms of state intervention. The northeast-Asian Tigers promoted exports through selective liberalization, while retaining considerable import protection and restrictions on inward investment. Later they gradually liberalized imports and FDI. Hong Kong returned to tariff-free trade and a fully open door to investment after the war. Singapore followed, though after a brief flirtation with protection (when part of the Malaysian federation). The other southeast-Asian Tigers (Malaysia, Thailand, Indonesia and the Philippines) liberalized significantly, on both trade and FDI, from the 1970s. The countries of

Indochina started gradual and halting market-based reforms in the 1980s. Vietnam accelerated trade-and-investment liberalization in the run up to its WTO accession in late 2006.

China's historic opening dates back to 1978, but major trade-and-investment liberalization took off from the early 1990s. Since then, China has swung from extreme protection to rather liberal trade policies, indeed very liberal by developing-country standards. The protective impact of classic non-tariff barriers (NTBs) has come down to less than 5 per cent; and the simple average tariff has come down from 42 per cent in 1992 to under 10 per cent after WTO accession – below the developing-country average. The crowning point of China's reforms was its WTO accession in 2001. Its WTO commitments are by far the strongest of any developing country in the WTO. This holds for tariff ceilings on goods (including agriculture); non-tariff barriers in goods and services (with big-ticket sectors like financial services, telecoms, retail, transport and a host of professional services thrown open to foreign competition); all manner of strong domestic regulatory disciplines to improve transparency and promote competition; and administrative and judicial-review procedures to ensure that WTO commitments are implemented domestically.

In south Asia, Sri Lanka pioneered external liberalization in the late 1970s. India's retreat from the 'licence raj' – its equivalent of Soviet-style central planning – began half-heartedly in the 1980s; but its decisive opening to the world economy dates back to 1991. The average tariff has come down to about 16 per cent from 125 per cent in 1991. Most border NTBs, internal licensing restrictions and restrictions on manufacturing FDI have gone. This still leaves high protection in agriculture and services. Pakistan followed in the late 1990s.

In Latin America, Chile pioneered radical external liberalization in the 1970s. Other Latin American countries followed in the 1980s (notably Mexico) and the 1990s (notably Brazil, Argentina and Peru). African liberalization was slow in the 1980s and faster in the 1390s. South Africa opened rapidly during and after the end of apartheid. The countries of east-central Europe and the Baltic states experienced a 'big bang' transition from the Plan to the Market after 1989, which included massive liberalization of trade and capital flows. This was less the case, and certainly more erratic, in Russia, other parts of the ex-Soviet Union and southeastern Europe. However, liberalization has recently accelerated in some of these countries, for example Romania, Bulgaria, Georgia and parts of the ex-Yugoslavia.

Finally, trade-and-investment liberalization in the old OECD countries has taken place in small steps since the 1980s – not surprising, since these are largely open economies in which the bulk of liberalization was done in the 1950s and 1960s. The exceptions are Australia and New Zealand. After over a century of protection, both opened decisively to the world economy in the 1980s.

THE POLITICAL ECONOMY OF TRADE-POLICY REFORM

The politics of economic-policy reform is as much about distribution as it is about wealth generation. This is true of international politics; it is even truer of domestic politics. Shifts in trade policy – from protection to openness or vice versa – trigger redistribution of gains and losses between regions (especially between rural and urban areas), sectors of the economy (agriculture, industry, services), classes (owners of capital, educated and skilled workers, semi- and unskilled workers), and even between ethnic groups. Such disruption, especially in the short-term, can be particularly unsettling in developing countries with political instability, corrupt elites, wide disparities in wealth and influence, meagre safety nets, ethnic divides and generally brittle institutions. Hence trade and other forms of liberalization take place in a snakepit of messy and sometimes poisonous politics.

What are the determinants of trade-policy reform, especially in the direction of liberalization? What follows is a simple taxonomy of relevant factors: a) circumstances, especially crises; b) interests; c) ideas; d) institutions; e) factor endowments.

Circumstances and Crises

> Events, dear boy, events. (Harold Macmillan)

> When a man knows he is going to be hanged in a fortnight, it concentrates the mind wonderfully. (Dr Johnson)

The practical politician, official or businessman knows that choices are dictated by responses to often unanticipated events. In reality, major episodes of economic-policy reform have mostly taken place in response to political and/or economic crises (Haggard and Williamson, 1993). A macroeconomic crisis, with symptoms such as extreme internal or external indebtedness, hyperinflation, a terms-of-trade shock, or a severe payments imbalance leading to a plummeting currency, provides the classic backdrop. This is when 'normal politics' is suspended, and when a period of 'extraordinary politics' can provide a window of opportunity for thoroughgoing reforms (that would not be possible in 'normal' political circumstances) (Balcerowicz, 1995). Examples are legion: Chile in 1973/4; Mexico in 1986;

Brazil and Argentina in the early 1990s; South Africa in the mid-1990s; Sri Lanka in 1977; India in 1991; eastern Europe and the ex-Soviet Union in the early 1990s; Australia and New Zealand in 1983/4.

But the crisis explanation cannot be taken too far. First, a crisis can precipitate swings both ways: sometimes towards liberalization; sometimes the other way, as happened during the Depression in the 1930s, and, to a lesser extent, in the 1970s after the first oil price shock. Secondly, different governments act in different ways in response to similar external shocks. Thirdly, a crisis might trigger some reforms, but it is no guarantee of the sustainability of those reforms, nor of further reforms down the line. That is one key difference between east-central Europe and the Baltic states, on the one hand, and Russia and other parts of the ex-Soviet Union, on the other. Lastly, there are counter-examples of gradual, but cumulatively substantial, reforms without a sudden crisis as a triggering mechanism. That is, roughly, the east-Asian record, and that of Australia's.

Why have some countries sustained reforms while others have not? Why have some gone farther than others? What happens to a reform programme post-crisis, when 'normal' political and economic conditions return? These questions demand supplementary explanations.

Interests

> A good cause seldom triumphs without someone's interest behind it. (John Stuart Mill)

Mainstream economists, following Adam Smith, tend to rely on an interest-group explanation of trade politics. Free trade is the optimal policy in most circumstances (they say), but protection more often the result, because organized rent-seeking interests demand protection, and politicians and officials supply it. The benefits of free trade are diffused over the broad majority of consumers, but its costs bear down disproportionately on minority producer interests. The latter, not the former, have the incentive to organize for collective action (Olson, 1971; Krueger, 1974).

In reality 'iron quadrangles' of politicians, bureaucrats, employers and unions imposed a straightjacket of protection in developing countries from the 1930s to the 1970s. Mostly this benefited capital-intensive, unionized, urban manufacturing industries producing for the domestic market, at the expense of agriculture and tradable sectors. India's licence raj was its most notorious incarnation. In many countries, a crisis was used to overcome interest-group opposition and push through liberalizing reforms (as happened in India in 1991).

But what role do interest groups play after an initial burst of external liberalization, and in post-crisis conditions when 'normal' politics returns? Here the picture differs across countries and regions. In some parts of the world, protectionist coalitions have halted or slowed down liberalization. This is the case with 'nomenklatura' coalitions in Russia, Ukraine and other parts of the ex-Soviet Union. Elsewhere, radical opening has triggered major economic shifts in favour of sectors exposed to the world economy. Traditional protectionist interests have been weakened, and countervailing coalitions have emerged. The latter comprise exporters, users of imported inputs, multinationals with global production networks, and cities and regions seeking to be magnets for trade and FDI. These interests lobby for the maintenance and extension of open trade and FDI regimes.[2] This has happened in strong liberalizing countries in east Asia, eastern Europe and Latin America. It happened in Australia and New Zealand from the early 1980s. It is also evident in India after the 1991 reforms.

Ideas

> It is the word in season that does much to decide the result. (John Stuart Mill)

> Madmen who hear voices in the air are distilling their frenzy from the academic scribblings of some defunct economist or political philosopher. Indeed the world is ruled by little else. (John Maynard Keynes)

It is difficult to gauge the influence of ideas (or ideology) in policy.[3] But practical observation teaches us that the prevailing climate of ideas, interacting with interests and events, can entrench or sway this-or-that set of policies. A policy consensus on import substitution, state planning and foreign aid was strongly embedded in developing-country governments and international organizations up to the 1970s. This was buttressed by a post-colonial political ideology of mercantilist state-building, and an interventionist consensus in development economics (Bauer, 2000a; Lal and Myint, 1996). This set of ideas was overturned by what came to be called the Washington Consensus, which reflected sea-changes in political ideology and in development economics. The latter returned to classical and neoclassical foundations, emphasizing market-based pricing, 'outward orientation', the prevalence of 'government failure' over 'market failure', not to mention a dose of aid scepticism.

Washington Consensus ideas took stronger hold in countries where reforms were substantial, especially in ministries of finance, central banks and presidential/prime-ministerial offices. These agencies tend to be the cockpits of policy reform. But now the climate of ideas has changed somewhat. This does not presage a return to full-blown pre-Washington Consensus thinking. The pendulum, however, is swinging towards more attention to market failure and government intervention, for example to ease back on further liberalization, expand 'policy space' and promote infant industries, defend 'food security' and increase foreign aid. The question is what effect this is having, and is likely to have, on trade policies.

Institutions

In the broad sense, institutions are the steel frame of the economy, its 'formal rules and informal constraints', according to Douglass North. The legal framework governing property rights and contracts, production and consumption, comes to mind. 'Formal rules' comprise bankruptcy laws, competition laws, regulations governing financial markets and corporate governance, and much else besides. 'Informal constraints' are (often non-legal) traditions and norms influencing the intersecting worlds of business, government and the law.

Evidently, 'institutions' are much broader and more difficult to pin down than 'policies'; and the two are of course intimately connected. Historically-conditioned institutions, domestic and external, set the scene for government action, interest-group lobbying and the influence of ideas. They are the arena for policy choices and their implementation. Making generalizations about institutional constraints on policy choice, and how this might explain differences in national and regional economic performance over time, is notoriously difficult. To what extent must 'good' institutions be in place before 'good' policies can take hold and work their magic? Conversely, to what extent are institutions the result, rather than the cause, of policy choices? These are chicken-and-egg questions.

In the narrow sense, institutions are the organizational map of decision-making at the junction where politics and public policy meet business and society. On trade policy, this map is much more complicated than it used to be. Trade policy, as we know, is no longer just about a clutch of border instruments, and the preserve of trade ministries. It is increasingly 'trade-related', a matter of non-border regulation reaching deep into the domestic economy and its institutions. That is reflected in more complex multilateral, regional and bilateral trade agreements. This brings in agencies across the range of government and many actors outside government as well. Now the management of trade policy involves: the division of labour between the executive, legislature and judiciary; the role of the lead ministry; the participation of other ministries and regulatory agencies on trade and trade-related policies; the WTO mission in Geneva; inter-agency coordination within government; the involvement of non-governmental actors, such as business and unions, and now including NGOs and think tanks; and the role of donors and international organizations.

Inasmuch as one can make generalizations about institutions and trade policy in developing countries, here are a couple. First, it is the more advanced developing countries (in terms of per-capita income and human-development indicators) that have liberalized more and plugged themselves better into globalization than other developing countries. They have lower trade and FDI barriers, higher ratios of trade and FDI to GDP, and better-performing tradable sectors of the economy. They also have stronger institutions in the broad sense: better enforcement of property rights and contracts (that is the rule of law), better-functioning judiciaries and public administration, better-regulated financial markets, a stronger competition culture, less corruption and so on (World Bank, 2002a; Michalopoulos, 2001). This is the divide that separates Chile and a few other Latin American countries, eastern Europe, the northeast-Asian and southeast-Asian Tigers, and a tiny handful of African countries (Mauritius, Botswana and South Africa), from the rest.

There are, however, two gigantic anomalies: China and India. Both are still low-income countries with weak institutions (going by some of the indicators mentioned above). Institutional improvements have taken place, but these have lagged well behind big policy shifts – not least lower trade and FDI restrictions – and fast-paced global integration. The World Bank's governance and business-climate indicators, for example, point to large institutional and policy differences among developing countries. That is predictable enough. But they also point to relatively weak institutions, as well as the high 'red-tape' costs of doing business, in China and India.

Second, looking at institutions in the narrower organizational sense, strong and sustained trade-policy and wider economic-policy reforms were driven, more often than not, by powerful presidential or prime-ministerial offices, ministries of finance and central banks, insulated from blocking pressures in other parts of government and outside government. This was more pronounced in advanced developing countries than elsewhere. These countries also have stronger capacity, in terms of qualified, experienced manpower and other resources, for formulating and implementing trade policy, whether done unilaterally or through international negotiations and agreements. Again, China and India are exceptional: they are low-income countries with relatively weak institutions (in the broad sense), but with relatively strong trade-policy capacity.

Factor Endowments

Explaining the trajectory of policy reforms is not complete without factoring in the relative mix of land (or natural resources), labour (including skills) and capital in an economy (Lal and Myint, 1996). We know from recent economic history that the star developing-country performers are east Asian. These countries had different starting positions, but, at a certain stage of development, relative labour abundance allowed them to break into labour-intensive manufactured exports, which became an engine of growth and in turn aided poverty reduction and human-welfare improvement. Of course this was not inevitable: it depended on the right policies and improving institutions. South Asia, with similar factor endowments, remained stuck on a low-growth, high-poverty path because it did not adopt market-based policies.

Latin American and African countries, on the other hand, are largely land- or resource-abundant and labour-scarce. Absent import-substitution policies, they are better able to exploit comparative advantage in land and resources – as Brazil, Argentina, Chile, Australia and New Zealand have done in agriculture since they liberalized, and as all the latter and many other countries are doing in the present China-driven commodities boom. Thus a simple story based on early twenty-first century comparative advantage would point to all-round gains from trade: for technologically-advanced and capital-abundant countries in the West; the labour-abundant countries of east and south Asia; and land and resource-abundant countries elsewhere.

But the political economy of factor endowments reveals a different and more problematic story. Arguably, land- and resource-abundant countries are at a structural disadvantage compared with labour-abundant countries. By plugging into global markets for manufacturing, and now labour-intensive services too, the latter seem to be on sustainable growth paths. Labour-intensive exports attract FDI (and the technology and skills that come with it), feed quickly into poverty-reducing, welfare-improving employment, and, more gradually, into better infrastructure and institutions. This creates and strengthens a constellation of interests to support open trade and FDI policies.

Land- and resource-abundant countries, given their relatively high price of labour, seem to be crowded out of global manufacturing markets by east-Asian (especially Chinese) competition (Wolf, 2004: 146–9). This leaves them dependent on cyclical and volatile commodities markets. FDI in resource-abundant countries tends to be capital-intensive and to generate big rents in not-so-competitive market segments. Often the result is an FDI enclave, without an employment, technology or wealth spillover to the rest of the economy, but with big profits to distribute among a corrupt local business and political elite. Most countries dependent on resources have the interest-group constellation to squander rents from resource booms, but not to spread wealth and improve governance and institutions. A retreat to protectionism, however, would repeat past mistakes and make matters worse. This is the dilemma inherent in the 'China-in-Africa' phenomenon. But there are notable exceptions to the 'resource-curse' rule: Chile has successfully exploited comparative advantage in agriculture and resources (mainly copper) through liberal trade policies, while diversifying the economic base and improving institutions. That is also true of Australia and New Zealand.

MULTI-TRACK TRADE POLICY

Another way of cutting into trade-policy reform is to look at it on several tracks. Some reforms are carried out unilaterally; others reciprocally through (bilateral, regional, multilateral) trade negotiations, or in agreements with donors. Most developing countries now do trade policy on all these tracks concurrently, though the relative balance differs from country to country.

Unilateral liberalization

> I trust the government … will not resume the policy which they and we have found most inconvenient, namely the haggling with foreign countries about reciprocal concessions, instead of taking that independent course which we believe to be conducive to our own interests … let us trust that our example, with the proof of practical benefits we derive from it, will at no remote period insure the adoption of the principles on which we have acted. (Sir Robert Peel, announcing the repeal of the Corn Laws, House of Commons, 1846)

> Liberalise first, negotiate later. (Mart Laar, former prime minister of Estonia)

Compelling political and economic arguments favour unilateral liberalization, with governments freeing up international trade and flows of capital and labour independently, not in the first instance via international negotiations. As any student of trade economics knows, welfare gains result directly from import liberalization, which replaces comparatively costly domestic production and reallocates resources more efficiently, and spurs capital accumulation, economies of scale as well as longer-run dynamic gains such as the transfer of technology and skills.[5] Similar and related arguments apply to the liberalization of inward investment and the cross-border movement of people.

Such gains come more quickly through own, unconditional liberalization than through protracted, politicized and bureaucratically cumbersome international negotiations. This Nike strategy ('Just Do It!') can make political sense too. Rather than relying on one-size-fits-all international blueprints, governments have the flexibility to initiate policies and emulate

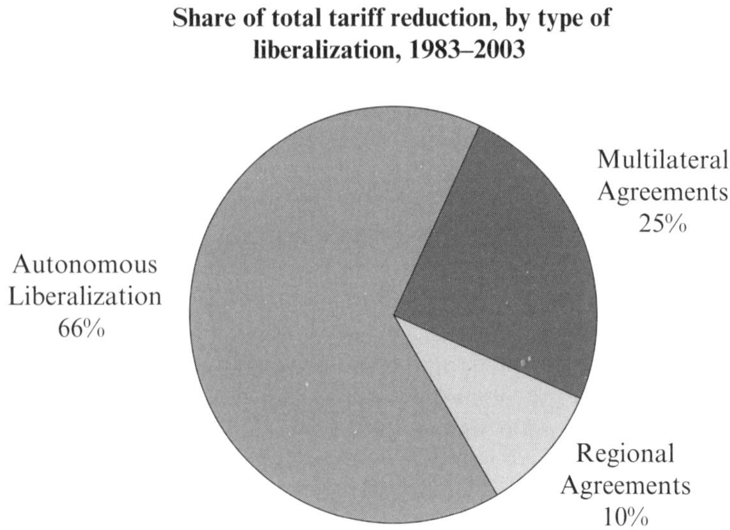

Source: World Bank http://siteresources.worldbank.org/INTGEP2005/Resources/GEP107053_Ch02.pdf

Figure 1.6 Source of liberalization, 1983–2003

better practice abroad in experimental, trial-and-error fashion, tailored to specific local conditions. In David Landes's words, it is 'initiated from below and diffused by example'. This was the preferred method of the classical economists from Smith to Marshall, and of the titans of mid-Victorian British politics (Sally, 1998).

In twentieth and twenty-first century conditions of democratic politics and vigorous interest-group lobbying, unilateral liberalization is of course a much more difficult proposition than it was in the nineteenth century. But observers often forget that the recent trade-policy revolution outside the West has come more 'from below' than 'from above'. The World Bank estimates that, between 1983 and 2003, about 65 per cent of developing-country tariff liberalization (a 21 per cent cut in average weighted tariffs) has come about unilaterally, with 25 per cent coming from the Uruguay Round Agreements and only 10 per cent from preferential trade agreements (PTAs) (Figure 1.6).

True, many governments liberalized reluctantly as part of IMF and World Bank structural adjustment programmes. But the strongest liberalizers have been unilateral liberalizers, going ahead under their own steam without the need for much external pressure. Prominent among them are the east-Asian countries, now led by China, as well as Chile, Mexico, the east European countries, Australia, New Zealand and South Africa. Nearly all of India's post-1991 liberalization has been done unilaterally.

Unilateral liberalization of trade and investment has been particularly strong in east Asia. China's massive opening is the most recent example, and was mostly done unilaterally, before WTO accession. Its extremely strong WTO commitments, and its generally constructive participation in the WTO since accession, are more the consequence than the cause of its sweeping unilateral reforms. China is in some ways today what Britain was in the second half of the nineteenth century: the unilateral engine of freer trade. It could well spur a pick-up in trade-and-FDI liberalization elsewhere, especially in Asia. Recently, India has accelerated its liberalization of tariffs and FDI – outside trade negotiations. Would this have happened, or happened as fast, if China had not concentrated minds? Probably not.

That is not to say that China-induced unilateral liberalization is a total solution. It is unlikely to induce further external liberalization in the developed world, and least of all in the USA, EU and Japan. In the developing world, its results will inevitably be patchy and messy. On its own it cannot slay protectionist dragons and solve international commercial conflicts – least of all in agricultural trade, where unilateral liberalization has been much more limited than in industrial goods and services. More importantly perhaps, it does not provide binding and enforceable rules for stable and open international commerce. That leaves room for reciprocal negotiations and international agreements, that is for the WTO and PTAs.

Multilateral Liberalization

> The great political virtue of multilateralism, far exceeding in importance its economic virtues, is that it makes it economically possible for most countries, even if small, poor and weak, to live in freedom and with chances of prosperity without having to come to special terms with some Great Power. (Jacob Viner)

> In recent years, the impression has often been given of a vehicle with a proliferation of backseat drivers, each seeking a different destination, with no map and no intention of asking the way. (The Sutherland Report)

Given the realities of modern politics – interest-group lobbying for protection, ingrained mercantilist thinking, the perception that liberalization hurts the poor and vulnerable – unilateral liberalization is often difficult to achieve in practice. The rationale of 'multilateralized reciprocity' is that GATT/WTO negotiations help to contain protectionist interests and mobilize exporting interests; and multilateral agreements provide fair, non-discriminatory rules for all. Perhaps the greatest utility of the WTO is that it provides a framework of rules to assist (mainly developing-country) governments that have strategically chosen to take their national economies in a market-oriented, globally-integrated direction. The accessions of China and Vietnam are textbook examples of how the WTO should work.

That said, the standard *raison d'être* for multilateral rules-based trade liberalization was easier said in the old GATT than done in the WTO. In many ways the WTO is the victim of its own success; of the successful conclusion of the Uruguay Round and the huge transition from the GATT to the WTO.[5]

Multilateral liberalization was successful during the GATT when the latter had a relatively slimline agenda, club-like decision-making dominated by a handful of developed countries (especially the USA and EU), and the glue of Cold War alliance politics. It has proved spectacularly unsuccessful in the WTO. Now, the WTO agenda, especially on non-border regulation, is technically more complicated, less amenable to the reciprocal exchange of concessions, administratively more burdensome and politically much more controversial; decision-making is a chaotic mess in a general assembly with near-universal membership; and the unifying glue of the Cold War has dissolved. The failure of the Doha round (as of the time of writing) probably shows that future multilateral liberalization will be elusive, and modest at best.

Arguably, the best the WTO can hope for post-Doha is to lock in pre-existing unilateral liberalization through binding commitments, and gradually improve the functioning of non-discriminatory multilateral rules. That implies scaling back ambitions and expectations. Market-access and rule-making negotiations should be more modest and incremental; and maybe trade rounds should become a thing of the past. Perhaps there should be more emphasis on the WTO as an OECD-type forum to share information and ideas, and to improve transparency through mutual policy surveillance, especially for developing countries. More attention should also be given to the technical, everyday task of administering trade rules.

Even achieving these objectives will be a tall order, given the present parlous state of the WTO. There is every prospect that multilateral trade rules will be undermined by major players seeking to evade them, and as a result of proliferating and discriminatory bilateral trade agreements. Weaker multilateral rules will be a much bigger cost for developing countries than the extra multilateral liberalization forgone as a result of Doha round failure.

Bilateral and Regional Liberalization

> We will work with can do, not won't do, countries. (Robert Zoellick)

By July 2005, 330 preferential trade agreements (PTAs) had been notified to the GATT/WTO, 206 of them since the establishment of the WTO in 1995. Over 180 are currently in force, with many more expected to be operational soon. Of the PTAs in force, 84 per cent are free trade agreements (FTAs), with customs unions (CUs) and partial-scope agreements making up the rest. Bilateral (country-to-country) agreements account for over 75 per cent of PTAs in force and almost 90 per cent of those under negotiation. The pace of PTA activity has increased since 1999/2000, and even more so since the launch of the Doha Round (WTO, 2006; Crawford and Fiorentino, 2005).

Eastern Europe, Africa and Latin America have long been involved in PTA activity. East Asia, which previously relied on non-discriminatory unilateral and multilateral liberalization, is now playing PTA catch-up, as is south Asia. All the major regional powers – China, India and Japan – are involved in Asian PTAs, as are the USA, EU, Korea, Australia, New Zealand, Hong Kong, other south-Asian countries and the ASEAN countries.

Why this rush? Proponents argue that small clubs of like-minded members can take liberalization and rules faster, wider and deeper than in the WTO, and act as 'building blocks' to further multilateral liberalization and rule-making. Sceptics say they are 'stumbling blocks', diverting attention from the WTO, creating 'spaghetti bowls' of discriminatory trade restrictions, and generally favouring powerful players at the expense of the weak (World Bank, 2004: ch. 6).

The reality is mixed. Unilateral and multilateral liberalization blunts the damaging effects of PTAs. There is little prospect of the world economy retreating to the warring trade blocs of the 1930s. Strong, 'WTO-plus' PTAs, that is with comprehensive sectoral coverage, more ambitious market-access and rules commitments than in the WTO, and simple, harmonized rules of origin, can also make sense. But these are rare. The EU, NAFTA and Australia–New Zealand CER are relatively strong PTAs. The record in developing-country regions, however, is not encouraging. South–South PTAs and most North–South PTAs tend to be driven by vague, muddled and trivial foreign-policy objectives with little relevance to commercial realities. Latin America and Africa have a messy patchwork of weak FTAs that do not liberalize much trade or improve upon WTO rules, but do create complications, especially through trade-restricting rules of origin, and divert attention both from the WTO and from unilateral reforms. This is also the emerging picture of FTAs in east and south Asia (Sally, 2006c).

The heart of the matter is that cross-border commerce in the developing world is throttled by the protectionist barriers that developing countries erect against their equally poor or even poorer neighbours. Will new PTAs make a big dent in these barriers and thereby spur regional and global economic integration? That looks doubtful.

The Role of Donors[6]

Foreign aid, with conditions attached by the IMF, World Bank and other donors, has clearly played a big part in driving Washington Consensus-type reforms in many developing countries. This has gone way beyond developing countries' (relatively weak) liberalizing commitments in the WTO and FTAs. Arguably, unilateral liberalization has not been truly 'unilateral' when it has depended on donor policy preferences and aid with strings attached. The record of IMF stabilization packages and World Bank structural adjustment packages has been mixed at best, and certainly disappointing compared with optimistic expectations in the 1980s (World Bank, 1998a; World Bank, 1998b). Often donor-driven reforms have proceeded in stops and starts, with reversals en route. Projected growth and poverty-alleviation effects have not materialized. The politics of aid is even more dubious than its economics. 'Conditionality' is empty rhetoric when self-serving interests at both ends of the pipeline ensure that aid continues to flow, even when promised reforms are not delivered. And the perception that Western donors are imposing reforms on otherwise reluctant countries is hardly sustainable: local 'ownership' is lacking (to borrow aid jargon), and it invites a backlash and reform-reversal at home (Bauer, 2000b).

The bottom line is that countries that have seen strong, sustained, unilateral liberalizing reforms are those whose governments have driven reforms ('from below', as it were) rather than having them imposed by donors ('from above'). Aid at its best has smoothed short-term adjustments; and donor conditionality has provided a 'good housekeeping seal of approval' – an international signal of reform credibility – more than anything else. In these countries (most in east Asia and eastern Europe, and a few in Latin America), aid has not been central to reform success. Where there has been more reliance on aid and donor conditionality, reforms have a far worse record. This applies to Africa in particular.

Seen in this light, the new conventional wisdom on aid is wrong-headed and dangerous. The UN Millennium Project and the Africa Commission Report both propose to double or even triple aid between 2005 and 2015, particularly with Africa in mind. The UN idea – or rather, Jeffrey Sachs's idea – is a new version of the old principle of aid: poor countries lack resources to invest, and donors have to fill this 'financing gap' with a 'big push' of investment if growth is ever to occur (UN, 2005; Sachs, 2005; Easterly, 1999). A sudden and massive increase of aid threatens to repeat past mistakes and provide extra incentives to delay and derail, not promote, market-based reforms. Available evidence shows that aid does not improve the productivity of investment; it diverts funds to stimulate government consumption and current spending; it has a negative impact on domestic savings; and, by expanding the role of already dysfunctional governments, it breeds waste and corruption. In short, this approach is misguided top-down intervention (Easterly, 2006).

A softer version of aid optimism, associated with the World Bank, assumes that countries are poor because of bad policy choices and weak institutions, and that aid can lock in already-accomplished reforms and facilitate additional reforms (World Bank, 1998a). This view is politically naive, though a convenient fiction for elites who profit from the aid business. The main objection is that aid has not and probably will not be a good midwife to market-based reforms. On the contrary, aid is given more often than not to support failed policies; and there is a high incidence of repeat lending to governments without a good track record of market-based reforms.

A particular version of the aid-to-reform idea is the 'aid-for-trade' scheme that is now discussed in the Doha round. No one has yet defined its modus operandi. Is it a structural adjustment programme, an unemployment insurance programme, a budget support programme, an industrial promotion programme, or something else? Whatever the purpose, the history of aid warns us of the perils of such a scheme. Moreover, the idea that countries should be protected from the market-based structural adjustment that trade liberalization entails is in direct conflict with the reality of development.

WHERE ARE WE GOING?

The naysayers, from the hard and soft left, and the conservative right, hold that liberalization has not delivered the goods. They argue for various forms of government intervention, at national and international levels, to tame 'market fundamentalism' and 'neoliberal globalization'. Interventionist ideas on trade (and aid) are not new; they hark back to pre-Adam Smith, 'pre-analytic' mercantilism (as Schumpeter called it). What they have in common is an age-old distrust of markets and faith in government intervention – what David Henderson calls 'New Millennium Collectivism'.[7] Such collectivist thinking is on the rise again. But it is still wrong and dangerous. It glosses over the damage done by interventionist policies in the past, and misreads the recent and historical evidence. The latter shows that external liberalization, as part of broad market-based reforms, has worked: countries that have become more open to the world economy have grown faster and become richer than those that have opened up less or remained closed.

There is much unfinished business. Barriers to trade, and the cross-border movement of capital and people, remain high, and more so in developing countries than in developed countries. But a combination of material circumstances and changes in the climate of ideas makes market-based reforms more difficult now than was the case a decade ago. Reform complacency has resulted from a post-crisis environment of buoyant growth and normal interest-group politics. There is dissatisfaction with previous reforms in parts of the developing world.

Moreover, the politics of 'second-generation' trade-policy reforms is proving much more difficult than that of 'first-generation' reforms. The former are all about complex domestic (though trade-related) regulation, such as services regulation, regulation of food-safety and technical standards, intellectual-property protection, public procurement, customs administration and competition rules. These reforms are technically and administratively difficult, and take time to implement. They demand a minimum of capacity across government, especially for implementation and enforcement. Above all, they are even more politically sensitive than border reforms, as they affect entrenched interests that are extremely difficult to dislodge.

The stakes, however, are too important for reform challenges to be avoided. While there is no imminent threat of global economic collapse, stalled reforms threaten to slow down globalization's advance, thereby depriving the world's least advantaged people of the life chances that globalization offers. That would reinforce strong pressures, from an alliance of old-style protectionist interests and new-style ideological forces, for overactive government to restrict economic freedom and the operation of the market economy. That is why new–old collectivist ideas need to be countered with full force. Reduction of what are still high barriers to trade, foreign investment and the cross-border movement of people holds the promise of higher growth, and significant poverty reduction and improvements in human welfare.

When thinking about the future reform agenda one should distinguish between 'first-division' and 'second-division' reformers. Second-division reformers, overwhelmingly in the low-income and least-developed bracket, have higher border barriers than first-division reformers, in addition to bigger domestic obstacles to trade and investment. They are less globalized. Their first priority should be to reduce border barriers and simple non-border barriers (such as some red-tape procedures that give them low rankings in the World Bank's Doing Business Report). They have less capacity than first-division reformers for implementing more complex second-generation reforms. These could wait until the easier reforms are done. The real dilemma is that countries at the bottom of this pile, especially among the LDCs, are mired in political instability and civil strife, with failed and failing states that do not perform the most basic public functions. Such countries do not have the capacity to implement even simple reforms. Aid-driven solutions have failed, but what is the substitute? This book provides some hesitant answers based on the experiences of the countries studied, but the 'transferability' of these lessons is difficult to know.

First-division reformers are the 20–25 developing countries – the 'new globalizers' – that have already gone far with macroeconomic stabilization, and internal and external liberalization. They have plugged themselves into the globalization process. Their task is to go further with dismantling border barriers to trade and opening the door to FDI. But their bigger challenge is to make much more progress on trade-related domestic reforms – the 'structural' and 'institutional' reforms where progress to date has been too slow. This entails tackling the second-generation issues mentioned above. What is needed is a culture of permanent, incremental reforms, mainly of the second-generation variety, that build on the foundations of first-generation reforms, so that the economy adapts flexibly to changing global conditions. That is easier said than done. The great difficulty lies in doing serious reforms in conditions of normal interest-group politics, without an economic crisis to concentrate minds. But the alternative is creeping sclerosis in times of plenty, and excessive reliance on a crisis for the next reform wave (Olson, 1982; OECD, 2007). That cannot be good for long-term political, social and economic health.

Fundamentally, required reforms boil down to restructuring the state, away from the large overactive state that intervenes badly across the range of economic activity, and towards the limited state that performs a smaller number of core functions well. The latter should focus on providing and enforcing a framework of rules for market-based competition. To use Michael Oakeshott's distinction, the state should be an 'umpire' of a 'civic association', not an 'estate manager' of an 'enterprise association'.

Thus it falls to friends of the market economy to make a strong case for further reforms, including external liberalization, and practically go about assembling reform coalitions. In the next seven chapters there is ample evidence to show how this might be both achieved and sustained.

NOTES

1. On the record of trade and FDI liberalization as part of larger packages of market-based reforms in developing countries and countries in transition, see Williamson, 1994; Kuczynski and Williamson, 2004; Lal and Myint, 1996; Dean, 1995; Drabek and Laird, 1998; Henderson, 1998; Michalopoulos, 2001; Bates and Krueger, 1993; Desai, 1997. On trade policy trends in Asia, see Sally, 2007, 2006b; Sally and Sen, 2005.
2. Ricardo–Viner and Hecksher–Ohlin models of comparative advantage are used to

explain interest-group activity pro and contra free trade in different countries with different factor endowments. See Rogowski (1990).

3. On 'ideational' approaches, see Goldstein (1994).
4. There is the theoretical possibility of (usually large) countries being able to exercise long-run market power in international demand for certain goods. This enables them to shift the terms of trade in their favour by means of an 'optimal tariff'. The corollary is that these countries should only lower tariffs if others reciprocate, in order to avoid worsening terms of trade. In reality, very few countries have such long-run market power. And retaliatory tariffs by other countries could nullify terms-of-trade gains. Thus – not for the first time – a neat theory turns out to have limited practical relevance. See Irwin, 1996: 106–115.
5. The following argument draws on Sally, 2006a.
6. This section draws on Erixon and Sally, 2006.
7. On the provenance and progress of these ideas, see Henderson (2001).

REFERENCES

Balcerowicz, Leczek (1995), *Socialism, Capitalism, Transformation*, Budapest: Central European University Press.

Bates, Robert and Anne Krueger (eds) (1993), *Political and Economic Interactions in Economic Policy Reform: Evidence from Eight Countries*, Cambridge, MA: Blackwell.

Bauer, P.T. (2000a), *From Subsistence to Exchange and Other Essays*, Princeton, NJ: Princeton University Press.

Bauer, P.T. (2000b), 'Foreign aid: abiding issues', in P.T. Bauer, *From Subsistence to Exchange and Other Essays*, Princeton, NJ: Princeton University Press.

Bhagwati, Jagdish and T.N. Srinivasan (1999), 'Outward-orientation and development: are revisionists right?', Yale University Economic Growth Center Discussion Paper no. 806, 17 September.

Chang, Ha-Joon (2002), *Kicking Away the Ladder: Development Strategy in Historical Perspective*, London: Anthem Press.

Crawford, Jo-Ann and Robert Fiorentino (2005), 'The changing landscape of regional trade agreements', WTO Discussion Paper No. 8, available at www.wto.org.

Dean, Judith (1995), 'The trade-policy revolution in developing countries', in S. Arndt and C. Milner (eds), *The World Economy, Global Trade Policy*, Oxford: Blackwell.

Desai, Padma (ed.) (1997), *Going Global: Transition from Plan to Market in the World Economy*, Cambridge, MA: MIT Press.

Drabek, Zdenek and Sam Laird (1998), 'The new liberalism: trade-policy developments in emerging markets', *Journal of World Trade*, **32**(5), 241–69.

Easterly, William (1999), 'The Ghost of the Financing Gap: Testing the Growth Model Used in the International Financial Institutions', *Journal of Development Economics*, **60**(2).

Easterly, William (2006), *The White Man's Burden: Why the West's Efforts to Aid the Rest Have Done So Much Ill and So Little Good*, New York: Penguin.

Erixon, Fredrik and Razeen Sally (2006), 'Trade and aid: countering New Millennium Collectivism', *Australian Economic Review*, **39**(1), 69–77.

Goldstein, Judith (1994), *Ideas, Interests and American Trade Policy*, Ithaca: Cornell University Press.

Grunberg, Isabel, I. Kaul and M. Stern (eds) (1999), *Global Public Goods: International Co-operation in the 21st Century*, New York and Oxford: Oxford University Press.

Haggard, Stephen and John Williamson (1993), 'The political conditions for economic reform', 1994, in Williamson, 1994, op cit., pp. 527–96.

Henderson, David (1992), 'International economic integration: progress, prospects and implications', *International Affairs*, **64**(4).

Henderson, David (1998), *The Changing Fortunes of Economic Liberalism: Yesterday, Today and Tomorrow*, London: Institute of Economic Affairs.

Henderson, David (2001), *Anti-Liberalism 2000: The Rise of New Millennium Collectivism*, London: Institute of Economic Affairs.

Henderson, David (2004), 'Globalisation, economic progress and New Millennium Collectivism', *World Economics*, **5**(3), July–September, 43–73.

Ingco, M.D. and J.D. Nash (eds) (2004), *Agriculture and the WTO: Creating a Trading System for Development*, Washington, DC: World Bank.

Irwin, Douglas (1996), *Against the Tide: An Intellectual History of Free Trade*, Princeton, NJ: Princeton University Press.

Krueger, Anne (1974), 'The political economy of the rent-seeking society', *American Economic Review*, **64**, 291–303.

Kuczynshi, P.P. and T. Williamson (eds) (2004), *After the Washington Consensus: Restarting Growth and Reform in Latin America*, Washington, DC: Institute for International Economics.

Lal, Deepak and H. Myint (1996), *The Political Economy of Poverty, Equity and Growth: A Comparative Study*, Oxford: Clarendon Press.

Little, I.M.D. (1999), 'Trade and industrialisation revisited', in I.M.D. Little (ed.), *Collection and Recollections*, Oxford: Clarendon Press.

Maddison, Angus (2003), *The World Economy: Historical Statistics*, Paris: OECD.

Messerlin, Patrick (2005), *Europe After the 'No' Votes: Mapping a New Economic Path*, London: Institute of Economic Affairs.

Michalopoulos, Constantine (2001), *Developing Countries and the WTO*, London: Palgrave.

Olson, Mancur (1971), *The Logic of Collective Action: Public Goods and the Theory of Groups*, Cambridge, MA: Harvard University Press.

Olson, Mancur (1982), *The Rise and Decline of Nations: Economic Growth, Stagflation and Social Rigidities*, New Haven: Yale University Press.

Organisation of Economic Cooperation and Development (OPED) (2007), *Economic Policy Reforms: Going for Growth*, Paris: OECD.

Oxfam (2002), *Rigged Rules and Double Standards: Trade, Globalisation and the Fight Against Poverty*, Oxford: Oxfam International, www.maketradefair.com.

Rodrik, Dani (1998), *The New Global Economy and Developing Countries: Making Openness Work*, Washington, DC: Overseas Development Council.

Rodrik, Dani (2001), 'Trading in illusions', *Foreign Policy*, March/April, www.foreignpolicy.com/issue_marapr_2001/rodrick.html.

Rogowski, Ronald (1990), *Commerce and Coalitions: How Trade Affects Domestic Political Alignments*, Princeton, NJ: Princeton University Press.

Sachs, Jeffrey (2005), *The End of Poverty: How We Can Make it Happen in our Lifetime*, London: Penguin.

Sachs, Jeffrey and Andrew Warner (1995), 'Economic reform and the process of global integration', *Brookings Papers on Economic Activity*, **1**.
Sally, Razeen (1998), *Classical Liberalism and International Economic Order: Studies in Theory and Intellectual History*, London: Routledge.
Sally, Razeen (2006a), 'Trade policy 2006: a tour d'horizon', *World Economics*, **7**(1), January–March, 49–71.
Sally, Razeen (2006b), 'Chinese trade policies in wider Asian perspective', in Yang Yao and Linda Yueh (eds), *Globalisation and Economic Growth in China*, London: World Scientific Publishing, pp. 181–233.
Sally, Razeen (2006c), 'FTAs and the prospects for regional integration in Asia', ECIPE Working Paper 1, www.ecipe.org/publications/2006/WPno1_06_Sally.pdf.
Sally, Razeen (2007), 'Trade policy in Asia', *ECIPE Policy Brief*, **1**, www.ecipe.org/pdf/Policybrief_0107.pdf.
Sally, Razeen and Rahul Sen (2005), 'Whither trade policies in southeast Asia? The wider Asian and global context', *ASEAN Economic Bulletin*, **22**(1), April, 92–115, Special Issue 'Revisiting trade policies in southeast Asia', Razeen Sally and Rahul Sen (eds).
Stiglitz, Joseph (2002), *Globalisation and its Discontents*, London: Allen Lane.
UN Millennium Project (2005), *Investing in Development: a Practical Plan to Achieve the Millennium Development Goals*, New York: Earthscan.
Wade, Robert Hunter (1990), *Governing the Market*, Princeton, NJ: Princeton University Press.
Williamson, John (ed.) (1994), *The Political Economy of Policy Reform*, Washington, DC: Institute for International Economics.
Winters, L. Alan (2004), 'Trade liberalisation and economic performance: an overview', *Economic Journal*, February.
Winters, L. Alan et al. (2004), 'Trade liberalisation and poverty', *Journal of Economic Literature*, March.
Wolf, Martin (2004), *Why Globalisation Works: The Case for the Global Market Economy*, New Haven: Yale University Press.
World Bank (1993), *The East Asian Miracle*, Washington DC: World Bank.
World Bank (1997), *World Development Report 1997: The State in Economic Development*, Washington, DC: World Bank.
World Bank (1998a), *Assessing Aid: What Works, What Doesn't, and Why*, New York: Oxford University Press.
World Bank (1998b), *1998 Annual Review of Development Effectiveness*, Washington, DC: World Bank Operations Evaluation Department.
World Bank (2002a), *Globalisation, Growth and Poverty: Building an Inclusive World Economy*, Washington, DC: World Bank.
World Bank (2002b), *Global Economic Prospects and the Developing Countries: Making Trade Work for the World's Poor*, Washington, DC: World Bank.
World Bank (2004), *Global Economic Prospects 2005: Trade, Regionalism and Development*, Washington, DC: World Bank.
World Bank (2006), *Doing Business in 2007*, Washington, DC: World Bank.
World Trade Organisation (2006), 'Regional trade agreements: facts and figures', www.wto.org/english/tratop_e/region_e/regfac_e.htm.

PART I

THE COMPREHENSIVE REFORMERS

2. Australia

Bill Bowen

INTRODUCTION

> If you go into a pet shop every parrot is screeching microeconomic reform, microeconomic reform, (Paul Keating, Bureau of Industry Economics, 1995: 44)

Australia is a case of ambitious, wide-ranging, unilateral trade liberalization having delivered very significant results. With other economic reforms, unilateral trade liberalization has delivered a more competitive, flexible and resilient economy.

In Australia's federal system the Commonwealth is responsible for trade policy. But in many key economic policy areas the states have the main responsibility. While this chapter is primarily concerned about trade policy reform, the Kennett and Greiner governments in Victoria and New South Wales implemented very significant economic reforms which were a central part of the overall reform effort.

The costs of reform are obvious, concentrated and incurred upfront. The benefits tend to be opaque, diffused and accrue downstream. A key issue is therefore how governments can compensate those who stand to lose from reduced protection so that the rest of the community can reap a reform dividend. Can social cohesion be maintained during ambitious reform? Can governments hold the line for long enough in the face of those arguing that the costs outweigh the benefits?

Australia's economic reforms, in particular its trade reforms, have transformed the Australian economy so fundamentally that the nature of the challenge is often forgotten – although not by the many economists who argue that the benefits from the comprehensive economic and trade reforms of the 1980s are dissipating and that Australia cannot afford to rest on its laurels. To understand the success of the outcomes a brief description of the nature of the Australian economy before the reforms is needed.

THE AUSTRALIAN ECONOMY IN THE 1970S: FIXED PRICE COUNTRY

The Australian economy in the 1970s and early 1980s reflected the cumulative failure of successive governments to address major structural rigidities. These rigidities, which earned Australia the name of 'fixed price country' by the end of the 1970s, were reflected in some very poor economic outcomes: high inflation; high nominal wages growth; high and rising unemployment; intractable industrial disputes (which imposed particular costs on the resources sector as they undermined its reputation for meeting contracted outcomes); low productivity; centralized wage determination, with pattern bargaining; low innovation and investment; high real and nominal interest rates; falling terms of trade (which had been underway for many years, and which needed to be counteracted by rising productivity); rising current account deficits; and a pessimistic siege mentality towards the competitiveness challenges from globalization, especially in East Asia.

How had Australia descended to such depths following the impressive economic performances of the 1960s? How would Australia compete with the industrializing economies of the Asia Pacific, especially Japan, Singapore, Hong Kong and Korea? Would the jibes from former Singaporean Prime Minister Lee, that Australia was on track to be the poor man of Asia and that its children would be washing dishes in Singapore, prove to be accurate?

Tariff protection underpinned the so-called Australian Settlement Compact. At its heart was the concept of 'protection all around' (and compensation for the agriculture sector from its consequences). Its champion was former Trade Minister, and leader of the (then) National Party, John McEwen. As he put it (in 1968), 'I have no doubt that if there were not a proper policy of protecting Australian industry we could not continue our migration policy or employ a rapidly growing work force within Australia.'[1]

Up to the mid-1960s this statement reflected the broad view of the Australian public. To the extent that they thought about it at all, protection was viewed as justified to underpin high wages and to enable Australian industry to compete in its domestic market. The costs and consequences of protection were not yet widely known. The economic prosperity of the 1960s had not yet evolved into the stagflation of the 1970s.

That the consensus in favour of protection should change so fundamentally in such a short time, and be replaced by the unilateral trade liberalization undertaken by Hawke and Keating in the mid-to late 1980s and early 1990s, is quite remarkable. One of the factors that underpinned that change in attitudes towards protection was a widespread perception that Australia's economic performance was deteriorating in the 1970s.

At the heart of the poor economic performance was a sclerotic set of industry policies. Protection was high. Manufacturing industries were more adept at seeking and keeping protection than they were at investing and being innovative. The economy was highly unionized. Wages were determined by collective bargaining rather than market forces.[2] One union (traditionally the metal workers, whose sector enjoyed very high protection) would take the lead in wage negotiations. Whatever wage increases it could extract would become the benchmark for the rest of the economy – and be validated by the Reserve Bank via an accommodating monetary policy. The inevitable outcome was wage/price inflation. By the late 1960s all this was under challenge – by the Tariff Board, by the Treasurer and his Department, and by a small number of other politicians and journalists.

The Whitlam government (1972–1975) came to power after 27 years of Coalition governments (comprising the Liberal Party and Country, subsequently National, Party). It had a mandate to address a range of social and infrastructure issues. It stuck to its mandate, irrespective of economic conditions.[3]

Though economic reform was not prominent in its platform, in 1973 the government announced a 25 per cent tariff cut. Whitlam explained that the prime reason was

> to reduce the growth of inflation: first, by allowing more imports to satisfy consumer and producer demands and thereby restrain upward pressure growth in prices of goods in short supply and, secondly, by restraining the growth in prices of imported goods. The long term aim was to facilitate the development of a more efficient economy. (Whitlam, 1985:192)

In a policy replicated in the 1980s by Hawke and Keating, Whitlam 'established a $25 million program of assistance to employees and firms who might have been adversely affected by the tariff reduction' (Whitlam, 1985: 192).

Many economists argue that while the 25 per cent tariff cut moved policy in the right direction, its suddenness and scale were very disruptive. The lesson was, however, not lost on Hawke and Keating and their Industry Minister, John Button, who opted for the policy of successive, small and pre-announced tariff reductions.

Whitlam laid the groundwork for the unilateral trade liberalization implemented by Hawke and Keating by establishing the Industries Assistance Commission, the successor to the Tariff Board. It 'extended to all industries, primary, secondary and tertiary, a system of assistance which for the previous 50 years had applied only to manufacturing.'[4]

Whitlam was also responsible for two other issues central to the political economy of trade and economic liberalization. First, his vision encouraged a wide range of talented people to enter Parliament, which Hawke inherited when he came to power in 1983. Second, there was a desire not to repeat the economic policy errors that had characterized much of the latter period of the Whitlam government.[5] The lack of economic discipline in Whitlam's latter years was instrumental in underpinning the determination of Hawke and his senior Ministers not to repeat those errors.

Whitlam was replaced by the Fraser (coalition) government in 1975. Fraser's government has been criticized as lacking the conviction of its free market principles. It did little to address underlying economic rigidities, especially the emerging understanding that protection lay at the heart of Australia's economic problems. Its main economic policy initiative was to implement a wages and prices freeze to address strong inflationary pressures. But this addressed the symptoms rather than the causes of inflation – which was an industrial relations system reliant on protection.

The former Chairman of the Tariff Board, Alf Rattigan, has noted that protection by manufacturers

> enabled the manufacturers to make the consumer pay for the industries' industrial peace. An increase in wages could be covered by an increase in prices without any loss of sales because the industries were well insulated from import competition . . . The fact that these industries were capable of absorbing, without a loss of profitability, an increased wage bill greater than the increase in productivity thus created the precedent, and the conditions, for increased wages throughout the economy in a way which was likely to increase inflation. (Rattigan, 1986: 79)

Others have noted that while the Fraser government did not widely increase tariffs, 'it did introduce further structural assistance to affected sectors (including by lowering import quotas), which substantially increased the effective rates of assistance to those industries and slowed structural adjustment'.[6]

At the end of Fraser's government effective rates of protection in Australia had not changed much, if at all, from the levels at the end of Whitlam's government. Snape, Gropp and Luttrall provide estimates of effective rates of protection for manufacturing and agriculture between 1969–69 and 2000–01 (Snape et al., 1998:13). By the mid-1970s, average effective protection in manufacturing in was about 28 per cent – down from 36 per cent in the late 1960s (Snape et al.,1998: 13).

A former Howard Government Minister, David Kemp, who was an adviser to Malcolm Fraser, has described the conditions Fraser inherited.

> To understand the course of policy in 1976 it is important to recognise the context of government and settled policy tradition within which Fraser operated. The Australian economy in 1976, and in the decades leading up to that year, was politically managed – it might be more accurate to say interfered with – by government to a degree that we would now think was incredible and almost

> unimaginable. While the Federation policy settlement – as Paul Kelly has called it – had already begun to be dismantled – White Australia by Holt and tariff protection by Whitlam – Fraser truly stood at the transition point in relation to the role of government in the economy, and 1976 was a year that saw several of the key turning points in the management of the economy. (Kemp, 1976)

Brennan and Pincus describe the outcome of the protectionist arrangements:

> Wages boards had increased pay rates on account of profitability, which was itself boosted by tariff rises granted on account of the cost disadvantage of Australian industry caused by high wages; and so on. There was an artificiality about the economy, and an inward-orientation that to many contemporary Australian and foreign observers seemed conducive to complacency. Both the Tariff Board and tariff inquiry warned of the dangerous inculcation of what now would be called 'rent-seeking' mentality: 'The most disquieting effect of the tariff has been the stimulus it has given to demand for government assistance of all kinds, with the consequent demoralizing effect upon self-reliant efficiency throughout all forms of production.' (Brennan and Pincus, 2002: 11–12).

A GROWING UNDERSTANDING OF THE COSTS OF PROTECTION

The three key factors in Australia's unilateral trade liberalization were:

- First, the Hawke/Keating governments, both Labour governments, were prepared to implement fundamental and wide-ranging economic reforms, including unilateral trade liberalization;
- Second, the role of the Tariff Board and is successor organizations (the Industries Assistance Commission and the Productivity Commission) in systematically identifying and publicizing the costs and consequences of protection; and
- Third, a media that took the results of the Tariff Board's work and informed an increasingly economically literate (and concerned) electorate of what this meant for future living standards – and facing the competitiveness threats from globalization generally and East Asia in particular. This meant that when Hawke and Keating were prepared to undertake significant unilateral trade liberalization they had the support of elite public opinion – which increasingly understood the need for reform if Australia was to regain lost competitiveness.

Hawke was able to build on the public perception that economically Australia was adrift – and losing competitiveness to regional countries such as Singapore, Korea and Japan. While elected on a mandate of 'bringing Australia together', Hawke and Keating lost no time in addressing economic reform. The first, and arguably one of the most significant reforms was floating the dollar and deregulating the financial system.

Hawke's economic adviser, (now) Professor Ross Garnaut, has described the background to the reforms in the following terms:

> The most important change in interest group behaviour, encouraged by the Hawke leadership style, was towards the emergence of economy-wide trade union and business groups ... Economy-wide perspectives gave greater weight to the national interest in liberal trade, significantly constraining the effectiveness politically of union and business groups advocating continued or increased protection of textiles, clothing, footwear and cars. In the new climate of opinion, more favourable to liberal trade, the NFF (National Farmers Federation) and AMIC (Australian Meat Industry Council) became more active in advocating trade liberalization. The Hawke government's freedom, and willingness, to press ahead with reductions in protection was encouraged significantly by the dominance of liberal approaches to trade within the opposition parties following the departure of Malcolm Fraser. (Garnaut, 1994: 240)

Hawke himself was quite explicit.

> We have to break loose from the notion, inherent in the negotiation framework, that one's own trade liberalization is a concession granted to others ... The freedom to act against one's own underlying interests is a freedom of little value ... The educative process on the costs of protection must ... come ... predominantly from within. (Snape et al.1998: 5)

The rising current account deficit was itself a major factor stimulating the need for reform. Keating's famous 'banana republic' statement (of 1986) is worth quoting.

> If in the final analysis, Australia is so underdisciplined, so disinterested in its salvation and its economic well being, [the] fall back solution is inevitable because you can't fund $12 billion [current account deficit] in perpetuity ... Then you have gone. You are a banana republic. (Snape et al.1998: 85)

This comment was widely reported. It came as a shock. It made people aware of their economic predicament. It helped make the public accept the need for reform – as long as the pain was shared in a socially acceptable way. It was reflected in a comment by John Button, Hawke's Industry Minister on the feeling of the new Hawke government: 'Most of us thought that Australia had slipped behind. There was a sense of wanting to get on with it, to get out of the economic recession and make some fundamental changes' (Button, 1998: 226).

Critical in this transformation was the change within the Australian Labour Party itself. Former Finance Minister Peter Walsh noted that:

> Most telling of all was the fact, finally driven into the (Labour) Party psyche, that protection at the same rate and on the same products had the same effect as sales tax on income distribution. Moreover, ABS (Australian Bureau of Statistics) Household Expenditure surveys showed that the proportion of income spent on clothing and footwear by the lowest income decile was nearly three times as high as that for the highest income decile. ...After this material was circulated in Caucus, the Left did not know how to deal with its dilemma – how to oppose consumption taxes that may or may not have been regressive, but simultaneously support protective measures which were demonstrably regressive. It still doesn't know because there is no answer. (Walsh, 1995: 34)

One of Australia's most eminent journalists, Paul Kelly, observed that the success of the Australian Labour Party, both nationally and at the state level, was underpinned by 'better leadership, Cabinet authority over the party, and internal unity which amounted to superior political skills.' (Kelly, 1994: 29)

THE ROLE OF THE TARIFF BOARD AND ITS SUCCESSOR ORGANIZATIONS

Party unity is a necessary but not always sufficient condition for successful reform. Institutional strength and quality are equally important. The institution with the greatest influence on dismantling Australia's high tariff levels was the Tariff Board and its successor organizations – the Industries Assistance Commission and the Productivity Commission.

Snape et al. have observed that

> to the extent that authorities such as the Tariff Board are established to deflect the direct pressure of vested interests away from governments, the more the authorities' decisions are overruled by the governments, the less useful they are to the government and the more likely governments are to attract the flak. The Tariff Board therefore could and did have a major role in tariff-making, a role that was not always in conformity with the Government's apparent wishes. (1998:22–3)

Snape et al. quote extensively from letters between former Trade Minister McEwen and Tariff Board Chairman Rattigan, which gives the flavour of the political pressures under which the Tariff Board operated in its early days.[7]

Kelly argues that

> The three greatest opponents of McEwenism had been Liberal Treasurer Billy McMahon, the chairman of the Tariff Board, Alf Rattigan, and Gough Whitlam. The final defeat of McEwenism was a triumph of a properly

> functioning democracy. It sprang from an irony, McEwen's misjudgement of Rattigan whom he appointed to head the Tariff Board only to discover that 'his man' became a convert to free trade. In 1966 Rattigan used the Tariff Board to embark upon a review of tariff assistance to every industry, the publication of the level of effective protection for each industry, and encouragement of a public debate about the costs of protection. Rattigan realized that once the true cost was laid on the bar of public opinion then protection was doomed. Secrecy was the lifeblood of Australian protection and Rattigan stripped it away in an epic battle with McEwen. (Kelly, 1994: 44)

Rattigan has provided some useful insights into how the Tariff Board managed to undertake its analyses and overcome political opposition from Trade Ministers McEwen and Anthony and the protectionist instincts of the major manufacturing industries. He refers to the consequences of 'excess protection', which were 'concentrated in the sections of the tariff protecting the production of machinery and fabricated metal products, and the Board's inquiries had shown that reductions of at least 50 per cent were necessary.' (Rattigan, 1986: 132)

In its 1966–67 Annual Report the Tariff Board noted that 'From its study of the structure and levels of protection the Board proposes to establish an initial classification of industries into those which have: (a) a high level of protection, (b) a medium level of protection, and (c) a low level of protection in relation to the overall structure of assistance which Australian import competing industries operate.' (Snape et al., 1998: 45) The Tariff Board went further in its 1967–68 Annual Report, arguing that it

> would usually regard new activities with low protective requirements – that is, 25 per cent or less in effective rate terms – as worthy of encouragement. ... The Board's attitude to new ventures requiring effective protection of from 25 to 50 per cent would be influenced by its assessment of their future prospects and the likely effects on other industries. On the other hand, it would be unlikely to recommend effective protection of more than 50 per cent on other than a short-term basis for any new venture, including an extension of existing production. (Snape et al., 1998: 46–7)

Rattigan singles out the lack of transparency behind high tariff levels:

> There was no possibility of replacing the huge amount of assistance the manufacturers received through the tariff with tax concessions or subsidies. Even if it were possible, the manufacturers would not want it because subsidies were regularly reviewed by the Parliament and tax concessions generally did not have the 'permanence' of Customs duties. (Rattigan, 1986: 135)

The Tariff Board had laid down a very clear set of markers for judging the merit of assistance: preference would be given to encouraging industries with lower protection against those requiring higher levels of assistance.

This was a major point of departure for tariff policy in Australia. By publicly revealing the levels of effective protection, and making the case strongly against allowing an expansion of industries that depended on high levels of protection, the Tariff Board had achieved two very significant outcomes. First, it had, as Kelly has observed, 'laid bare' the costs of protection. Second, it had provided the information for a vigorous public debate on the costs and benefits of protection.

Rattigan puts the issue succinctly:

> Because of the great complexity of many government measures used to assist industries in all sectors of the economy, only an organization capable of obtaining from various sources a wide range of data and carrying out sophisticated analyses can provide worthwhile information on the costs and consequences of industry assistance. To ensure, as far as possible, that the information produced is objective, the organization should be divorced from the normal government administration and its investigations and reports should be open to public scrutiny. (Rattigan, 1986: 276)

A reading of Rattigan's battles with protectionist Ministers emphasizes the validity of his conclusion – and demonstrates that without an independent Tariff Board and a media prepared to propagate its key conclusions, unilateral tariff reform in Australia would not have occurred when and on the scale that it did.

Newspapers, especially the *Australian Financial Review*, *The Australian* and *The Age*, vigorously promoted a debate about the costs of protection. The Tariff Board's reports, and those of its successor organizations, received extensive media coverage. Opinion pieces by academic economists reinforced an understanding of the costs of protection. From around the late 1960s, the costs of protection were becoming increasingly understood – not only by elite opinion but among the general public. As Rattigan has observed, 'Immediately after the Board's [1969–70 annual] report was released, and for a long time afterwards, the press highlighted the figure of $2700 million [as the total cost of protection]. (Rattigan, 1986: 78)

Snape et al. observed that

> Over the next few years industry and protection policy was a battleground. On the one side were ranged many of the heavily protected industries and their industry associations ... and the Trade Ministry; on the other were the Tariff Board, much of the economic press, most academic economists with interests in international trade and primary industry organisations – though not the leadership of the political party that represented farmers, the Country Party – and a lone politician, Bert Kelly. One of the main weapons of those in the freer trade camp was to bring the battle into the open. 'Public scrutiny' or 'transparency' of policy became the banner under which the Tariff Board and its successor, the IAC, were to fight. (1998: 21)

DISMANTLING PROTECTION

The story of the dismantling of protection in Australia is one of governments progressively responding to the challenges of globalization – and the realization that protection was not only not succeeding in creating the dynamic and competitive industries that Australia required, but was, on the contrary, imposing high costs on the most competitive areas of the economy: agriculture and mining.

The first major step was the 25 per cent tariff cut by the Whitlam government in 1973. There is general agreement that while a move in the right direction, the size and unexpected nature of this decision made the adjustment costs higher than they could or should have been. This decision informed the gradualist approach adopted by the Hawke–Keating governments.

The next major policy development was the May 1988 Economic Statement by the Treasurer, Paul Keating – which received the strong support of Industry Minister Button, who demonstrated a steely determination to confront those sectors which stood to lose from lower protection.[8] This statement announced that 'over a transitional period to 1992, tariffs greater than 15 per cent are to be phased down to that level, except for textiles, clothing, footwear and passenger cars; tariffs between 10 per cent to 15 per cent were to phase down to 10 per cent; and a "revenue duty" of 2 per cent was abolished'. (Snape et al., 1998: 29)

It is worth quoting from Hawke's statement of 12 March, 1991, in which he announced a further substantial tariff reduction programme:

> Right from the start, this Government deliberately and determinedly set about pulling down the tariff walls. By 1992 our existing programs will have slashed the nominal rate of assistance to the manufacturing sector by over one third, from 13 per cent to 8 per cent, and the effective rate from 22 per cent to 12 per cent. Tariff cuts presented Australian manufacturers with a major challenge. To their credit, many of them are meeting that challenge. Their endeavours are too rarely appreciated and their success too often underestimated. (Snape et al., 1998: 94)

Hawke went on to announce further tariff reduction plans. The general level of assistance was reduced from 10 per cent and 15 per cent in 1992 to 5 per cent by 1996. Tariffs on passenger motor vehicles were phased down from 35 per cent in 1992 in annual steps of 2.5 percentage points to 15 per cent in 2000. Tariff reductions on textiles, clothing and footwear were accelerated so that the maximum tariff was 25 per cent by the year 2000; the termination of quotas was brought forward two years to 1 March 1993. Finally, general agricultural assistance was reduced in line with the pace of tariff reform in manufacturing.

It should be noted that under Hawke tariffs were reduced *unilaterally*.

They were not tied to GATT negotiations. This reflected recognition that the benefits of reform flowed to the liberalizer.[9]

Michael Emmery has noted that

> The … announcements in 1991 were accompanied by some of the strongest statements made by Australian politicians in favour of trade liberalisation. Interestingly they were made at a time of economic recession and high unemployment. Prime Minister Hawke stated: 'Mr Speaker, the most powerful spur to greater competitiveness is further tariff reduction. Tariffs have been one of the abiding features of the Australian economy since Federation. Tariffs protected Australian industry by making foreign goods more expensive here; and the supposed virtues of this protection became deeply embedded in the psyche of the nation. But what in fact was the result? Inefficient industries that could not compete overseas; and higher prices for consumers and higher costs for our efficient primary producers. Worse still, tariffs are a regressive burden – the poorest Australians are hurt more than the richest.'
>
> Treasurer Keating was equally damning of the tariff: 'The package of measures announced today ends forever Australia's sorry association with the tariff as a device for industrial development. By turning its back on tariffs, Australia will be further propelled in its quest for international trade and efficiency, a search begun with the opening up of the economy in 1983 when we floated the dollar and abolished exchange controls. As in all nations before it, the pursuit of trade and competition has instilled in Australia a thirst for greater efficiency at home and a larger dominion abroad.'[10]

It is true, as Emmery has observed, that these statements were made during a recession. But this recession accentuated the need for such unilateral trade liberalization; the public came to the view that the costs of retaining protection were just too high.

Emmery notes further the complementary reforms introduced by the government.

> The recession continued through 1992 and Prime Minister Keating introduced a range of measures to facilitate business growth and generate employment. These were outlined in his *One Nation* statement on 26 February 1992 and the *Investing in the Nation* statement on 9 February 1993. Measures announced in these packages included accelerated depreciation for plant and equipment, reduction in the company tax rate, measures to facilitate major projects and a number of incentives to encourage exports and innovation, as well as a range of initiatives to assist training and job creation. These positive measures no doubt helped to detract attention from the critics of trade liberalisation and the across-the-board program to reduce tariffs announced in 1991 continued to operate as scheduled. (Emmery, 1999: 2)

In commenting on the tariff cuts, Snape et al. have observed that

> In an Australian context this was a bold and decisive move – comparable with the 25 per cent tariff cut in 1973. The explicit justification for it was more firmly

> based on economic theory and international experience than that earlier cut, tariffs being more directly relevant to economic efficiency than macroeconomic performance (though the two are not unconnected). The government had accepted – and had decided that voters would also accept – that the costs of transition were smaller than the costs of inaction. Many observers have identified the 'Banana Republic' comments by the Treasurer, on 14 May 1986, as a key factor in turning public perceptions, and were somewhat surprised that there was no significant policy action at that time. (1998: 29–30)

Central to the industry accepting reductions in protection were the accompanying adjustment assistance arrangements. These budgetary assistance measures, which accompanied the structural adjustment programmes that came with tariff liberalization, fell into three broad categories:

- output bounties (which currently apply to books and shipbuilding, and previously to computers, machine tools, textile yarns and steel mill products)
- export incentives to specific industries, namely passenger motor vehicles (PMV), textiles, clothing and footwear (TCF) and pharmaceutical industries and also general grants for Export Market Development, and
- incentives and other support for R&D, innovation, small and medium sized enterprises and world best practice programmes.

Emmery provides data on the average nominal and effective rates of assistance for the total manufacturing sector, and for three of the more highly protected industries (textiles, clothing and footwear, and motor vehicles and parts; see Figures 2.1 and 2.2).

Emmery's conclusions regarding the trends in assistance to manufacturing between 1990 and 2000 are as follows:

> - The trade liberalisation process in Australia started with the 25 per cent across-the-board tariff cut in July 1973. This reduced the average nominal rate of assistance for manufacturing from 22 to 17 per cent and the average effective rate from 35 to 27 per cent.
> - The next decade from 1974–75 to 1984–85 witnessed a stable average level of protection for the manufacturing sector as a whole but some marked changes in the assistance afforded different industries within the sector.
> - Assistance to the textiles, clothing and footwear and passenger motor vehicle industries blew out over this period under a regime of tariff and quota arrangements and the local content plans for passenger motor vehicles. The average effective rate for textiles increased from 39 per cent in 1974–75 to 75 per cent in 1984–85; the corresponding rate for clothing and footwear rose from 87 per cent to 250 per cent over this period; and for passenger motor vehicles and parts, from 54 per cent to 143 per cent.

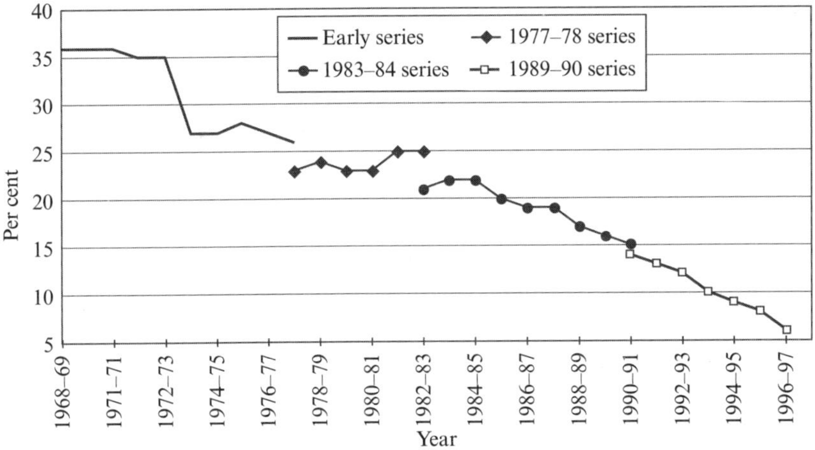

Source: Industry Commission, 'Assistance to Agriculture and Manufacturing Industry', Information Paper, March 1995, as reproduced in Emmery (1999).

Figure 2.1 Average effective rates of assistance to manufacturing, 1968–69 to 1996–97

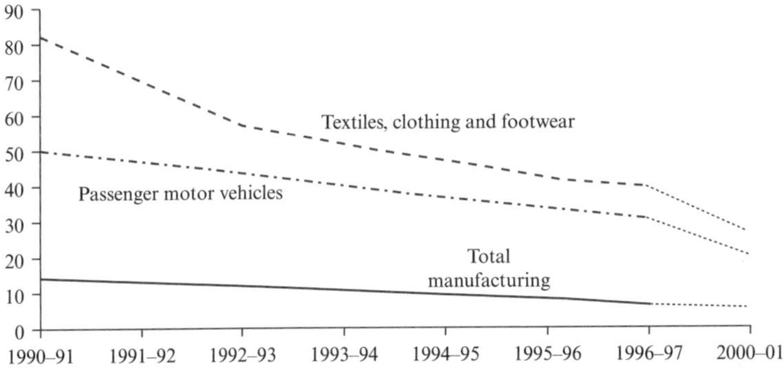

Source: Productivity Commission, Trade and Assistance Review, 1997–98.

Figure 2.2 Average effective rates of assistance to manufacturing PMV and TCF, 1990–91 to 2000–01

- The large increases in assistance to the above three industries were offset by declining assistance to a wide range of other manufacturing industries as part of the Tariff Review Program.
- The subsequent period from 1984–85 to the present and continuing to 2000–01 has seen a continuous, almost linear, decline in the level of assistance to the manufacturing sector and in this period, textiles, clothing and

footwear and motor vehicles have been key elements of the trade liberalisation process.

The final point, which Emmery and others have identified, is that there are important differences between industry assistance delivered via tariffs, and assistance delivered via less specific measures such as R&D support and export and innovation incentives. The latter are sector-neutral, and more transparent. Tariffs, on the other hand, lack transparency, and are less contestable than direct budgetary assistance (including R&D support), which must be defended in annual budgets. (Emmery, 1999: 6–7)

A former senior public servant observed to the author that the dismantling of protection induced demands for the wider microeconomic reforms undertaken by Hawke and Keating. Industry representatives argued strongly to senior Ministers that as they had lost their tariff protection, the Government had an obligation to pursue further microeconomic reform. The argument was that the economy needed to become as efficient as possible to enable firms that had lost tariff protection to be able to compete. Industry argued that input costs for manufacturing needed to be lowered via more vigorous competition policy – and especially for key inputs such as gas and electricity.[11]

Australia's unilateral tariff reductions could only succeed if they happened progressively in small, pre-announced, increments. In the auto sector, for example, the slow pace of tariff reduction was informed by an understanding that fixed costs were large and investment horizons long. Time was needed for the capital stock to adjust to lower tariffs. This also meant there was a consensus that there needed to be structural adjustment programmes, especially retraining, for those who had lost their jobs. Retraining programmes were complemented by programmes to encourage investment in new technology and research and development. The objective was to encourage firms to move up the value chain.

STRUCTURAL ADJUSTMENT ASSISTANCE AND EQUITY

How to absorb the labour released by lower tariffs was a major preoccupation. Peter Walsh has put the issue succinctly:

> An IAC report in 1977 showed that far from being the decentralized industries they purported to be, they (textiles, clothing and footwear) were heavily concentrated in capital cities, in the south-east, and particularly in Melbourne. Claims that these industries were essential for the employment of otherwise unemployable females were confounded by the fact that female unemployment

> in such states like WA (Western Australia), with virtually no such industry, was no higher than in Melbourne or elsewhere.[12]

Garnaut emphasizes equity issues: 'The Australian compulsory-voting democracy required market-oriented reform to be taken forward within wider policies that acknowledged traditional Australian concern for equitable distribution' (2002: 7). Garnaut draws a wider conclusion about the importance of matching economic reform with distributive equity:

> Prime Minister Hawke's Economic Statement of March 1991 announced the reduction of tariff protection to below the low levels in place at the beginning of the century. Considerable flexibility in wage determination was introduced under the Labour Governments and extended by the Howard Coalition after 1996. In wages policy, however, neither the shift nor the extension extended to 'safety net' minimum wages, which after a period of moderation within the (wages and incomes) Accord rose more rapidly in real terms in the last 5 years of the century than over any comparably long period from the original adoption of the Harvester (wage) Judgment approach (in 1905), excepting only the years of the Whitlam Labour Government in the mid-1970s. (2002: 7)

A concern for equity had other implications. Garnaut argues that

> The policies of 'protection-all-round' owed a great deal to the Australian concern for horizontal equity. Tariff protection for manufacturing industries and fiscal subsidies of various kinds had a large and inequitable effect on the vertical distribution of income, but were broadly accepted as being fair to the extent that they seemed to be applied equitably across producers of various goods. (2002:15).

The need to compensate the losers from structural adjustment was made very clear by Hawke in his 1991 Statement – Building a Competitive Australia:

> Throughout my public life it has been my firm conviction that if the community believes that change is necessary in the interests of the community as a whole, then that belief carries with it a necessary corollary – that the community must not leave those individuals or groups who are adversely affected to bear the whole burden of change. It must itself be prepared to share that burden of change, as well as reaping the benefits of change. Accordingly, we will establish labour adjustment programs to assist displaced workers in our car and textiles, clothing and footwear industries with relocation, training and wage subsidies for redeployment to other jobs. This will cost at least $90 million over the life of the programs. (Snape et al., 1998: 95–5)

Hawke reflected on reform and equity after his political career ended:

> As with the approach to tariff reductions, the readiness of the community to accept change, and continuing macro and micro economic reform more

> generally, will be a function of its perception that the rewards of growth are equitably distributed. This was the point of the Accord processes. Under those processes the tendency towards a widening dispersion of market income was offset by a combination of more progressive tax scales and means-tested cash transfer systems. I do not assert that we got everything right nor do I argue for a revival of the Accord. But I do assert that those basic objectives remain indispensable to growth with cohesion. (1999a)

SOME WIDER POLITICAL AND POLICY ISSUES

The wide-ranging microeconomic reforms, which were started by Whitlam, were in limbo during Fraser's government, accelerated by Hawke and Keating, and taken further by Howard (for example in industrial relations and tax policy), need to be seen in the context of the internationalization of the Australian economy. Tariff reductions did not take place in isolation.

It is widely accepted in Australia that it would have been better off if tariffs had been lowered during the 1960s when growth was strong. But history, both in Australia and elsewhere, suggests that unilateral reform does not happen when times are good. It takes a sense of economic crisis to make the public accept the pain of reform for the longer-term benefits reform delivers.

The tariff and other microeconomic reforms need to be seen in the context of the Australian community waking up to their predicament: the prosperity that appeared never ending in the 1960s came to a shuddering halt by the mid-1970s. East Asia was growing strongly and posing a major challenge to the heavily protected manufacturing sector. The current account deficits, as reflected in Keating's 'banana republic' remarks, jibes by Singapore Prime Minister Lee, stagflation and the growing perception that Australia could not afford to stand still in the face of the Asian challenge were also instrumental in preparing the ground for major change.

What had been so conspicuously lacking under previous governments was political courage. Hawke and Keating and their talented team of Ministers and advisers were the spark needed to take advantage of the political conditions that had gradually emerged over the previous 15 years – and reflected in a public looking for a new direction and willing to reward rather than punish governments prepared to undertake economic reform.

Hawke's political skills were critical. He was elected with a vague mandate of 'bringing Australia together'.[13] He did not have a mandate for radical economic reform. What he did have was a capacity to relate to the Australian people. And he had close links with the trade union movement from his previous experience as President of the Australian Council of Trade Unions.

Observers have argued that it took someone with the Cold War political credentials of former Presidents Nixon and Reagan to establish a dialogue with China and Russia respectively. The same can be said of Hawke and the trade union movement: it would have been much more difficult for a conservative politician to persuade workers in protected sectors that they needed to give up their privileged position for the good of the wider community – and to accept the significant decline in real wages under the Accord with the trade unions that was required to increase the profit share and hence underpin investment.

This was achieved by persuading workers to satisfy wage demands in the form of government superannuation contributions rather than as nominal wages. There is near universal agreement among economists in Australia that this was instrumental in breaking the back of wage inflation and in enabling a substantial shift to profits. Other commentators have argued that in the end the Accord acted as a constraint on reform as it effectively allowed the trade union movement a seat at the Cabinet table – and gave them a veto on reform initiatives.

The Reserve Bank of Australia has concluded that 'The wage pause and the Prices and Incomes Accord restrained real wages, encouraging a shift in the capital/labour ratio. (Reserve Bank of Australia Bulletin, 1995: 41) Hawke's own assessment is worth noting:

> Increases in money wages need not be seen as the only mechanism by which to achieve this goal of equity. Under the Accord which operated throughout the period of my Prime Ministership, the trade union movement accepted restraint in movements in money wages in return for improvements in the social wage, particularly but not exclusively, in the areas of education and health. While these benefits had a more general application, the government and the trade unions accepted that because of the application of means-testing provisions, the greatest beneficiaries were those at the lower end of the wage scale. (Hawke, 1999b)

Similar credit needs to be given to Keating's political skills. He gave the Australian public a crash course in the need for microeconomic reform – as reflected in his quotation presented at the start of this chapter. To take Keating's saying to its logical conclusion, parrots were able to speak about microeconomic reform as they had heard so much of it from Keating himself. As former Industry Minister Button has observed, 'Keating talked as if it was some sort of natural meritocracy. I remember his finger jabbing the air somewhere in front my chest. "You've got to remember, mate, we're here because we're the best"' (Button, 1998: 226) Paul Kelly argues that in retaining John Stone as Treasury Secretary, 'Keating, alive to the Whitlam legacy, was sending a message: this Labour administration believed in harnessing the support of the economic institutions.' (1994: 58)

Former Finance Minister Walsh has emphasized Keating's highly effective political skills:

> Apart from two lapses, one rhetorical and the other substantial, Keating has maintained the commitment to free trade and an open economy which he developed in the 1980s. In late 1992 his rhetorical flourishes, which were supported by what remains of the once formidable protection lobby, blew the modest difference between the Opposition and the Government tariff policy out to a life or death matter. (1995: 252)

Finally, the role played by Hawke's advisers, principally Ross Garnaut, deserves mention. In his writings on economic reform in Australia, Garnaut does not acknowledge his own contribution. This despite Paul Kelly's observation that, 'Ed Visbord [an economic adviser in Hawke's office] said later "Hawke never took advice on a single economic issue unless it coincided with that of Ross Garnaut"'. Kelly concludes that 'Garnaut was a strategic thinker whose influence on Hawke was never remotely matched by any subsequent economic advisor.' (1994: 58)

THE POLITICAL ECONOMY OF UNILATERAL TRADE LIBERALIZATION

A precondition for persuading the public of the need for trade liberalization is to inculcate an understanding of the costs and consequences of protection. The Tariff Board and its successor organizations, together with a media that was prepared to take the results of this research and educate the public, played a pivotal role in preparing the ground and changing public attitudes. It is important to understand that Tariff Board reports were credible in the public eye, as they came from an independent body. There was no question of the Government 'leaning on' Tariff Board authorities to come to particular conclusions – despite considerable tension between the Board and particular Ministers in the early years. This demonstrates clearly the value of having an independent organization undertake research on the costs of protection.

The Chairman of the Productivity Commission, Gary Banks, has observed that the vast majority of Australia's reforms have 'stuck' over the longer term, citing tariff liberalization and the development of a competition policy as the two prime examples. This durability is attributed to independent, credible, and transparent policy research and formulation. 'The institutions and implementation strategies ... were devised to promote an awareness of the benefits from reform, to help build political support, weaken resistance and promote adjustment'. (Banks, 2005: 28) Banks concludes that 'Political leadership is critical to structural reform, but its influence on policy in the longer term can be ephemeral. Its most enduring legacy may well come from more fundamental actions to entrench institutions and processes that can facilitate ongoing reform beyond the life of any one government' (2005: 29)

Nevertheless, reforms along the lines undertaken in Australia require impressive political and communication skills. Australia was fortunate that Hawke and Keating came to power when they did. The ground had been prepared by independent research, communicated through an effective media, to the extent that by the time Hawke and Keating came to power and were prepared to undertake necessary reforms, they were 'pushing on an open door'. But there was nothing inevitable about what they did. It took very considerable political courage to undertake the wholesale trade and economic reforms there were implemented progressively from 1983 onwards.

Central to that political management was an acceptance that the losers from reform needed to be compensated. Equity is deeply engrained in the Australian psychology. Appropriately designed adjustment assistance, especially retraining but also programmes to encourage investment, innovation and research and development expenditure, were central to the reform effort. Yet the Australian experience also demonstrates that adjustment packages need to be carefully designed, sequenced and targeted. It is easy to waste resources and to over-compensate losers.

There is now no argument in Australia that there should be a return to protection, albeit that the need for a more interventionist 'industry policy' never dies. It can be argued that the demise of protection has been aided in Australia by timing: to have reformed the Australian economy in time to take advantage of the commodities boom from the rapid increase in global growth from China and India. Luck played a part. But Australia made its own luck by ambitious unilateral trade liberalization and complementary microeconomic reform.

NOTES

1. Snape et al. (1998: 53).
2. Union wage-negotiating behaviour flowed from the so-called 'harvester judgment' in 1905, whereby the wages required to keep a family at a decent standard of living were determined in a court.
3. Whitlam would reportedly turn to his election manifesto after Cabinet meetings and tick off commitments.

4. Whitlam (1985: 192) 192. A former senior public servant has observed to the author that Whitlam threatened to resign if his Caucus (the members of the Federal Parliamentary Labour party) refused to agree to the establishment of the IAC.
5. Whitlam was well aware of the problems flowing from the wage-setting mechanism in Australia. 'The chief economic failure of my Government resulted from the wage explosion of 1974. In part, our failure was a failure of communication, our failure to persuade the trade union movement to accept the central concept of Labour's program ... The specific origins of the wages explosion of 1974 can be traced to the decisions of the 1960s under Australia's unique system of industrial relations established before World War I ... The main cause of industrial conflict was not disputes over wages but disputes over managerial policy and physical working conditions'. (Whitlam, 1985: 198).
6. de Brouwer (2003: 3). The effective rate of protection includes the additional benefit that industries which enjoy protection have from securing access to imported inputs at low or zero tariff rates.
7. Snape et al. quote a letter from Tariff Board Chairman Rattigan to Trade Minister McEwen: 'I submit that if the Board were to accept a directive which is not apparent to all interested parties a situation would be created where the Board would appear to have formulated its recommendations on the basis of its examination of the evidence presented at its inquiry whereas the recommendations would in fact reflect a view reached by the Government of the Minister before the Board's inquiry – a view which might in some cases be contrary to the weight of evidence presented at the inquiry and the Board's judgement based on that evidence. Would this situation not constitute a danger to the whole Tariff Board system?' Snape et al., 1998: 51.
8. Button was instrumental in securing agreement to various industry 'plans'. They reflected the reality of sunk costs – and that if capital-intensive industries such as automotive were to become more competitive they needed time to adjust and structural adjustment assistance – especially for re-training.
9. A former senior official in the (then) Ministry of Trade has advised the author that the prospect of using the unilateral tariff reductions as part of Australia's multilateral trade diplomacy did not inform the Government's approach to unilateral tariff reductions. Ministry of Trade officials subsequently used the reductions in the Uruguay Round. But Ministry of Trade officials played no role in designing the tariff reduction programme. Another official has advised the author that unilateral tariff reductions gave Australia the credibility to lead the Cairns Group. This official contrasted this approach with Trade Ministers returning from negotiations in the Tokyo Round and earlier declaiming publicly how they had successfully resisted pressures to reduce tariffs.
10. Emmery (1999). A useful summary of the other microeconomic reforms can be found in an article by Productivity Chairman Banks: 'Structural reform Australian-style: lessons for others?' pages 6 and 7, at http://www.pc.gov.au/speeches/cs20050601/cs20050601.pdf, page 6. These are summarized by Banks as capital markets, infrastructure, labour markets, human services, 'National Competition policy' reforms, macroeconomic policy and taxation reform.
11. This is an interesting counterpoint to the tariff compensation argument that prevailed prior to the dismantling of tariff protection – whereby agriculture needed to be compensated for the higher costs of tariff protection.
12. Walsh (1995: 35). One of the arguments in favour of protection is that without it there would be no TCF industry – which was a major employer of migrant women who lacked other skills. This argument carried significant weight in public opinion until the Tariff Board and its successor organizations published estimates of the costs of providing protection to sustain these jobs.
13. An insight into Hawke's consensual approach to politics, which was one of the factors that enabled him to persuade the public of the need for unilateral trade liberalization, can be seen from the following observation he has made: 'government should not regard one side of the industrial relationship as "the enemy". The unprecedented decline in industrial disputes during our period of office was not simply a function of our

co-operation with the trade union movement. We made the employers equal partners in the work of the Economic Planning Advisory Council and our doors were always open to them. Some groups and individuals on both sides have often acted with scant regard for the public interest but the reality is that trade unions and employer organisations are central and legitimate parts of our economic and social fabric.' (Hawke, 1999b)

REFERENCES

Banks, G. (2005), 'Structural reform Australian-style: lessons for others?', available at http://www.pc.gov.au/Speeches/cs20050201.pdf.

Brennan, G. and J. Pincus (2002), 'From the Australian settlement to microeconomic reform: the change in twentieth century policy regimes', Discussion Paper No. 0213, July Centre of International Economic Studies.

Bureau of Industry Economics (1995), 'Setting the scene: monitoring microeconomic reform', December, at http://www.pc.gov.au/bie/report/96-01/96-01.pdf.

Button, John (1998), *As it Happened*, Melbourne: the Text Publishing Company.

de Brouwer, G. (2003), 'Economic reform and growth in Australia', paper prepared for the Australian Studies Association of Japan Symposium in Nagoya, 14–15 June.

Emmery, Michael (1999), 'Australian manufacturing: a brief history of industry policy and trade liberalisation', at http://www.aph.gov.au/Library/Pubs/rp/1999-2000/2000rp07.html.

Garnaut, Ross (1994), 'Trade and tariffs in Australian business', in Randall G Stewart (ed.) *Government and Business Relations in Australia*, St Leonards, NSW: Allen and Unwin.

Garnaut, Ross (2002), 'Equity and Australian development: lessons from the first century', at http://rspas.anu.deu.au/economics/publish/papers/garnaut/2002_0726_Equity.pdf.

Hawke, R.J.L. (1999a), Opening address to the Australia Unlimited Conference', Melbourne, 4 May at http://www.unisa.edu.au/hawkecentre/library/speeches/1999_may_unlimited.asp.

Hawke, R.J.L. (1999b), 'Speech in honour of Sir Richard Kirby', at http://www.unisa.edu.au/hawkecentre/library/speeches/1999_april_kirby.asp.

Kelly, Paul (1994), *The End of Certainty: Power, Politics and Business in Australia,* St Leonards, NSW: Allen and Unwin.

Kemp, David (1976), *Australian Government, National Archives of Australia,* '1976 Cabinet Records', Advisors and Decisions, http://www.naa.gov.an/collection/explore/cabinet/by-year/1976-advisers-decisions, aspx

Rattigan, Alf (1986), *Industry Assistance: The Inside Story,* Carlton, Victoria: Melbourne University Press.

Reserve Bank of Australia Bulletin (1995), 'Productivity and Growth', at http://www.rba.gov.au/PublicationsandResearch/Bulletin/bu_oct95/bu_1095_5.pdf.

Snape, R., L. Gropp and T. Luttrell (1998), *Australian Trade Policy, 1965–1997: A Documentary History*, St Leonards, NSW: Allen & Unwin.

Walsh, Peter (1995), *Confessions of a Failed Finance Minister*, Milsons Point, NSW: Random House.

Whitlam, Gough (1983), *The Whitlam Government: 1972–1975*, Melbourne: Viking.

3. Chile

Sebastián Herreros[1]

INTRODUCTION

Chile is widely seen today as an example of a country that has successfully liberalized its economy, both internally and externally. In the area of trade policy, this process started with the radical reforms undertaken in the mid-1970s. While the broad thrust of Chilean trade policy shows substantial continuity over the last three decades, there have been significant changes in the relative emphasis of that policy. Between 1973 and 1989 it was based almost exclusively on unilateral opening (along with participation in multilateral negotiations), whereas since 1990 it has evolved towards a 'multi-track' approach. The latter combines further unilateral opening with a continued commitment to multilateralism and a growing emphasis on bilateral and regional negotiations. This chapter attempts to explain the evolution of Chilean trade policy since the mid-1970s, in the context of a political economy analysis. This will include the economic rationale for the reforms, as well as the role played by foreign policy considerations, international actors, ideology and interest groups. The evolution of other economic policies, especially those affecting foreign investment, is examined as relevant context for the trade policy reforms.

The second section briefly reviews Chile's economic policies during the import-substitution stage. The third and fourth sections examine the trade and complementary reforms implemented during the period of military rule (1973–89) and under democracy (1990 to the present). The fifth section looks at the impact of these reforms on the overall performance of the Chilean economy. The sixth section identifies the main challenges Chile faces in order to continue benefiting from its integration into the world economy. In the final section some conclusions are drawn, including on the relevance of the Chilean case for other developing countries.

THE IMPORT-SUBSTITUTION PERIOD

The Great Depression of the 1930s had such a negative impact on the Chilean economy[2] that it caused a radical change in its development pattern: from an outward-oriented economy, heavily dependent on mineral exports (nitrate and later copper), to an inward-oriented one, with a focus on industrialization. This shift was reinforced by the scarcity of imported goods caused by the Second World War (Meller, 1996). Over the next decades, Chile resorted to a host of tools in order to promote industrialization, such as exchange controls, multiple exchange rates, high import tariffs, export taxes, import licences, import quotas, import prohibitions, credit rationing and different types of subsidies. This was often done at the expense of the agricultural and mining sectors, which were subject to high taxes and fixed prices.

The United Nations Economic Commission for Latin America (ECLAC), created in 1948 and headquartered in Chile's capital Santiago, was very influential in spreading the paradigm of industrialization through import-substitution across the region. The best known exponent of this 'development from within' paradigm in the Latin American context was the Argentinean economist Raul Prebisch, who was also ECLAC's Executive Secretary from 1950 to 1963.

Fontaine (1993) labelled Chile's socio-economic model prior to 1973 'the redistributive State' and argued that the country was during this period a typical case of a rent-seeking society. From a distributive point of view, the model had a clear pro-urban bias. It favoured urban consumers through capped prices for basic agricultural products. Import-substitution policies also favoured industrial entrepreneurs and workers, especially those unionized, who were also urban dwellers. This pattern was consistent with the political landscape during most of the import-substitution period, characterized by a small electorate dominated by urban voters.

In Chile, the import-substitution model delivered only modest GDP growth, averaging 3.8 per cent a year between 1940 and 1970 (Meller, 1996). It was also characterized by high inflation, chronic fiscal deficits, frequent balance of payments crises and an overgrown public sector. While the share of manufacturing in GDP climbed from 13 per cent in 1925 to about 25 per cent in 1970, large segments of Chilean industry were internationally uncompetitive. Import-substitution was especially unsuitable for a country like Chile with a small internal market. Moreover, it led to the stagnation of the agricultural sector and discouraged exports (Eyzaguirre et al. 2005).

The evidence suggests that the 'easy stage' of import-substitution was over in Chile by the mid-1950s (De la Cuadra and Hachette, 1988; Stallings and Brock, 1993). However, the overall model was by and large maintained since then by successive administrations of different political sign.[3] This is explained in good measure by the fact that most entrepreneurs either adhered to or acquiesced with the concept of a 'mixed economy', in which the State has an entrepreneurial role and also promotes economic activity (Valdés, 1995). This was obviously especially the case for industrial entrepreneurs who benefited most directly from import-substitution policies. As Fontaine argues, the model enjoyed a significant 'social consensus' during the 1940s and 1950s (Fontaine, 1993).

The social consensus gradually began to unravel towards the end of the 1950s, as a consequence of two big trends: a massive increase in the electorate, with the entry of previously disenfranchised segments such as women and illiterate peasants,[4] and a deceleration of economic growth due to the numerous distortions produced by the import-substitution model.[5] The result was that, at the same time that large, poor and mostly rural segments of society entered the political game for the first time, the capacity of the system to deliver on their demands was drastically reduced. This led to a radicalization of the social and political process, especially in the late 1960s, which in turn brought about a hardening of positions by the entrepreneurial movement and the increased unity between its different components.

In particular, the process of Agrarian Reform launched under President Frei Montalva's Christian-Democrat administration (1964–70) sparked a process of defensive organization across the different entities representing the entrepreneurial sector (agriculture, industry, mining, commerce). These left their considerable differences aside and formed a common bloc aimed at the defence of private property (Valdés, 1995).

In 1970 Salvador Allende, from the Socialist Party, took office as President, having obtained only 36 per cent of the votes in the elections that year. He was backed by the Popular Unity left-wing coalition, whose economic programme aimed at a massive collectivization of the means of production. Under President Allende the number and magnitude of distortions in the trade regime (as in the whole economy) grew enormously. The following is a brief summary of the situation at the time of the 1973 military coup (Meller, 1994):

- Import tariffs ranged from 0 to 750 per cent, with an average of 105 per cent.
- 50 per cent of tariff lines had tariff rates above 80 per cent, while only 4 per cent had tariff rates below 25 per cent.
- However, import taxes were only 26 per cent of import value in 1971, as a result of widespread exemptions and special regimes.

- For more than 60 per cent of imports there was a 90-day, non-interest-bearing prior deposit of 10 000 per cent of the imported goods' value.
- Almost 50 per cent of tariff lines required the Central Bank's approval for importing the goods.
- There were eight official exchange rates, with a 1000 per cent differential between the maximum and the minimum.

This system of protection did not result from any specific development objective. The disorganization prevalent not just in trade policy but in economic policy as a whole led to the stagnation of manufacturing production, the disappearance of economic growth, and a severe contraction of the fledgling non-traditional export sector (Agosin, 1999). When in September 1973 the military staged the coup that put an end to President Allende's Socialist experiment, Chile was in the middle of an economic (and political) crisis of enormous proportions. Serious economic mismanagement had brought about hyperinflation (606 per cent in 1973), a massive fiscal deficit (21 per cent of GDP) and crippled productive capacities (Dornbusch and Edwards, 1994).

Before proceeding to the reforms of the military regime, it is important to note that for all its shortcomings, the import-substitution model had some positive aspects. For example, during the 1960s the State promoted research and the creation of human capital in the areas of forestry, fishery and agriculture, all of which would later become leading exporting clusters. The action of the State was also instrumental in developing the physical and telecommunications infrastructure essential for the subsequent export boom (Meller, 1996; Agosin, 1999; Ffrench-Davis, 2003).

THE REFORMS OF THE MILITARY GOVERNMENT

When it seized power in September 1973, the military junta led by General Augusto Pinochet had no definite government project (Valdés, 1995), let alone an economic blueprint. However, it quickly chose a long-term 'foundational' scheme over a 'restoration' one. In other words, the military saw themselves as leading a transformation project for Chilean society, rather than just restoring order and providing the bridge to a civilian administration. According to the military government's Declaration of Principles of March 1974, what was required was 'profound and prolonged actions to change Chilean mentality' (Valdés, 1995).

Although the junta's leaders were all strongly anti-communist, the military's nationalistic tendencies connected well with a protectionist view in economic matters (Fontaine, 1993). Lacking themselves both experience in government and technical expertise in economics, the military resorted to a group of young, liberal economists who had been secretly working since 1972 in an alternative economic programme, in anticipation of Allende's overthrow. The military approached this group partly because of its image of technical competence and partly because of the seriousness of the economic crisis facing the country. Here a brief digression is in order, because that group of economists, who would later come to be known as the 'Chicago Boys', would play a central role in the implantation of a free market model in Chile.[6]

Most of the Chicago Boys were alumni of the Catholic University's Economics Department. All of them followed graduate studies in Economics at the University of Chicago under a cooperation programme between both universities that ran from 1956 to 1964. This programme, known as the Chile Project, was funded by the government of the United States through its International Cooperation Administration (later known as the Agency for International Development, AID). It was deliberately conceived as a means to counter the influence in Chile of the structuralist views then prevalent both in ECLAC and in the national university (the University of Chile). Most Chicago Boys returned to academic life in the Catholic University's Economics Department, which they eventually came to dominate. They also gradually began partaking in debates on economic policy, at the same time as Chilean politics became increasingly polarized.

The group was characterized by a strong *esprit de corps* and by heavily ideological views on social life. All Chicago Boys shared an absolute belief in economic science – in its neoclassical stream – as the best provider of answers to most questions concerning the organization of society. Consequently, they dismissed the role of other social sciences. They also criticized openly not just democratic politics but actually the very notion of politics, which they saw as inherently corrupt and obstructing market forces (Valdés, 1995). Although this discourse made them natural allies of the military, it was inconsistent with their stated aim of building a 'free society' through the reforms of the military government.

During roughly the first two years of the military regime, the Chicago Boys struggled for influence. Not all members of the economic team shared their radical views. In fact, many favoured a more gradualist and less ambitious approach, aimed mainly at correcting the imbalances created under Allende. In the words of the then Finance Minister Jorge Cauas, speaking in July 1974, the goal was to create 'a modern, mixed economy'.

The massive balance of payments crisis of 1975 provided the opportunity for the Chicago Boys to secure the backing of General Augusto Pinochet, with their proposals for a radical adjustment programme. From then onwards, they embarked on an ambitious process of reforms, ultimately aimed at transforming Chile into a truly market-driven economy. The main elements of their platform were liberalization, deregulation and privatization. The Ministry of Finance took on the lead role, especially after December 1976, with the appointment as Finance Minister of Sergio De Castro, widely seen as the Chicago Boys' natural leader.

The First Trade Reform: 1974–1979

Liberalization of the trade regime was essential for the success of the new strategy. The first reform, started in parallel with an adjustment programme aimed at bringing down inflation (Meller, 1996), was radical in its depth and speed. By the time it was completed, in 1979, 'the Chilean import regime could be considered one of the most open in the world. There were no quantitative restrictions, no prohibitions, no anti-dumping or countervailing duties, no subsidies on exports, and a uniform nominal tariff of 10 per cent for all imports except automobiles' (De la Cuadra and Hachette, 1988). Essentially all discretion was removed from Chilean trade policy (Ffrench-Davis, 2003).

This first trade policy reform experienced significant changes along the way, reflecting the tensions between the more pragmatic and the more orthodox positions within the government. In a first stage, from early 1974 to mid-1975, all quotas and official approvals for imports were eliminated, all quantitative restrictions were replaced by tariffs, and the different exchange rates were unified. The simple tariff average was cut from 105 per cent to 57 per cent, although some tariffs still reached 120 per cent. In May 1974 the authorities announced that by 1977 no tariff would exceed 60 per cent. However, this target was subsequently revised downwards, and in August 1975 it was replaced by a range from 10 per cent to 35 per cent, to be achieved during the first half of 1978. The envisaged cuts were implemented faster than had been announced, with the new target range being reached in August 1977. This was seen as the end of the tariff-reduction process (French-Davis, 2003). Up to that point, it was quite an ambitious reform, but one that retained some differentiation in protection levels depending on the degree of sophistication of the products concerned. However, only four months later, in December 1977, the Minister of Finance announced a new tariff reduction plan, aimed at reaching by mid-1979 a uniform tariff of 10 per cent for practically all products. This new target was reached, as foreseen, in June 1979. The more orthodox sector, represented by the Chicago Boys, had clearly prevailed.

The new strategy resulted in Chile's withdrawal from the Andean Pact in 1976.[7] The decision was based both on discrepancies with that bloc's restrictive treatment of foreign investment and on Chile's unwillingness to maintain the high protection levels demanded by the bloc's common external tariff.

By mid-1979 Chile's trade policy had become unique. The 10 per cent protection level was then unusually low among economies at a similar development level, and the lack of any selectivity was (and continues to be) exceptional, even among developed countries. The flat tariff presents several advantages. First, from an economic point of view, it is consistent with the principle of neutrality, or equal treatment to all sectors. The new economic team was of the view that by ostensibly granting the same level of protection to all sectors, the undisturbed market forces would determine the most efficient allocation of economic resources. Second, from a political economy point of view, it minimizes the incentives of individual firms or sectors to lobby for protection. Third, it simplifies customs administration substantially.[8]

Consistent with the new economic strategy, an export promotion agency, ProChile, was set up in 1974, first within the Ministry of Economy and after 1979 under the Ministry of Foreign Affairs. Since its inception ProChile has been an important actor in the efforts to diversify Chilean exports and to increase the number of exporting firms.

The radical character of the first trade reform (as well as of the ones implemented in many other areas) can only be understood within its historical context. First, the economic crisis facing the country was of such magnitude that it provided the right environment for radical reforms. Secondly, the military junta exercised absolute political control. All political parties were outlawed. The National Congress was closed. Left-wing parties were violently repressed, with many of their leaders and members killed, tortured or exiled. The power of labour unions was drastically reduced. Business leaders, most of whom supported the overthrow of Allende, were initially very enthusiastic about the military regime and supported the removal of quantitative restrictions and the early tariff cuts (Stallings and Brock, 1993).[9] Those entrepreneurs who felt negatively affected by the reforms were not heeded. The military granted the economic team isolation from any interest group pressure (Stallings and Brock, 1993). In short, the ideologically-driven Chicago Boys were given the space to implement their policies in almost laboratory-like conditions.

In the multilateral sphere, Chile also broke new ground. In the Tokyo Round of 1973–79, the country bound its entire tariff book, the first GATT member to do so. All tariffs were bound at a flat 35 per cent. The Chilean example of full binding (but not the flat tariff) would be followed by a number of developing countries, especially in Latin America, a decade and a half later in the Uruguay Round.

Investment and Labour-market Reforms

The economic authorities considered it very important to attract foreign investment so that it could flow to the sectors where Chile had comparative advantage, in the context of the new open-economy model. Liberalization of the foreign investment regime was therefore another of the early reforms of the military government. It was explicitly aimed at restoring foreign investors' confidence after the difficulties of the 1970–73 period.

The Foreign Investment Statute, which entered into force in 1974, was instrumental in opening Chile's foreign investment regime. This instrument, still in force, is the main channel through which foreign direct investment (FDI) enters the country. Under its provisions, the foreign investor signs a legally binding contract with the State of Chile for the transfer of capital or other forms of investment and receives a number of specific guarantees and rights. The contract cannot be modified unilaterally by the State or by subsequent changes in the law. However, investors may, at any time, request the amendment of the contract to increase the amount of the investment, change its purpose or assign its rights to another foreign investor.

The Foreign Investment Statute guarantees non-discriminatory and non-discretionary treatment of foreign investors. Therefore, foreign investors enjoy the same rights and guarantees as local ones. It also guarantees investors the right to repatriate capital one year after its entry and to remit profits at any time.[10] Once all relevant taxes have been paid, investors are assured access to freely convertible foreign currency without any limits on the amount, for both capital and profit remittances. The repatriation of all capital invested is devoid of any tax, duty or charge up to the amount of the originally materialized investment. Only capital gains over that amount are subject to the general regulations contained in the tax code. The Foreign Investment Statute allows investors to lock in the tax regime prevailing at the time an investment is made.

Labour market reforms pointed in the same direction as the overall shift in economic policy. Along with the loss of power experienced by labour unions, regulations were made more flexible so as to facilitate the firing of personnel, and there was a reduction in employer-financed pension charges and more generally in non-wage labour costs (Meller, 1996). Labour market reforms also included the removal of entry barriers to some occupations, such as port workers (Fontaine, 1993). However, not all labour-market reforms were in the direction of increased flexibility: a system of wage indexation based on past inflation was put in place in 1973 and retained until 1982.

The 1982 Crisis and the Populist Interlude

Chile's access to international capital markets improved towards the mid-1970s. Starting in 1976, limitations on international capital movements were systematically eliminated, ending with the complete liberalization of international capital flows in 1981.

By the end of the 1970s, there was already talk of the 'Chilean miracle' (Meller, 1996). Average GDP growth was around 8 per cent a year between 1976 and 1981. Exports grew from US$1.3 billion in 1973 to US$4.7 billion in 1980. However, the strong real appreciation of the peso since 1976, along with the reactivation of growth from 1977 onwards and continuing tariff liberalization, led to a large import surge and the emergence of unsustainable current account deficits, financed by private foreign capital.

In June 1979 (that is, at the same point at which the flat 10 per cent tariff was reached), Chilean authorities fixed the exchange rate against the US dollar, in an effort to fight inflation. The same nominal exchange rate was maintained for three years, until June 1982. As inflation came down slowly, this brought about a 31.3 per cent real appreciation of the Chilean peso over this period (French-Davis, 2003), fostered by large capital inflows. This in turn led to a loss of competitiveness for both exporting and import-competing sectors. The tradable sectors of the economy contracted, while the non-tradable ones expanded.

The way in which the domestic financial markets were liberalized aggravated the situation. The 1975 reforms included the privatization of banks, the elimination of ceilings on interest rates, the reduction of the compulsory reserve requirements applicable to banks, and the elimination of all restrictions on credit. At the same time, barriers to entry into banking and financial activities were sharply reduced. Moreover, prudential regulation of banks and other financial institutions was weak. As a result, the financial sector grew enormously, financial operations replaced real investments, and interest rates soared from negative levels to extremely high levels in real terms (Agosin, 1999). This hit both the exporting and import-competing sectors, already affected by the real overvaluation of the peso.

When the debt crisis arrived in 1982, the Chilean economy was the worst hit in Latin America (French-Davis, 2003). Gross Domestic Product dropped by 14.1 per cent, while official unemployment reached 26 per cent (Meller, 1996). As foreign capital dried up, the authorities reacted to the need to generate current account surpluses to service the external debt by successive devaluations that continued well into that decade. The Chicago Boys fell from grace and were replaced by new economic authorities with more heterodox views.

Between 1982 and early 1985 Chile experienced a populist interlude. The government adopted a number of unorthodox measures. Among the most visible was the intervention in a large part of the banking system in January 1983, effectively rescuing those banks from bankruptcy. Moreover, the Central Bank, which would only become independent in 1989, purchased risky portfolios and set a preferential exchange rate for debts in dollars, thereby sheltering those debtors at least partially from the devaluation of the peso.

In the area of trade, there was a partial reversal of the previous reform. Tariffs were raised to 20 per cent in March 1983 and to 35 per cent (the maximum level bound in the Tokyo Round) in September 1984.[11] In addition, temporary tariff surcharges were authorized in 1982 for sectors in special difficulty (mostly industrial ones), and a mechanism to compensate for external price instability – the price band system – was introduced in 1984 for wheat, sugar and vegetable oil. However, the flat tariff policy remained in place (with the exception of the price band system), and there was no recourse to quantitative restrictions.

The tariff increases were aimed at generating additional fiscal revenue at a time when the international price of copper was low, but they were also a response to mounting social pressures. After 1982 opposition groups, although formally proscribed, began organizing massive rallies to protest against the deteriorated economic and social situation, and in favour of a return to democracy. The survival not just of the Chilean free market experiment but even of the military regime itself was seriously questioned (Fontaine, 1993). Moreover, the measures adopted in favour of the financial sector were resented by other entrepreneurs, who were experiencing massive bankruptcies. These business sectors thus became much more vocal than in the past, demanding more active government action to encourage economic recovery (Stallings and Brock, 1993; Campero, 1992; Valdés, 1995). Increased tariff protection was part of the government's answer.

Not all business associations favoured the tariff increases. In fact, by 1984 the main ones had come to be dominated by exporters. These included the National Agricultural Society (where the traditional grain producers were gradually replaced by export-oriented fruit entrepreneurs), the National Mining Society (a traditional export sector in Chile), and the National Chamber of Commerce (dominated by importers). Opposition to free trade was led by some segments of the manufacturers' lobby *Sociedad de Fomento Fabril* (SOFOFA) and by representatives of small and medium enterprises (Fontaine, 1993).

In 1982–83 the Chilean economy faced both internal and external disequilibria. The internal disequilibrium had to do with the very high unemployment rates and the deterioration in workers' wages. The external one had to do with the scarcity of foreign exchange due to the heavy burden of servicing the external debt.[12] After some hesitation, the authorities chose to reduce the external imbalance even at the cost of aggravating the internal one. The political logic behind this decision seems to have been that the military could control domestic unrest by sending soldiers into the streets, but had no leverage to prevent multilateral financial institutions and international banks from cutting the provision of credit to the country. It was therefore decided to 'invest in reputation' by following a non-confrontational strategy vis-à-vis foreign creditors (Meller, 1996).

From 1983 Chile entered into several adjustment programmes with the International Monetary Fund. The Fund identified substantial reduction of the external debt as Chile's most urgent priority. To that effect it prescribed a quick reduction in the current account deficit, to be achieved through restrictive monetary and fiscal policies. The IMF also prescribed a strategy of growth based on the expansion of exports, whose proceedings would allow an orderly servicing of the debt (Meller, 1996).

The Second Trade Reform

The reversal of the trade opening of the 1970s was short-lived. Once the external disequilibrium was reduced, a new economic team led by Hernán Büchi launched the second trade reform in 1985, in line with IMF prescriptions. There was a drastic initial reduction in tariffs from 35 per cent to 20 per cent in just four months, with a further reduction to 15 per cent in January 1988. These tariff reductions were supported by the majority of Chile's business associations, thereby reflecting the ascendancy of a free trade constituency within Chile's business sector.

A key difference with the first reform was the continuous real depreciation of the peso that took place from 1982 to the end of that decade, compensating for the tariff reductions and improving the competitiveness of both exporting and import-competing sectors.[13] This was facilitated by the abolition in 1982 of the mechanism of automatic wage indexation according to inflation that had been put in place in 1973. This resulted in real wages falling by nearly 20 per cent between 1981 and 1987 (Meller, 1996), thereby countering the effect of the successive nominal devaluations on the price level.

From the mid-1980s several mechanisms aimed at promoting non-traditional exports were put in place. The general drawback, introduced in 1988, allows all exporters to be reimbursed for import duties paid on imports incorporated or consumed in the production of exported goods. The simplified drawback, introduced in 1985, was targeted at 'non-traditional' exports (less than US$ 7.5 million a year at the time). It established a refund equivalent to a percentage of the value of a company's exports of a given product (up to 10 per cent), depending on the country's total exports of that product (the higher the country's total exported value, the smaller the refund in percentage terms). This mechanism, which benefited mostly industrial products, could on some occasions have an export subsidy component, as there was no link between the refund and the imported content of exported items (Agosin, 1999). Both drawback programmes are still in force, although the simplified drawback was modified and reduced as a result of Chile's commitments under the WTO Agreement on Subsidies and Countervailing Measures.

The Automotive Statute, which entered into force in 1985, allowed the exemption of customs duties on imports of vehicles for assembly in Chile, to the extent that they were offset by exports of domestic components of an equivalent value, within a period of 12 months following the importation. This provision was among the types of practices prohibited by the WTO Agreement on Trade-Related Investment Measures and was eliminated in 2003.

Starting in 1987, and with a view to promoting technological innovation and stimulating the purchase of capital goods, Chile also allowed for the deferred payment of import duties on imports of capital goods for up to seven years.[14] Moreover, there could be a partial or total remission of the amount due on the deferred import duties if the company concerned had used the capital goods to produce exports. These debt reductions amounted in effect to export subsidies. They were therefore phased out gradually, starting in 1998, as a consequence of Chile's commitments under the WTO Agreement on Subsidies and Countervailing Measures.

ProChile, the State's export-promotion agency, also began to play a more active role in the 1980s. Its main activities include disseminating information on foreign markets, promoting Chilean exports through generic publicity and participation in international fairs, and working to resolve administrative problems faced by exporters through its network of offices abroad.

In short, Chilean trade policy, as indeed the management of the whole economy, presented during most of the 1980s a much more pragmatic, less orthodox character than prior to the 1982 crisis. This was reflected in the deliberate efforts made to preserve a high (that is depreciated) real exchange rate, as well as in the granting of different types of export incentives and of product-specific, temporary protection via surcharges. Real interest rates were reduced substantially as a result of Central Bank intervention, from an average of 38 per cent between 1975 and 1982 to 13 per cent in 1983–85 and 8 per cent in 1986–88 (Ffrench Davis, 2003). This contributed to a more favourable environment for the productive sectors and therefore for economic recovery. In the words of a sympathetic observer, the key to the success of Chile's economic policies in the second half of the 1980s rested in their 'pragmatic orthodoxy' (Fontaine, 1993). This stands in contrast with what has been termed 'the naive phase' of reforms, from 1974 up to the 1982 crisis (Valdés, 1995; Eyzaguirre et al., 2005).

The Trade Reforms of the Military: Overall Assessment

Chile was an early reformer, in trade policy as in other areas. It began implementing autonomously most of the 'Washington Consensus' reforms a decade before the debt crisis gave the IMF and World Bank the leverage to push those reforms in other Latin American countries. Moreover, as it has been widely noted, its reforms predated the 'neoliberal revolutions' of Thatcher in the United Kingdom and Reagan in the United States.

During the period of military rule Chile experienced two separate trade reforms, with one interlude (and partial reverse) in between. The first reform was more ambitious than the second one, but less successful. The lack of coherence between trade and macroeconomic policies, as well as the lack of sound regulation in the financial sector, led to economic collapse and the brief reversal. Moreover, an important part of the existing manufacturing capacity in 1974 was destroyed, rather than being re-oriented towards the exporting sector. Agosin (1999) and Ffrench Davis (2003) have noted that the period corresponding to the first trade reform was characterized by exchange rate instability (and since June 1979 by a strong real appreciation of the peso), very high real interest rates, depressed domestic demand following the 1975 recession, and high unemployment. Against this background, Ffrench-Davis argues that the first trade reform was too fast and too deep. Many entrepreneurs, used to decades of import substitution and government-fixed prices, struggled to make the right decisions in the context of a rapidly liberalized economy. On the positive side, the first reform was instrumental in eliminating the strong anti-export bias of the economy before 1973, and in re-directing resources towards the country's sectors of comparative advantage.

The second reform was much more successful than the first one in promoting export-led growth and the diversification of Chilean exports away from copper. Between 1985 and 1990, exports grew at an average 16.9 per cent per year (Meller, 1993). They benefited from a favourable exchange rate, lower real interest rates, a much more activist trade policy, the existence of substantial spare capacity in the form of a vast pool of unemployed or underemployed labour, and very favourable terms of trade between late 1987 and 1992. Agosin (1999) and Ffrench-Davis (2003) argue that the simplified drawback programme was instrumental in increasing both the number of exported industrial products and the value of those exports.

A few figures illustrate how successful the trade reforms of the 1970s and 1980s (and other associated economic reforms) were in inducing export growth. Exports climbed from US$ 1.1 billion in 1970 (16 per cent of GDP) to US$ 8.3 billion in 1990 (34 per cent of GDP). An important diversification also took place: the share of copper in Chilean exports fell from 80 per cent in 1970 to less than 45 per cent in 1990, although in aggregate Chile's exports continue to be overwhelmingly concentrated in natural resources. Export success stories such as wine, salmon and fruit date to the second half of the 1980s, along with the emergence of a new generation of Chilean entrepreneurs with a global outlook. In sum, the reforms of the 1970s and 1980s laid the foundations for the export-led growth that Chile has experienced almost without interruption since the mid-1980s.

In contrast with its good external performance, Chile's growth record in the 1974–89 period was quite poor: at an average of 3 per cent a year, it was below the 3.8 per cent average of the import-substitution era. Chile also presented a very erratic growth pattern, including two major recessions, in 1975 (with a drop in GDP of 12.9 per cent) and 1982 (drop in GDP of 14.1 per cent), but also two periods of average GDP growth above 6 per cent (1976–81 and 1985–89). The main reason for the country's poor growth performance under the military was the low levels of investment: between 1974 and 1989, investment accounted on average for only 15.6 per cent of GDP (Ffrench-Davis, 2003).

The reforms and adjustment under the military had a big social cost, especially in the years following the 1982 crisis. Unemployment was at double-digits during practically the whole period of military rule, topping at 31.3 per cent in 1983 and staying at effective levels above 20 per cent between 1982 and 1985. Real wages fell by about 20 per cent between 1981 and 1987. In the same period, per capita social spending fell between 6 per cent and 12 per cent, depending on the item (Meller, 1996). Many social indicators worsened markedly.[15] Poverty reached 45 per cent of the population in 1987, several years after the collapse of 1982–83. Income inequality also increased significantly.[16]

The pain from the adjustment process of the 1980s was far from evenly spread. On the one hand, the severe contraction of per capita social spending hit especially hard the poorest and most vulnerable segments of society, which rely disproportionately on the public provision of health, education, housing and – ultimately – a social safety net. On the other hand, the economic authorities strayed from laissez faire on several occasions to subsidize privileged, mostly upper income, groups. Meller (1996) illustrates this by pointing out that while 600 000 people received an unemployment subsidy equivalent to 1.5 per cent of GDP, less than 10 000 debtors in dollars received support equivalent to 3 per cent of GDP. A further 400 000 unemployed did not receive any unemployment subsidies.

The handling of macroeconomic policy during the years of military rule is also widely seen as deficient, especially in the 1974 to 1985 period (Eyzaguirre et al., 2005; Agosin, 1999; Meller, 1996). This is particularly evident in the failure to bring inflation down to single-digit levels.

TRADE REFORMS UNDER DEMOCRATIC RULE: 1990–2005

After winning the December 1989 elections, Patricio Aylwin took office in March 1990 as Chile's first democratically elected President after almost 17 years of military rule.[17] The broad centre-left coalition he led, the Concertación, has been in power without interruption until today, winning the Presidential elections of 1993, 1999 and 2005, as well as all parliamentary and municipal elections.[18]

The successive democratic governments have faced the challenge of both achieving dynamic economic growth and spreading its benefits more evenly across society. This was a major challenge, considering the enormous social frustration accumulated during both the closed-economy period and the military regime (Eyzaguirre et al., 2005).

The new economic authorities – most of them trained in the United States – chose to stick to the market-economy, outward-oriented model. This had to do with a number of factors. First, the economy had been growing by more than 6 per cent a year between 1985 and 1989, with exports growing even faster and unemployment finally coming back to a single-digit figure. Second, by the early 1990s there was widespread and vocal support for the model among Chile's business sectors, which made even a partial reversal almost inconceivable. An influential 'free trade constituency' had emerged among entrepreneurs, made up – among others – of exporters in booming sectors such as salmon, wine and agro-industry, as well as of Chilean firms interested in investing in other Latin American countries. Third, the main parties in the new ruling coalition, and their technocratic elites, had gone through their own processes of reassessing the role of markets during the 1970s and 1980s. These processes are briefly discussed below.

For many leaders of the Chilean left, the experience of exile meant first-hand exposure to European social democracy at work, as well as to the failure of 'real socialism' in the Soviet Union, Eastern Europe and elsewhere. This led to their gradual reappraisal of the role of markets in economic life, and to the emergence of 'renewed', social democrat sectors within the main left-wing parties (the Socialist Party and the Party for Democracy). These groups have become increasingly influential over time.

The other main partner in the Concertación coalition, the Christian Democratic Party, was historically not as hostile to markets as the left parties. However, its roots are not economically liberal either, as they are heavily influenced by corporatism and the Catholic Church's social doctrine. Its shift towards a more market-friendly approach was spearheaded by CIEPLAN, a mostly economic think tank created in 1976.[19] CIEPLAN grouped a number of Chilean economists, most of them associated with the Christian Democratic Party and with graduate studies in prestigious US universities. Their research provided a critique of the military government's economic policies that was both analytically rigorous and grounded on standard economic theory. CIEPLAN thus greatly influenced the Concertación's government programme in the late 1980s, and after 1990 many of its best known academics have occupied top economic posts in the successive democratic administrations.

Under the Concertación governments, some of the structural reforms initiated by the military regime have been modified, but not repudiated. For example, some changes to labour laws were introduced in 1991, restricting the grounds for firing employees, increasing the compensation that firms had to pay to lay off employees, and restricting employers' recourse to lockouts. While these and other changes marked a break with the authoritarian regime, they did not amount to a major alteration of the labour-market regime.

Trade Policy

Chilean trade policy under the Concertación administrations can be described as following a 'multi-track' or 'lateral' approach (Sáez and Valdés, 1999). The policy of unilateral opening started during the military regime has not only been maintained, but actually deepened. At the same time, the country has been an active player at the multilateral level, both during the Uruguay Round and in the current Doha Round. Finally, a new and growing emphasis on bilateral and regional agreements was added. This 'lateral' strategy is based on the concept of 'open regionalism'. This concept was enshrined – although not defined – as a fundamental principle of the Asia Pacific Economic Cooperation (APEC) since its creation in 1989, and was later popularized in Latin America by ECLAC.[20] According to the Chilean authorities' own vision, open regionalism 'seeks to ensure that no trade agreement limits the freedom [of Chile] to negotiate further agreements or creates more obstacles *vis-à-vis* other trading partners'

(WTO, 1997). Mirroring these changes, the Foreign Ministry – through its specialized Trade Directorate – has assumed a leadership role in trade negotiations.

Although the focus of this book is on autonomous trade liberalization, free trade agreements have become such a prominent feature of Chile's trade policy since 1990 that it is relevant to look at the causes of this trend. Several forces were at play (see Box3.1).

BOX 3.1 THE ROOTS OF CHILEAN TRADE REGIONALISM SINCE 1990

Chile's steady move into bilateral and regional trade agreements since 1990 results from a number of factors. A first precondition was obviously the country's emergence from dictatorial rule. Moreover, by the early 1990s there was a certain consensus among the economists associated with the incoming Concertación coalition that it was time to move beyond an exclusive focus on unilateral opening (Butelmann and Meller, 1993; Agosin, 1993; Velasco and Tokman, 1993; Ffrench-Davis, 1996). The substantial unilateral opening of the 1970s and 1980s had allowed the Chilean economy to reap substantial efficiency gains. However, the open trade regime that Chile already had in the early 1990s meant that the additional efficiency gains from further unilateral opening would be much smaller.

A third element was the desire to promote exports with higher value-addition, reflected in the discussions about a 'second exporting phase'. To achieve this, improved access to foreign markets for more sophisticated products was required. This could not be obtained via unilateral opening. Therefore, a new strategy incorporating some element of reciprocity appeared necessary.

Fourth, the world economy had by the early 1990s moved clearly towards regional agreements, with the Canada–USA Free Trade Agreement (later NAFTA), the Single Market project in the European Union, and the creation of APEC and MERCOSUR. This trend provided an additional, defensive rationale for a small country like Chile to either join or negotiate FTAs with the main blocs. The substantial geographical diversification of Chilean exports made this argument especially compelling.

Fifth, during most of President Aylwin's administration there was uncertainty about the outcome of the Uruguay Round. Therefore, Chile – along with many other countries – took some form of 'insurance policy' in the form of bilateral agreements (Sáez and Valdés, 1999).

Sixth, the Uruguay Round did not achieve as much liberalization as Chile expected in several areas, such as agriculture. Indeed, Chile acknowledges that the liberalization that can be achieved at the multilateral level is necessarily limited. Therefore, the country has negotiated faster and more comprehensive liberalization with countries that were prepared to do so. A clear example is the elimination of antidumping duties in the Chile–Canada and Chile–EFTA FTAs, something that is inconceivable in the WTO. Moreover, multilateral liberalization is not a continuous process. The launch and conclusion of every trade round are difficult processes, highly dependent on the political and economic conditions in the major trading powers. A small country like Chile, highly dependent on exports, cannot simply 'wait until the next round' – or even until a round in progress is completed – while its competitors are negotiating preferential deals in all its most important markets. Furthermore, Chile's experiment with bilateralism has neither stopped unilateral liberalization nor resulted in a lack of attention to the multilateral sphere.

Seventh, Chile's flat and relatively low tariff ensured that bilateral agreements would not create significant trade diversion (Velasco and Tokman, 1993). One of the reasons behind the decision to unilaterally reduce the MFN tariff between 1999 and 2003 was to further reduce the scope for trade diversion caused by free trade agreements.

Finally, the re-democratization process that took place across Latin America in the 1980s and early 1990s, coupled with increased convergence in economic policies along market-based lines, created the conditions for a renewal of the integration drive. Within the region, integration agreements have often had an important political logic. For Chile this is particularly clear about its relations with its neighbours: Argentina, Peru and Bolivia. These have traditionally been characterized by tensions (two wars with both Peru and Bolivia in the nineteenth century, a near-war situation with Argentina as late as 1978). Chile has seen a reinforced institutionalized integration with its neighbours, including trade but going well beyond it, as a means to promote peaceful and cooperative relations.

There has been a substantial degree of continuity between the trade policies of the successive democratic administrations. However, it is possible to distinguish three phases in it, which broadly coincide with the stints of Presidents Aylwin (1990–1994), Frei (1994–2000) and Lagos (2000–2006).

The Aylwin administration (1990–94)

The most important trade measure adopted by President Aylwin's administration was to lower Chile's applied Most Favoured Nation (MFN) tariff from a uniform 15 per cent to a uniform 11 per cent in June 1991. This was intended to ease the tendency towards appreciation of the Chilean peso resulting from increased capital inflows (Jara, 2005). The Government's tariff reduction plan was approved unanimously in Congress.

The newly democratic Chile chose neither to return to the Andean Pact (later renamed Andean Community) nor to join the new Common Market of the South (MERCOSUR), created in 1991.[21] This decision responded to several reasons. First, at the time several members of both blocs were still experiencing important levels of macroeconomic instability. Second, both groups are customs unions with (incomplete) common external tariffs that differ from Chile in that they are not uniform and are on average higher than Chile's. Third, both integration projects aim at common policies or regimes in several areas of economic policy, which are not necessarily compatible with Chile's own policies. Therefore, joining either group would have meant for Chile surrendering its autonomy in trade policy and in other areas of economic policy, as well as in trade negotiations. Instead, Chile obtained 'associated member' status in both groups.

Chile's independent-minded policy has attracted criticism within South America (and occasionally within Chile itself). However, it has proved beneficial, as it has allowed it both to go faster with its own reforms and to exploit opportunities that would not have been available to it as a member of one of the two main integration schemes in the region. Chile's FTAs with the United States, European Union, Korea and China are clear examples.[22]

During the Aylwin administration Chile negotiated its first free trade agreement, with Mexico in 1991. At Chile's request, the agreement provided for the elimination of tariffs on almost all products. Therefore, it represented a significant departure from the traditional approach in Latin America, based on partial product coverage and tariff reduction rather than elimination. However, its scope was limited to trade in goods. The agreement with Mexico was followed in 1993 by two others, along the same lines, with Venezuela and Colomba.

The new democratic administration was very keen to reassure international investors about its intention of keeping unaltered the liberal economic policies implemented by the military government. This was a key factor behind the strong priority Chile gave from the early 1990s to either joining NAFTA or negotiating a bilateral FTA with the United States. Arguably the importance of this motivation fell over time, as successive democratic administrations proved their commitment to a liberal economic model.

The end of the Aylwin administration coincided with the conclusion of the Uruguay Round. Chile committed to reduce its bound MFN tariff from 35 per cent to 25 per cent for practically all products by 2000, in fulfilment of the agreed cuts for developing countries.[23] In addition, Chile made commitments in several service sectors within the context of the General Agreement on Trade in Services (GATS).[24] Those commitments essentially bound the policy framework in place at the time (WTO, 2003).

Summarizing, the main objective of Chilean trade policy during the first post-Pinochet democratic administration was twofold. First, to send a clear message of continuity with the fundamentals of the 'Chilean model' to economic agents both in Chile and abroad. And second, to put the country again on the Latin American map after a long period of diplomatic isolation. The first goal was achieved by locking in – and in the case of tariffs, deepening – the country's openness levels to trade and foreign direct investment. This was done both unilaterally and multilaterally (through Uruguay Round commitments). The second goal, which had at least as much to do with foreign policy as with trade, was pursued through the negotiation of bilateral agreements.

The Frei administration (1994–2000)

During the administration of President Eduardo Frei Ruiz-Tagle, Chile continued to extend its net of bilateral and regional agreements in Latin America, while at the same time it began venturing further afield. In 1994 it joined APEC and was invited to join NAFTA (this offer never materialized, however, due to the Clinton Administration's lack of 'Fast Track' authority). New FTAs were added with Ecuador (1994), MERCOSUR (1996), Canada (1997) and Peru (1998). The FTA with Canada, Chile's first free trade agreement with a developed country, was also the first in which the country undertook commitments in areas such as services and investment. Both parties also agreed not to apply antidumping duties to each other. Chile was also an active participant in the FTAA (Free Trade Agreement of the Americas) negotiations, launched in December 1994.[25]

On the multilateral front, Chile advanced its Uruguay Round bound tariff reduction schedule from 2000 to 1996, as a result of commitments in APEC. It also publicly and continuously supported the launch of a new round of multilateral trade negotiations in the WTO.

Two important events took place in domestic trade policy. First, a law was passed in 1998 providing for a further reduction of five percentage points in Chile's applied Most Favoured Nation (MFN) tariff, from 11 per cent to 6 per cent, to be implemented uniformly in the same number of years. The rationale for this decision was twofold: to improve the overall competitiveness of the economy, and to reduce the room for trade diversion that could arise as the result of the country's various free trade agreements. This tariff reduction plan was more controversial than the one of 1991, as the first effects of the Asian crisis had begun to be felt, as well as increased flows of cheap imported manufactures (Jara, 2005; Silva, 1999). This was compounded by increased agricultural imports from MERCOSUR following the 1996 agreement and which hit Chile's politically influential import-competing agricultural sector.

In this context, to make possible the approval in Congress of the tariff reduction plan, the Government committed to introduce draft legislation allowing the application of safeguard measures. This legislation, which entered into force in May 1999, is stricter than the WTO's Agreement on Safeguards. For example, it only allows for safeguard measures to last one year, renewable for up to one additional year, instead of the 'four plus four' years allowed by the WTO. The effectiveness of the general safeguards regime as a protection tool is further eroded by provisions in several of Chile's free trade agreements that set strict conditions for safeguards to be applied to FTA partners.

The Lagos administration (2000–2006)

During the administration of President Ricardo Lagos, the implementation of the unilateral tariff reduction plan approved in 1998 was concluded. Also during the 2000–2006 period Chile modified several trade-related laws (such as on customs procedures, trade-related investment measures in the automotive sector, and protection of intellectual property rights) pursuant to Uruguay Round commitments. In the multilateral sphere, Chile enthusiastically supported the launch of the WTO's Doha Round in 2001, and has been an active participant in it. However, the most prominent feature of Chilean trade policy during this period was the conclusion of free trade agreements with several of the world's 'mega markets': the European Union (November 2002), Korea (February 2003), the United States (June 2003) and China (November 2005).[26]

An ambitious, trade-related reform was undertaken with the entry into force of the Government Procurement Law in 2003. The law sets out the principles of public procurement for all governmental and other public institutions, including regional governments and municipalities, but excluding public works and state-owned enterprises. Its objectives are to achieve maximum transparency in public procurement, to allow savings for the State and to promote the use of e-commerce. It makes public tendering compulsory for all contracts exceeding US$ 62 000 (as of May 2007). The law does not provide for different treatment of national and foreign goods, services, or suppliers. The law also establishes a tribunal for public procurement, which deals with infringements of procurement procedures, including for public works (WTO, 2003).

In the area of trade facilitation, Chile has been continuously streamlining its import procedures since 1997, *inter alia* through the introduction of an electronic processing and payment system. Imports are usually cleared the same day they arrive at port (WTO, 2003).

IMPACT OF THE REFORMS

Protection Levels

Chile's bound tariff rate since the end of the Uruguay Round is a flat 25 per cent, with a handful of exceptions in agriculture (see note 22). As a result of its last unilateral tariff reduction, Chile's applied MFN tariff has been a flat 6 per cent since 1 January 2003, again with roughly the same exceptions as for the bound rate. Taking into account Free Trade Agreements, the country's average applied tariff level is much lower, at around 2 per cent (and going down). This reflects the fact that the countries with which Chile has subscribed such agreements account for 79.4 per cent of the country's trade (as well as for 76.6 per cent of the world's produce).[27] Chile maintains only one multilateral tariff-rate quota, for sugar, although it has negotiated some others under bilateral agreements, usually for sensitive agricultural products.

Except for a handful of import-competing agricultural commodities (sugar, wheat and wheat flour, dairy and poultry), the tariff level has almost ceased to be a relevant variable. Today productive sectors in Chile (both exporters and those competing with imports) tend to care more about the exchange rate. Trade remedies are also used very scarcely, with the exception of safeguards for the agricultural commodities already mentioned.

Chile follows a general policy of no permanent a priori exceptions in its free trade agreements. Sensitivities are dealt with through longer tariff phase-out periods. The only exceptions respond to reciprocity considerations (that is, when a partner in an FTA permanently excludes items of exporting interest to Chile from tariff elimination). Chile also maintains the policy that its FTAs must have the widest thematic coverage possible, including trade in services, investment, government procurement and other 'second generation' areas. It has accordingly been expanding and updating its network of FTAs within Latin America, which originally covered only trade in goods.

Trade and Investment Performance

Chile's total merchandise trade reached a record US$ 95 billion in 2006, explained by exports of US$ 59 billion and imports of US$ 36 billion. Its ratio of merchandise trade to GDP was 63.4 per cent in 2005, and 76.4 per cent if trade in services is included (World Bank, 2007). Chile's trade is geographically well diversified. In the case of exports, in 2006 Asia absorbed 34 per cent, the European Union (EU-25) 27 per cent, the NAFTA countries 22 per cent, and Latin America 13 per cent. In the case of imports, 34 per cent came from Latin America, 20 per cent from both Asia and the NAFTA countries, and 15 per cent from the EU-25.

While in 1975 Chile exported 200 products by 200 companies to 50 destinations, in 2004 it exported 5238 products by 6636 companies to 171 destinations.[28] Despite this successful diversification effort, Chile remains highly dependent on copper exports. Copper's share in total exports, after being brought down to around 40 per cent in the 1990s, has rebounded strongly in the last years, reaching nearly 55 per cent in 2006. This reflects the currently very high international price, caused among other factors by soaring demand in China.

Foreign direct investment has also played a crucial role in fostering Chile's integration with the world economy. The Chilean FDI regime accords National Treatment to foreign investors with only a few sectoral exceptions (international land transport, maritime cabotage, fisheries, and radio and print media).

Chile's FDI stock reached 64.6 per cent of GDP in 2005, up from just 30 per cent in 1990. By comparison, in 2005, the average world figure was 22.7 per cent, and 27 per cent for developing countries (UNCTAD, 2006). For the past ten years, the ratio of FDI to GDP has averaged 6–8 per cent, higher than the OECD average and any other Latin American country.

Between 1974 and 2006, materialized FDI in Chile totalled US$ 84.1 billion. It is worth noting that 90 per cent of this amount entered the country after 1990. This suggests that foreign investors have rewarded the increased political, social and macroeconomic stability that has characterized the country since regaining democracy. In recent years, foreign investment has increasingly been taking place not just to supply the Chilean market but also other markets, especially within Latin America, taking advantage of Chile's network of free trade agreements.[29] In this context, a large number of multinational companies currently have operations in Chile.[30]

In terms of composition, between 1974 and 2005, the mining sector was the main receptor of FDI, accounting for 33.1 per cent of gross inflows under the Foreign Investment Statute. It was followed by services (19.6 per cent), utilities (19.2 per cent), manufacturing (12.7 per cent) and transport and communications (11.6 per cent). Since 1990 the share of mining in total FDI has decreased (it represented 47 per cent until that year) and other sectors have expanded, notably transport and communications and utilities. This was mainly the result of privatizations in the energy and telecommunications sectors and of increased competition following the deregulation of mobile and long-distance telephone services. An infrastructure concessions programme, launched in 1995, opened the way for the participation of private capital, mostly from abroad, in the construction and operation of roads and airports. Water privatizations and a concessions programme for water treatment services have also attracted important FDI inflows in recent years.[31]

Chile has also become an active foreign investor, especially within South America. It is estimated that between 1990 and 2006 Chilean investment abroad exceeded US$ 38 billion, with Argentina, Brazil, Peru and Colombia accounting for 80 per cent of the total. However, there are registered Chilean investments in countries as far as Spain, Australia, Croatia or the United Arab Emirates. Most Chilean FDI concentrates on energy, forestry, manufacturing and a wide variety of services (especially financial and retail services, but also other emerging sectors such as engineering, information technology and even air transport).[32]

The Services Sector[33]

Services are the most important sector of the Chilean economy in terms of contribution to GDP and employment (52.7 per cent and 62.8 per cent respectively in 2002). Conditions for foreign participation in Chile's services sector are far more liberal than implied by its GATS commitments. Foreign participation in Chile's services sector is substantial, especially in financial services and telecommunications. Since the early 1990s, Chile's telecommunications sector has been fully privatized. There is substantial presence of foreign companies in the sector.

State involvement in the provision of commercial services is limited. The State retains ownership of one bank (BancoEstado), the postal and railway services, and one public television channel. It also owns major seaports and airports; however, these have been increasingly given in concession to private operators. State involvement in any of these sectors does not preclude private participation.

Equity caps only exist in the maritime transport sector, where more than 50 per cent of the capital of a shipping company must be owned by Chileans. Maritime cabotage is also reserved by law for Chilean enterprises. There are also limits on the proportion of foreigners allowed to work in a company established in Chile: according to the Chilean labour code, foreign natural persons cannot make up more than 15 per cent of the total staff employed in Chile. This provision does not apply to highly specialized personnel with skills that cannot be procured in Chile.

Chile's banking system includes a large number of foreign-owned or controlled banks. Foreign banks incorporated in Chile and branch offices are allowed to undertake the same range of activities as national banks and are subject to the same regulations. Foreign financial services providers that wish to establish a commercial presence in Chile must obtain authorization from the Superintendent of Banks and Financial Institutions (in the case of banking services) and from the Superintendent of Securities and Insurance (in the case of insurance services). Authorization depends on market conditions.

Chile's air transport policy is based on the principles of open skies, free competition between airlines, and freedom of price-setting. Chilean and foreign airline companies are allowed to supply commercial air transport services both domestically and internationally. However, by law the participation of foreign companies is allowed only on the basis of reciprocity. Chile's airports are state-owned, but their construction and administration, including the provision of terrestrial auxiliary services, has been given in concession to private enterprises. With the exception of traffic control, the State is not involved in the provision of air transport or auxiliary services.

Macroeconomic and Growth Performance

Chile shows a strong growth record in the last 20 years. Even accounting for the 1998–2003 slowdown, its GDP grew at an average of 5.8 per cent between 1987 and 2006, the fastest rate in Latin America. Agosin (1999) argues that Chile since the mid-1980s is a case of export-led growth rather than one of 'growth-induced exports'. He identifies export expansion and growth in investment as the Chilean economy's twin engines of growth in this period.[34] Since 1990, investment has represented between 22 and 27 per cent of GDP, well above the levels it reached during the period of military rule (Ffrench-Davis, 2003). This has allowed higher and more sustained growth.

In spite of being a very open economy, Chile is today less vulnerable to external shocks than it historically was. This is explained in large part by its solid macroeconomic policies since 1990. Inflation, still at 26 per cent in 1990, was brought down to single-digit levels by 1995. The Central Bank, made autonomous towards the end of the military regime in 1989, adopted in 2000 an inflation-targeting policy, with a target band of 2 to 4 per cent. Inflation levels have been within this band in all years since 1999. In other words, Chile presents since the late 1990s inflation levels comparable to those in OECD countries.[35] The consolidated net public debt (central government and Central Bank) represented less than 6 per cent of GDP in 2004, down from nearly 34 per cent of GDP in 1990 (OECD, 2005).

In 1999 the Central Bank abandoned the policy of targeting the nominal exchange rate that had been pursued since 1984 and let the peso float freely. In so doing, it has allowed the exchange rate to play a greater role in the stabilization of activity in response to external shocks.

Fiscal policy has assumed a counter-cyclical stance since the introduction in 2001 of the structural surplus rule. This rule stipulates that the calculation of the annual budget should produce a surplus of 1 per cent of GDP, assuming a level of activity consistent with the economy's trend output growth. In so doing it allows an expansionary fiscal policy in periods of low economic activity, without interfering with the country's monetary policy or raising the risk perception of foreign investors.[36] The responsibility for estimating the values of the two key variables in this calculation – the economy's trend output growth and the medium term copper price – has been delegated to expert panels, therefore reducing the risk of political interference (OECD, 2005).

During most of the 1990s Chile maintained some capital controls. These were a response to the great abundance of foreign capital the country experienced during most of that decade, and to the desire to prevent such inflows from inducing an excessive appreciation of the peso. The authorities therefore put in place measures to discourage inflows of short-term capital,[37] while continuing to welcome FDI (Agosin, 1999). The development of hedging instruments together with the increased maturity of the Chilean financial system and the credibility of its macroeconomic policies made it possible to eliminate these restrictions in 2001 (WTO, 2003).

While in the past copper prices had a big effect on the country's macroeconomic stability, this effect has been moderated since the creation of the Copper Stabilization Fund. This fund was set up in 1986 in the context of a structural adjustment programme with the World Bank. It allows the Chilean State (the only shareholder of CODELCO, the world's largest copper producer) to maintain a stable spending pattern in spite of fluctuations in copper's international price. It does so by providing for the collection of surpluses in times of high prices and their withdrawal when prices are lower.

Employment

Unemployment was at double-digits during practically the whole period of military rule. Although there are no comparable figures available for the national unemployment rate before 1986, the series compiled by the University of Chile on unemployment in Greater Santiago since 1960 provides a good proxy.[38] It shows that unemployment reached particularly high levels following the recession of 1975 (over 16 per cent in that year and 1976) and especially the one of 1982 (exceeding 22 per cent in that year and 1983). Moreover, the figures for the 1980s substantially underestimate the extent of the problem, as they exclude the emergency employment programmes put in place after 1982 and that essentially amounted to masked unemployment.

The national unemployment series available since 1986 shows a brighter picture. Starting at 12.1 per cent in that year, the unemployment rate finally reached a single-digit level in 1988 (9.7 per cent) as a result of economic recovery in the second half of the 1980s. It continued to decrease gradually in a context of high and sustained growth, reaching its lowest level (an average of 6.3 per cent) in the 1996 to 1998 period. It rebounded again in 1999, the only year since 1983 in which the Chilean economy has experienced negative growth (-0.7 per cent). This took place in the wake of the Asian and Russian crises and in a context of high interest rates that choked economic activity. Unemployment remained at 9 to 10 per cent levels until 2005, finally beginning to ease off towards the end of that year. The average for the first half of 2007 was 6.8 per cent, suggesting that the economy is finally close to the levels of the mid-1990s.

Poverty Reduction

Since regaining democracy, Chile has experienced a massive reduction in poverty, from 38.6 per cent of the population in 1990 to 13.7 per cent in 2006 (14 per cent in urban areas and 12.3 per cent in rural areas). Extreme poverty (that is, destitution) has been reduced from 13 per cent in 1990 to 3.2 per cent in 2006.[39] This record is unparalleled in Latin America. Poverty reduction has been matched by improvements in social indicators, including enrolment in primary education, youth literacy, infant mortality and life expectancy, with these indicators reaching levels close to those in advanced economies. According to the OECD, infant mortality, which stood at 78 children per 1000 live births in 1970, had fallen to 17 children by 1990 and 7.6 by 2004. Life expectancy at birth has also risen steadily and in 2004 stood at 78 years.

It is widely recognized that strong and sustained economic growth, complemented by much increased social spending in areas such as health and education, has played a key role in the above achievements. It is also broadly accepted that the openness of the Chilean economy has contributed strongly to the country's robust economic performance. It can therefore be argued that this openness has also helped to reduce poverty and to otherwise improve social indicators.

CHALLENGES AHEAD

> As in previous years, **Chile,** ranked 27th, leads the rankings in Latin America and the Caribbean. Chile's position reflects not only solid institutions – already operating at levels of transparency and openness above those of the EU on average – but also the presence of efficient markets that are relatively free of distortions. The state has played a supportive role in the creation of a credible, stable regulatory regime. Extremely competent macroeconomic management has been a critical element in creating the conditions for rapid growth and sustained efforts to reduce poverty. The resources generated by Chile's virtuous fiscal policy have gone to finance investment in infrastructure and, increasingly, education and public health. Given Chile's strong competitive position, the authorities will have to focus attention on upgrading the capacity of the labour force with a view to rapidly narrowing the skills gap with respect to Finland, Ireland and New Zealand, the relevant comparator group for Chile. (The Global Competitiveness Report 2006–2007, World Economic Forum)

Chile is now an upper-middle income country. Its per-capita gross national income, of US$5870 in 2005 (US$11470 in purchasing power parity terms), exceeds those of all Latin American countries except Argentina, is similar to the levels in Russia and South Africa, but lower than in all OECD countries except Mexico and Turkey. Notwithstanding two decades of rapid growth, per capita incomes are still less than half the OECD average.[40]

Today Chile shows much improved social indicators and a solid record of macroeconomic stability, with low inflation, a structural fiscal surplus and a strong reserve position. It has the lowest country risk in its region, and along with Mexico, is the only sovereign borrower in Latin America to enjoy an investment-grade credit rating.

Chile is widely considered the freest economy in Latin America and the Caribbean.[41] Moreover, it is widely considered to have transparent institutions and a generally effective regulatory framework.[42]

Arguably Chile's main challenge over the coming decade will be to cross the development threshold, catching up with the lower-rung members of the OECD. This will imply, as the OECD itself has put it, 'lifting the economy's growth potential' (OECD, 2005).[43]

Chile is a clear example that natural resources are not necessarily a curse. However, doubts remain as to whether 'more of the same' will be enough to cross the development threshold, and if so, when. In particular, it has been pointed out that there are countries with natural resource endowments similar to Chile's, but with a more abundant and cheaper workforce, and closer to the world's big 'centres of consumption'. The vulnerability of comparative advantages based on exhaustible natural resources has also been highlighted, as well as the catching-up effect as other developing countries undertake the same reforms in which Chile was a pioneer (Eyzaguirre et al., 2005). Chile also has a low research and development intensity by international standards (0.7 per cent of GDP, about one-third of the OECD average). And despite the significant progress made since 1990, especially in terms of coverage, Chile's educational performance remains poor in comparison with OECD countries (OECD, 2005).

Against this background, it has been argued that Chile must embrace 'the knowledge economy' more aggressively, while maintaining its specialization in the natural resource areas where it has comparative advantage. The preconditions for this qualitative jump are already in place: the rule of law, macroeconomic and institutional stability, a market-based economy (including liberal trade and investment regimes), reasonably good public infrastructure, a well-regulated and expanding capital market, and notable improvements in educational coverage (Eyzaguirre et al., 2005; OECD, 2005).

A prerequisite to benefit fully from the knowledge economy is to develop the country's human capital. In policy terms, this requires improving the quality of education (especially in the public system, which caters for the majority of the population) and fostering innovation (Eyzaguirre et al., 2005; OECD, 2005). In the microeconomic area, it will be important to improve access to capital for small and medium enterprises and start-ups, as well as finding ways of increasing the very low participation rate of women in the labour force (for example, through the expanded availability of childcare and pre-school education).[44] Other challenges ahead are improving environmental standards, so that Chilean products are not discriminated against by governments or customers in developed country markets, and securing stable and diversified energy sources.[45]

Despite Chile's success with poverty reduction, its income distribution has shown little improvement from the maximum levels it reached towards the end of the military rule period. Today it remains very unequal even by world standards. This issue has become increasingly prominent in the public debate, as the latter gradually shifts from how to eradicate extreme poverty to how to ensure a fair distribution of the fruits of economic growth. Therefore, another major challenge for the political sustainability of the 'Chilean model' is bringing these persistently high levels of income inequality closer to OECD levels.[46]

In the context described above, the role of trade policy in the coming years is less obvious than it was in the last three decades. With an average applied tariff level around 2 per cent (and going down), few gains can be expected from new unilateral tariff reductions, except to simplify customs procedures. The Chilean services regime is also recognized as generally very open. On the other hand, Chilean exporters enjoy today free, or at least preferential, access to the world's biggest and most dynamic economies. The main challenge in the area of trade policy is now to exploit these opportunities fully. This will require a big public effort to disseminate information on the markets concerned and on the opportunities opened through the FTAs.

Summing up, Chile's economic references in the coming years will be those developed countries that have been able to prosper by adding value to mostly natural resource-intensive exports (Australia, Canada, New Zealand) and those that, being relatively small economies, have succeeded by adopting the right policies in areas such as education, innovation and fostering entrepreneurship (Ireland, Scandinavia).

CONCLUSION

For an outside observer, if there is one common thread in Chile's trade policy over the last three decades, it is a consistent commitment to trade liberalization. Aside from a brief policy reversal right after the economy's near-collapse in the early 1980s, both the right-wing Pinochet dictatorship and the successive centre-left administrations led by the Concertación have pursued freer trade almost relentlessly. All avenues have been explored: unilateral liberalization (in the second half of the 1970s, in the second half of the 1980s, in the early 1990s and again in the late 1990s), multilateral commitments in the GATT/WTO, and most visibly now, free trade agreements since the early 1990s. Chile has experimented both with 'big bang' reforms under dictatorial rule and gradualist reforms in democracy (see Table A3.1 in the Appendix for a chronology of Chile's trade and investment reforms).

How did this come to pass? It certainly was not a foregone conclusion in September 1973. There was no reason to expect that the military, once in power, would preside over a period of such radical economic reform. Many other military dictatorships in Latin America and elsewhere chose to leave the import-substitution model essentially in place.

In the Chilean case, it was a very specific set of circumstances that allowed events to happen the way they did. The seriousness of the country's crisis in 1973 provided the conditions for radical reform. But equally crucial was the symbiosis that took place between the military's 'national re-foundation' project and the ideological vision of the Chicago Boys. The military gave the Chicago Boys a free hand to implement their preferred policies. Equally importantly, they carried on with the reforms in spite of the high social cost, buying time for them to finally begin to pay off from the mid-1980s. In a 'normal politics' situation, it is very likely that the social and economic cost of the reforms (including trade liberalization) would have been considered excessive, and the reforms abandoned or at least partially reversed. The result was that, by the time the country regained democracy, the open economy model had been showing positive results for half a decade, both in terms of growth and employment. Moreover, an influential pro-market, pro-free trade constituency had emerged among entrepreneurs. Finally, the leaders of the incoming coalition had just witnessed the collapse of 'real Socialism' in the Soviet Union and elsewhere. In short, there was no turning back the clock.

The military government was responsible for implanting the market economy model in Chile, and for convincing entrepreneurs of its virtues. However, it failed in one crucial aspect: gaining popular support for the model.[47] This task was left for the future democratic administrations. The process was remarkably quick. As one author sympathetic to the military government observed in the early 1990s, the free market model only began to be accepted by the Chilean population at large under democratic conditions (Fontaine, 1993). Writing only two years later, Valdés asserted that export orientation and the opening-up of the economy to foreign competition had 'become articles of faith for Chilean society in general' (Valdés, 1995).

Chile experienced an average growth rate of 6.4 per cent during the first three years of President Aylwin's administration, coupled with falling inflation, rising investment and a fall in unemployment. This good performance in the critical first years of democracy probably explains in good part why the market economy model quickly began to legitimize itself among the wider population. Another, very important part of the explanation lies with the more 'social democratic' nature of the new social compact. After 1990, long-repressed social demands were met through policies such as the introduction of a minimum wage and of an unemployment benefit scheme, as well as through increased social spending in the areas of public health and education, long neglected by the military. In this way, a basic social protection net was created (in some cases, reconstructed). Finally, the search for consensus further reinforced the legitimacy of economic policies among the wider population. In sum, democracy allowed 'a social pact between government, business sectors, and workers' (Valdés, 1995).

Against the predictions of many supporters of the military government (including some prominent Chicago Boys), democracy has not only proved not to be a problem for the working of the open economy model: it has actually reinforced it. The overall performance of the Chilean economy improved dramatically since 1990, in a context of political and social stability, coupled with greater policy coherence, better macroeconomic management and a strengthened regulatory framework. This has of course been greatly facilitated by the near consensus that exists across the Chilean political spectrum on the fundamentals of a market-based, outward-oriented economy.

A number of lessons can be distilled from the rich experience Chile has accumulated in over thirty years of trade-related reforms. While some of them are more specific to the Chilean context than others, all of them have some level of applicability to other developing-country situations. Following are some of the most important.

When launching a trade reform, it is important to eliminate quantitative restrictions first, as Chile did in the first stage of its reform between 1974 and 1975. This is so because quantitative restrictions are the most distorting kind of trade barriers, as they inhibit response to price signals – and therefore the reallocation of resources – more than tariffs. Anyway, this particular recommendation has lost most of its relevance, as the vast majority of developing countries have by now committed under WTO rules not to maintain quantitative restrictions.

The near-collapse of the Chilean economy in 1982 illustrates the importance of policy coherence during reform. Specifically, governments should try to avoid real exchange rate appreciation while simultaneously reducing tariff protection, so as to avoid a 'double whammy' effect on import-competing sectors. The 1982 crisis also points at the importance of proceeding cautiously when opening the capital account, and of putting in place a sound regulatory framework for the financial sector before doing so.

The Chilean experience also shows the importance of macroeconomic stability, including low inflation, to allow economic agents to assess adequately where to channel resources in response to price – including trade – liberalization. High inflation and macroeconomic stability in the first years of reforms made it difficult for economic operators to assess the comparative competitiveness of different industrial sectors. Investment in Chile's sectors of comparative advantage picked up significantly in the second half of the 1980s, and especially from 1990 onward, in the context of increased macroeconomic stability and lower inflation.

The Chilean experience suggests that a gradual approach to trade reform is in principle preferable to a 'big bang' one, as it allows a more orderly adjustment by the productive agents, thereby minimizing economic and social costs. As it has been shown, the second trade reform under military rule delivered better results than the first, in spite of being less ambitious. However, an assessment of the relative merits of each approach will necessarily depend on the circumstances. For example, Chile arguably needed some sort of 'big bang' to kick-start reforms in the highly distorted economic environment prevailing after the military coup. In contrast, all subsequent trade reforms took place in a much less distorted environment, therefore allowing for more gradualism and fine tuning. Moreover, a large part of the explanation regarding why the first trade reform ended in collapse had to do with inadequate policies in other areas and a general lack of policy coherence, rather than with the depth or speed of trade reform per se.

Chile's experience with an essentially flat tariff structure has been largely positive. While being an extreme case, the Chilean experience points at the benefits of a simple tariff structure that avoids large tariff dispersion. These benefits accrue through a less distorted allocation of economic resources, more transparency and predictability for economic operators, fewer incentives for lobbying, and a simplified customs administration. Moreover, the low and uniform tariff has allowed Chile to negotiate bilaterally with different partners, by reducing substantially the scope for both trade diversion and incoherence among the different agreements.

Chile's successful second trade reform highlights the benefits of pragmatism, as shown in the use of different types of export incentives (including some export subsidies). It is worth recalling, however, that some of those export incentives are no longer legal under WTO rules. Increasingly intrusive multilateral rules mean that developing countries have less 'policy space' now than in the 1980s.

In this new international context of reduced policy space, the role the State can play in fostering exports through WTO-consistent, horizontal mechanisms becomes even more important. In particular, the experience of ProChile highlights the benefits of an active export-promotion agency in gathering and disseminating information on foreign markets and in encouraging small and medium enterprises to associate and cooperate to explore those markets.

The most important lesson that can be drawn from the Chilean experience is one that has already been mentioned: democracy is in no way intrinsically detrimental to trade reform or to economic growth in developing countries. Ultimately, trade reforms – indeed, any reforms – need political legitimacy if they are to be preserved in the long run. The specific type of export model Chile developed under the military, based on low wages and an aggressive exploitation of the country's natural resources, could not be sustained indefinitely. For their part, the continued large inflows of foreign investment since 1990 strongly suggest that investors put a premium on stability, not just economic but also political and social. At the same time, it cannot be ignored that trade policy-making under democratic politics has been greatly facilitated in Chile by the country's near consensus on the benefits of free trade.

NOTES

1. The views expressed in this article are those of the author and do not necessarily reflect those of the Chilean government.
2. Compared with the average of the 1927–29 period, in 1932 Chile's gross domestic product (GDP) had fallen by 38.3 per cent, its exports by 78.3 per cent, its imports by 83.5 per cent, and its per-capita GDP by 42 per cent (Meller, 1996).
3. Populist (Ibáñez, 1952–58), Conservative (Alessandri, 1958–64), Christian Democrat (Frei, 1964–70). Several, largely unsuccessful, attempts to reform the trade regime were made in 1956, 1959–61 and 1968–70 (De la Cuadra and Hachette, 1988).
4. Until the early 1950s, the electorate accounted for only 10 per cent of the population. Women were allowed to vote in 1950 and the illiterate population only in 1970. As a result of these and other electoral reforms, the electorate grew from 1.28 million in 1957 to 3.24 million in 1969 (Fontaine, 1993).
5. Between 1950 and 1970, Chile's per capita GDP grew at a yearly average of 1.4 per cent, compared with an average of 3.1 per cent 6 per cent for the group of developing countries with a comparable income level, and with 3.3 per cent for the industrialized countries (Fontaine, 1993).
6. An excellent reference on the Chicago Boys is Valdés (1995).
7. The Andean Pact (now Andean Community), created in 1969, is an integration scheme comprising trade and other policies. Its other members at the time Chile abandoned it were Peru, Bolivia, Colombia, Ecuador and Venezuela.
8. Although the importance of a tariff structure with low dispersion is widely accepted among Chilean economists, the flat tariff policy has attracted some criticism. One example is Ffrench-Davis (2003).
9. This may have had to do with the high tariff level at the beginning of the reform, which meant that the early reductions were only eliminating redundant protection (Meller, 1994; Ffrench-Davis, 2003).
10. Chile's Foreign Investment Committee argues that in practice the one-year capital lock-in has not represented a restraint since most productive projects – in areas such as mining, forestry, fishing and infrastructure – require more than a one-year start-up period (see www.cinver.cl).
11. Jara (2005) presents evidence in the sense that, had it not been for the Tokyo Round binding, tariffs would have been increased beyond 35 per cent.
12. Between 1982 and 1987, Chile's external debt was bigger than its gross domestic product and four times higher than its exports (Meller, 1996).
13. The Chilean peso depreciated 130 per cent in real terms between 1982 and 1988 (Ffrench-Davis, 2003).
14. Purchasers of Chilean-made capital goods were entitled to a tax credit equivalent to 73 per cent of the customs duty on the net invoice value of the goods.
15. There were some exceptions. For example, during the 1980s Chile achieved one of the lowest infant mortality rates in Latin America (0.84 per cent). This probably responded to some extent to the efforts made by the military regime to target some social programmes at the most vulnerable groups (Meller, 1996).
16. There are no comparable figures on income inequality at the national level before 1987. However, there are older series based on occupation polls conducted by the University of Chile in the Greater Santiago area. These show that the Gini coefficient, which measures income inequality, climbed from a value of 0.476 in the 1958–63 period to a maximum of 0.570 in 1987–90.
17. The Constitution that entered into force in 1980 envisaged a referendum in 1988 on the continuity of the military regime for a further eight years. Following the victory of the 'No' option with nearly 55 per cent of the votes, presidential elections took place in December 1989. These were won by the Concertación's candidate, Patricio Aylwin of the Christian Democratic Party, over the right-wing candidate Hernán Büchi (who had served as Finance Minister between 1985 and 1989).

18. Arguably the main strength of the Concertación has been its broad character. It includes forces such as Socialists, Social Democrats and Christian Democrats that, while all in opposition to the Pinochet regime, were in opposite camps during the Allende period. This inclusiveness has provided successive administrations with a broad base of popular support and legitimacy.
19. See www.cieplan.cl.
20. See ECLAC (1994).
21. MERCOSUR's current members are Argentina, Brazil, Paraguay and Uruguay. Venezuela, which withdrew from the Andean Community in 2006, is in negotiations to become a full MERCOSUR member.
22. The argument can be summed up as 'the advantage of being single (and small)'. Chile is an economy small enough not to threaten the viability of any productive sectors in its FTA partners (even in agriculture). This is obviously not the case for MERCOSUR, for example, which contains agricultural powerhouses such as Brazil and Argentina.
23. Wheat, wheat flour, sugar, vegetable oils and dairy products were bound at 31.5 per cent. The sugar bound tariff was raised in 2001 to 98 per cent. This product is subject to the price band system, created in the 1980s. The price band provides for a higher tariff the lower the international price. In 1999–2000, very low international sugar prices resulted in Chile's tariffs for that product largely exceeding the bound level, which led to the decision to re-negotiate that level upwards in the WTO.
24. The sectors are business services, leasing and rental services, telecommunications, financial services, tourism and travel-related services, and auxiliary air transport services.
25. These talks did not result in convergence, however, and were frozen indefinitely in 2005.
26. A 'partial scope' agreement was subscribed with India in March 2006, providing for tariff preferences on a number of products. Under the current administration of President Michelle Bachelet, an FTA with Japan was signed in March 2007 and entered into force in September of this year.
27. See the website of the Ministry of Foreign Affairs' Economic Directorate, at www.direcon.cl.
28. ProChile (Chile's export promotion agency). See its English language website at http://www.chileinfo.com/index.php?accion=info_comercial
29. Chile's Foreign Investment Committee. See www.cinver.cl (available in English).
30. For a list, see the English language website of Chile's Foreign Investment Committee, at http://www.cinver.cl/index/plantilla2.asp?id_seccion=1&id_subsecciones=100.
31. Chile's Foreign Investment Committee. See www.cinver.cl (available in English).
32. Ministry of Foreign Affairs' Economic Directorate. See http://www.direcon.cl
33. This section is based on WTO (2003).
34. Agosin identifies two main channels through which exports induce growth in a small and developing economy such as Chile's. First, they potentially represent – unlike the domestic market – a nearly infinite source of demand. Second, they promote technological change by financing imports of capital goods, which tend not to be produced domestically.
35. The expected inflation rate for 2007 is around 7 per cent, as a result – among other factors – of increased energy and food costs.
36. Ministry of Finance's website, at www.minhda.cl.
37. FDI was required to remain in Chile for at least one year and a non-interest-bearing reserve on short-term external credit was imposed.
38. It is worth noting, however, that the unemployment rate in the Greater Santiago area tends to be above the national figure in 'bad years' and below it in years of high economic activity. This is probably because Santiago concentrates a disproportionate share of Chile's industry and other activities, such as construction, that are very sensitive to the economic cycle.
39. The poverty line used in Chile corresponds to twice the cost of a basic food basket. In 2006, it was equivalent to about US$90 per person per month in urban areas (US$60

in rural areas). Destitution is defined as income below the cost of one basic food basket. For more details on the methodology used and the evolution of poverty since 1990, consult the Planning Ministry's website: http://www.mideplan.cl/final/categoria.php?secid=25&catid=124.

40. World Bank (2007).
41. Chile is ranked 11th among 162 countries according to the 2007 Index of Economic Freedom, published jointly by the US-based Heritage Foundation and *The Wall Street Journal*. As on previous occasions, it ranked first in Latin America and the Caribbean. See http://www.heritage.org/index/countries.cfm.
42. In 2006 Chile was ranked best in its region in Transparency International's Corruption Perceptions Index (and twentieth overall). See http://www.transparency.org/policy_research/surveys_indices.
43. Last May, the OECD formally invited Chile to start negotiations conducive to full membership.
44. At 40.9 per cent in 2005, Chile's labour force participation rate for women is well below the world's average (57.9 per cent), and is lower than that of any region except for the Middle East, North Africa and South Asia (World Bank, 2007). This very low figure probably responds to a host of reasons, including not just inadequate coverage of child-care and pre-school education, but also entrenched cultural patterns. Chile is widely seen as Latin America's most socially conservative country.
45. Chile is highly dependent on foreign energy sources (oil and natural gas). In recent years it has experienced growing difficulties to secure an adequate and stable supply, especially from neighbouring countries. This in turn puts a question mark on the Chilean economy's growth prospects.
46. Although high even by Latin American standards, Chile's income inequality levels are reduced significantly when State transfers to the poorest segments of society are considered. In 2006, the income ratio between the richest 10 per cent of the population and the poorest 10 per cent fell from 31.3 times to 12.1 times when such transfers were considered (Ministry of Planning, www.mideplan.cl).
47. Fontaine (1993) provides data supporting this view, based on polls conducted in 1988 in Chile's capital Santiago. Just as an example, according to those polls, 54.8 per cent of Santiago's population favoured income redistribution policies as the best means to eradicate poverty, against only 37.6 per cent who preferred economic growth.

REFERENCES

Agosin, M. (1993), 'Beneficios y costos potenciales para Chile de los acuerdos de libre comercio'. *Estudios, Públicos*, **52**, (Spring).

Agosin, M. (1999), 'Comercio y crecimiento en Chile' (also published in English as "Trade and growth in Chile'), *CEPAL Review*, **68**, August, available in http://www.eclac.cl/publicaciones/xml/3/20203/agosin_i.pdf.

Butelmann, A. and P. Meller (1993), 'Tópicos centrales en una estrategia comercial chilena para la década de los 90', in A. Butelmann and P. Meller (eds), *Estrategia Comercial Chilena para la Década del 90*, Santiago de Chile: CIEPLAN.

Campero, G. (1992), 'Entrepreneurs under the military regime', in Paul W Drake. and I. Jaksic (eds), *The Struggle for Democracy in Chile*, Lincoln, NE: University of Nebraska Press.

De la Cuadra, S. and D. Hachette (1988), 'The timing and sequencing of a trade liberalization policy: the case of chile', working paper no. 113, Instituto de Economía, Pontificia Universidad Católica de Chile.

Dornbusch, R. and S. Edwards (1994), 'Exchange rate policy and trade strategy', in B. Bosworth, R. Dornbusch and R. Labán (eds), *The Chilean Economy. Policy Lessons and Challenges*, Washington, DC: The Brookings Institution.

ECLAC (United Nations Economic Commission for Latin America and the Caribbean) (1994), 'Open regionalism in Latin America and the Caribbean', Santiago: ECLAC.

Eyzaguirre, N., M. Marcel, J. Rodríguez and M. Tokman (2005), 'Hacia la economía del conocimiento: el camino para crecer con equidad en el largo plazo', *Estudios Públicos*, **97**, (Summer).

Fontaine, J.A. (1993), 'Transición económica y política en Chile: 1970–1990', *Estudios Públicos*, **50**, (Autumn).

Ffrench-Davis, R. (1996), 'Comentarios, in "Panel: ¿Son el NAFTA y el MERCOSUR el camino hacia la integración del Hemisferio?"', in R. Lipsey and P. Meller (eds), *NAFTA y MERCOSUR. Un diálogo canadiense-latinoamericano*, CIEPLAN/DOLMEN.

Ffrench-Davis, R. (2003), *Entre el Neoliberalismo y el Crecimiento con Equidad. Tres Dácadas de Política Económica en Chile*, 3rd edn, Santiago: Comunicaciones Noreste, second edition published as *Economic Reforms in Chile. From Dictatorship to Democracy*, University of Michigan Press, 2002.

Jara, A. (2005), 'Las virtudes de la promiscuidad (La apertura comercial de Chile)', in A. Estevadeordal and R. Torrent (eds), *Regionalismo Global: Los Dilemas para América Latina*, Barcelona: Fundación CIDOB.

Labán, R. and P. Meller (1997), 'Trade strategy alternatives for a small country: the Chilean Case', in Richard Lipsey and Patricio Meller (eds), *Western Hemisphere Trade Integration*, London: Macmillan Press.

Meller, P. (1993), 'Economía Política de la Apertura Comercial Chilena', *Serie Reformas de Política Pública*, ECLAC.

Meller, P. (1994), 'The Chilean trade liberalization and export expansion process 1974–90', in Gerald Helleiner (ed.), *Trade Policy and Industrialization in Turbulent Times*, London: Routledge.

Meller, P. (1996), *Un Siglo de Economía Política Chilena (1890–1990)*, Santiago: Editorial Andrés Bello.

OECD (Organization for Economic Cooperation and Development) (2005), *Economic Survey of Chile, 2005*, Paris: OECD Policy Brief.

Sáez, R. (1995), 'Estrategia comercial chilena: ¿Qué hacer en los noventa?', *Colección Estudios CIEPLAN*, no. 40, March.

Sáez, S. and J.G. Valdés (1999), 'Chile y su política comercial "lateral"' (also published in English as 'Chile and its "lateral" trade policy'), *CEPAL Review*, **67**, April, available at http://www.eclac.cl/publicaciones/xml/5/19935/saezvaldes.pdf.

Silva, V. (1999), 'Política comercial y relación público-privada en Chile durante los noventa', unpublished draft.

Stallings, B. and P. Brock (1993), 'The political economy of economic adjustment: Chile, 1973–90', in R. Bates and A. Krueger (eds), *Political and Economic Interactions in Economic Policy Reform*, Oxford: Blackwell.

UNCTAD (United Nations Conference on Trade and Development) (2006), *World Investment Report 2006: FDI from Developing and Transition Economies: Implications for Development*, Geneva; available at http://www.unctad.org/en/docs/wir2006annexes_en.pdf.

Valdés, JG. (1995), *Pinochet's economists. The Chicago School in Chile*, Cambridge: Cambridge University Press.

Velasco, A. and M. Tokman (1993), 'Opciones para la política comercial chilena en los 90', *Estudios Públicos*, **52**, (Spring), 53–99.
World Bank (2007), *World Development Indicators 2007*, Washington, DC: World Bank.
World Economic Forum (2006), *The Global Competitiveness Report 2006–2007*, Geneva, available at http://www.weforum.org/en/fp/gcr_2006-07_highlights/index.htm.
World Trade Organization (1997), *Trade Policy Review Chile 1997*, Geneva: WTO.
World Trade Organization (2003), *Trade Policy Review Chile 2003*, Geneva: WTO.

APPENDIX

Table A3.1 Chronology of Chile's trade and investment reforms, 1974–2003

Year/period	Event
1974	The Foreign Investment Statute enters into force: liberalization of the FDI regime
1974–75	First stage of the first trade reform: quantitative restrictions are eliminated, the different exchange rates are unified, tariffs are reduced from an average of 105% to an average of 57%
1975–77	Second stage of the first trade reform: tariffs are reduced to a range from 10% to 35%
1976–81	Elimination of capital controls
1977–79	Third stage of the first trade reform: tariffs are reduced to a flat 10% (except for automobiles)
1979	Tokyo Round: Chile binds all its tariffs at 35%
1982	Debt crisis and near-collapse of the economy
1983–84	Partial reversal of trade reforms: tariffs are raised to 20% (March 1983) and then to 35% (September 1984)
1985–88	Second trade reform: tariffs are reduced to 30% (March 1985), then to 20% (June 1985) and finally to 15% (January 1988)
1991	Unilateral tariff reduction, from 15% to 11%
1991	Capital controls are introduced (on short term capitals)
1991 to the present	Negotiation of several free trade agreements
1994	Uruguay Round: Chile binds practically all its tariffs at 25%[1] and undertakes some commitments on Services
1999–2003	Unilateral tariff reduction, from 11% to 6%
2001	Capital controls are eliminated

Note: 1. Wheat, wheat flour, sugar, vegetable oils and dairy products were bound at 31.5%. The sugar bound tariff was raised in 2001 to 98%.

4. New Zealand

Ron Sandrey

INTRODUCTION

The economic reforms in New Zealand from 1984 onwards rapidly became a benchmark for similar reforms in other countries to be judged against. However, coming from a small and somewhat isolated part of the world one must place these in perspective and recognize that many other countries, such as those of the former Soviet Union and China at one extreme, and economies such as those in this book, have also undergone reforms. However, what sets the New Zealand reforms apart from others was the comprehensive nature and speed of the reforms. While this chapter examines the trade policy reforms, these cannot be viewed in isolation from the overall package, a package that covered the full stabilization and liberalization spectrum of reforms in:

- financial markets
- trade policy
- agricultural and industry support
- research and development
- the labour market
- taxation and taxation policies
- monetary policies
- fiscal policies
- the welfare state itself
- corporatization and eventually privatization
- government departments

Many of these policies are inexorably linked (you cannot have a trade policy without an agricultural policy, for example), and even after a period of nearly a quarter of a century it is hard to clinically assess the overall effects of the package, let alone the effects of an individual component of the package. Arguments continue over the sequencing versus comprehensiveness of the reforms and their associated human cost, but the New Zealand of today is a much different place from that of the early 1980s.

THE BACKGROUND

By the 1950s New Zealand had become one of the richest countries in the world on a per capita basis, with this prosperity based upon agricultural exports. The UK absorbed most of the produce New Zealand could supply; in 1960 the UK was the destination of 53 per cent of all New Zealand's merchandise exports, and such was the dominance of pastoral agriculture that wool (33 per cent), meat (24.2 per cent) and dairy (23.9 per cent) comprised 81.1 per cent of total global exports. New Zealand was regarded as a British farm.

From there the dream started to end, and by the early 1980s New Zealand had become a highly regulated economy, with extensive government involvement in most areas. This was especially so in agriculture, where by 1984 assistance to the sector had doubled over a very short three-to-four year period to reach 30–34 per cent of the final value of most pastoral farm output. Since then the economy in general has evolved to one of the most open in the world, and the agricultural sector is held up as the classical 'farming without subsidies'[1] example.

By the late 1960s, faced with growing balance of payment problems, successive governments sought to maintain New Zealand's high standard of living and full employment rate with increased levels of overseas borrowing and increasingly protective economic policies. The government introduced controls (quotas) for manufactured goods, increased tariffs, and undertook a huge capital works programme, building roads, houses, hospitals, power stations and telecommunications. The inevitable result was an inefficient manufacturing base, economic stagnation and increased government management of the economy.

With export markets for agricultural produce guaranteed, increasing production became the name of the game. A turning point came around 1973 when the UK entered the European Common Market and the cosy agricultural market arrangements ceased,[2] and the first international oil crisis hit, a crisis that New Zealand did not respond well towards, to its medium-term detriment.

By 1984 there was wide acceptance that a change in direction was required, and a number of acute problems had to be addressed:

- The fiscal deficit, which had reached 9 per cent of GDP.
- A growing public debt problem, with borrowing often being used to support consumption. Government net debt as a proportion of GDP had risen from 9 per cent in 1976 to 41 per cent by the mid-1980s.
- A persistent current external deficit, which was complicating overseas debt management[3] and putting pressure on the exchange rate.

- Persistent inflationary pressures, with the consumer price index (CPI) reaching almost 20 per cent before price controls were imposed in 1982.
- A lax monetary policy, which, because of the government's suppression of interest rates, had led to excessive monetary growth.
- A growing unemployment rate, which had reached 7 per cent by 1983.
- A real GDP per capita growth between 1976 and 1984 that averaged only 1.15 per cent per annum.

A 'snap' election in 1984 brought to power the Labour Party, with a Finance Minister committed to a less interventionist approach and with strong support from his senior colleagues. For a traditionally left-wing democratic party, this approach was inconsistent with their general policy stances, and this contradiction demonstrated how far the previous government had drifted into intervention, the general disenchantment with intervention, and the need for radical reform.

Looking back it is difficult to understand why New Zealand continued to rely upon border protection after the end of the Second World War, and increasingly pursue an import-substitution policy in the manufacturing sector over this period. The general rationale for such a policy is to ensure that employment is preserved and grown, but in New Zealand's case at one stage during the 1950s the official unemployment rate was around 0.1 per cent.[4] The problem was, perversely, that these protectionist policies were generally considered to be the reason for the low unemployment, and this disguised the 'cost excess' burden[5] of protectionism upon the export sector for many years during and after the commodity boom of the 1950s.

Right through to around the early 1970s, a period of another commodity boom and the first oil crisis, New Zealand seemed to be 'I'm OK mate' with respect to economic policies. The economy continued to grow, and it was only when the relative growth was set against other rich countries that warning signs became apparent. New Zealanders were losing ground on a relative basis. From there until the 1984 crisis the economy deteriorated.

During the period leading up to 1984 steps were taken to address the fundamental problems, but these were often slow and faltering. For example, to free up the economy the first moves towards the Closer Economic Partnership (CER) with Australia were taken (the original agreement was signed in 1982), and protectionist measures such as the import licensing scheme were moved towards a tariffs-only system (albeit with these tariffs at a high level). On the other hand, from the late 1970s the infamous 'Think Big' import substitution programme for expanding domestic industries (car assembly and steel production) and energy production (petrol from natural gas) was launched, complemented with an ambitious export subsidy programme.

The latter, by definition of the role of agriculture in the export mix of the time, concentrated upon agricultural products, many of which were becoming increasingly protected in overseas markets. This accentuated New Zealand's already substantial problems. Attempts by the government of the time to remedy things resulted in what was referred to as 'hydraulic policies' – an attempt to patch one problem through intervention merely increased the pressure on another weak point, causing yet another problem. This was the situation at 1984.

THE REFORMS

The striking feature of the reforms from that point was their dramatic nature; attention focused on stabilization of the inflation rate, government deficits and overseas debt, and deregulation through reforms of commercial policies, the taxation system and the financial sector, and government trading policies. Trade policy reforms were an integral part of the overall package, and had a major impact on exports. But they were one element of a fully comprehensive package. So comprehensive that the New Zealand experience is often compared with 'Thatcherism' in the United Kingdom. However, since the UK, being part of the European Union, has neither its own trade nor agricultural policy, such a comparison is inaccurate.

Since agriculture was such a large component of total exports, reforms on the supply (export) side cannot be viewed independently of reforms on the demand (import) side. Agriculture became a central part of the overall reform effort partly because of its importance to the economy and partly because it was such a visible target. These agricultural reforms also enjoyed political support from the Labour Party's traditionally somewhat 'anti-farmer' worker base.

However, reform of the agricultural sector also had many supporters within the sector itself. The situation was widely regarded as unsustainable, and farmers expected certain macroeconomic reforms to benefit their sector. In particular, they expected that, given agriculture's dominance in total production and trade, the newly-floated exchange rate would closely follow the agricultural terms of trade. This would then in turn provide a counter-cyclical compensation in the form of a lower New Zealand dollar and therefore higher farm gate returns during these periods of lower agricultural prices on world markets.

On the latter they were somewhat misled; the reforms to agriculture took place much faster than many reforms elsewhere, and, contrary to conventional wisdom, the nominal exchange rate (and consequently the real exchange rate) actually appreciated strongly. Both accentuated problems for the sector and delayed its eventual recovery.

A few months prior to floating, the New Zealand dollar (the 'Kiwi') was devalued. A number of other changes were introduced over a very short period of time. Export assistance was discontinued, import protection was lowered, the tax base was widened and made more indirect, government trading activities were privatized, and the public sector was reformed.

Agricultural subsidies were withdrawn and by 1991 their value had reduced to around 2 per cent of output from the 1983 figure of 33 per cent. The 1991 levels have remained more or less unchanged since then, with the remaining minimal support concentrated upon research and extension, animal health and quarantine, and assistance in times of adverse events. Concessionary farm loans were progressively brought into line with market rates for the government-owned Rural Bank (although some debt write-off was introduced by way of compensation, the only real compensation provided to the sector). User fees were introduced for most government services and farm input subsidies were terminated. In addition, the reform of domestic marketing regulations resulted in complete deregulation of the wheat and egg sectors and a partial deregulation of the town (domestic) milk sector (the export milk sector deregulation proved to be much more difficult). All of this happened over a short two-to three-year period between 1986 and 1988, and, as mentioned, very limited compensation occurred.

Labour market reforms were also significant, and were critical to the success of the overall package, in particular New Zealand's trade performance. Although the Labour Party government upheld compulsory unionism during their 1984 to 1990 regime, they altered the nature of wage bargaining in one important respect – the government was no longer going to be involved, as was previously the case. It was often claimed that it wasn't until advent of the 1991 Employment Contracts Act, following the change of government in 1990, that real reform took place. These placed labour contracts on the same footing as other commercial contracts, and employees were free to choose their own agents, agents that may or may not have been trade unions.[6] However, some analysts (including this author) consider that the preconditions for labour market reform were in fact set by the Labour Party government's Labour Relations Act (LRA) of 1987, and that by 1991 the full significance of the changes introduced in that Act had not been in place long enough to be widely appreciated.

Associated with the labour market reforms was the Corporatization and Privatization process, whereby much of the government involvement in commercial activities was both initially corporatized to improve efficiency and then often privatized. This dual process was designed to end the drain on the public purse that many operations had become. Examples of where this influenced trade included the railways and the ports, both of which saw massive labour shedding, which contributed to unemployment initially, but the resultant efficiencies later meant lower transaction costs to the productive sector.[7]

Government departments were also the focus of many changes, both in their operational procedures and in their mandate. Departments such as Agriculture, for example, saw many of their previous operations in areas such as product inspection and research and development moved to State Owned Enterprises. Indeed, the Ministry of Works (formerly the Public Works department), was abolished entirely, partly because its role in major public projects was reduced markedly, and partly because during 1987 they remained critical of the reform process, in particular its architect, Finance Minister Roger Douglas.

The Political Economy of The Period

There is much discussion in New Zealand about the importance of sequencing reforms appropriately. While many commentators argued that New Zealand's case proves the dangers of ignoring this consideration, I would argue that comprehensiveness and certainty of 'staying the distance' were more important, from a political economy perspective. The speed of reforms certainly lessened opportunities for lobbyists, who were effectively unable to keep apace with policy changes, let alone influence them. The NZIER (2006) use the phrase 'crashing through the fog of war' to describe how Roger Douglas 'crashed through before opposition could organise itself'. In the desire to maintain momentum little consideration was given to adjustment costs, and it became difficult for anyone (and especially opponents of the reforms) to keep track of individual reforms, let alone the whole package.

The fascinating feature of the New Zealand reforms is that for the initial period leading up to the 1987 elections there was strong support from both major political parties. The governing Labour Party's position was, however, masked by the developments within the party itself; the reforms were effectively rammed through by a small cabal of perhaps ten to twelve senior Cabinet Ministers, with many other Parliamentarians in the party (the traditionally left-wing group) marginalized. The National Party opposition, a party that had mostly drifted towards the left itself, based their 1987 election campaign on the notion that 'we will do what they are doing, but we'll do it better'. There was a general sense of economic well-being leading through to the 1987 election, albeit one not reflected on the farms. The financial sector was booming, along with a very bullish share market that was, along with the appreciating dollar, seen as a vindication of economic policies. Several of the other economic indicators were registering good news also.

Following the 1987 election, however, things began to unravel. First, the global share market crashed in 1987, and the New Zealand market suffered more than many others as the speculative bubble burst. This, together with continuing unemployment, caused confidence in the reforms to waver.[8] Reform architect Finance Minister Douglas and sometimes reluctant supporter Prime Minister Lange visibly fell out in early 1988, and this rift continued to place enormous pressures on the party and the economic reform policies.[9] Despite this the economy actually started to do somewhat better, but the 1990 election saw a change of government to one that many voters considered was more capable of continuing the reforms. The National Party fought the 1990 election saying that while they were generally in favour of the economic reforms there was a need for more thought to be given to the human consequences. Their leader and new Prime Minister Jim Bolger spoke of 'the Decent Society' during the campaign, but after the election the incoming Finance Minster Ruth Richardson wished to expand and not retreat from the reforms. Once again the electorate felt betrayed.

The Intellectual Basis of the Reforms

It is difficult to say where the intellectual basis of the reforms came from. Certainly they were consistent with the so-called Washington Consensus of the time, and what can be thought of as the Chicago school of right-wing economists. But they were just as much a case of 'kiwi' pragmatism in realizing that something had to change dramatically.

For the narrower tariff reforms, the intellectual concept of the true rates of assistance to specific sectors, and the recognition of the cost-excess implied for the export sectors resulting from high tariffs, were important. A report by the Australian consulting firm SYNTEC (1984) provided the initial intellectual support for the first of the three or four tariff reviews conducted over the next 15 years. This was augmented by some computable general equilibrium (CGE) modelling in the 2003 tariff review. This highlighted the high and often uneven nature of industry protection, and clearly illustrated how much protection of the import substitution sector created inefficiencies for the export sector by artificially raising costs (Duncan et al., 1992). While this intellectual basis was not as powerful an influence as it was in Australia (and the astute reader will note that the dates here are largely after the initial reform thrust) it nonetheless was influential. This was especially so in the case of the tariff reforms, where the reductions were more measured and signalled in advance.

Using a broader base, the concepts of public choice theory, agency or principle–agent theory, and transactions cost theory were widely used to seek improvements in economic efficiency. The instruments were deregulation, liberalization, commercialization, and public service management (Bale and Dale, 1998). Critics such as Hazledine (2002) have argued that this foundation was inappropriate and indeed may have actually served to reduce economic efficiency as monitoring and enforcement costs rose to counter increasing non-cooperation among the agents. As the New Zealand economy stagnated during much of the late 1980s to early 1990s he may have a valid argument.

Other critical commentators include Easton (1994), who argued that while the New Zealand reforms were motivated partly by orthodox economics and the desire to apply its precepts to government, they were also influenced by the political 'New Right'. This latter approach sought, on philosophical grounds, a smaller role for the public sector than perhaps could be justified from conventional economic theory alone. The Treasury blueprint was the 1984 and 1987 post-election briefing papers that are prepared after each election as an economic vision for the short-term future, but these documents are based upon what the Treasury considers needs to be done rather than an intellectual framework.

Later (Easton, 1998), argues that

> the overt theory was essentially that which is known in Australia as 'economic rationalism', the consistent application of modern neo-classical market theory. At the practical microeconomic policy level this has been the withdrawal of government interventions which preferred one firm, industry, or sector (relative to others), in favour of market regulation of economic activity. Thus import licences have been abandoned, tariff levels steadily reduced, subsidies and tax incentives withdrawn, the tax regime made more uniform with exemptions, barriers to entry eradicated, corporatisation and privatisation of government trading activities, and greater reliance on competition law.

Easton's arguments find support in that independent clinical analysis of the reforms became difficult to find for an extended period. Those in support proclaimed that any downside was caused not by the reforms but by the failure to pursue them far enough and fast enough, while those railing against them tended to do so in a more emotional than analytical manner. It is only relatively recently that there has emerged a more objective analysis. There are of course some exceptions to this, with Easton for example being a balanced critic over an extended period of time. Indeed, Easton (1998) outlines the following general arguments put forward to justify the poor economic performance of New Zealand over the 1988 through to around 1993 period:

- The reforms were fundamentally flawed.
- The promise that the benefits of the reforms are yet to come has been a constant theme of the pro-reformers since 1985, with a constant shifting into the future of the date at which any benefits will become apparent.
- The economic record would have been even worse without the reforms.[10]
- Any counterfactual scenario needs to take into account the international environment (terms of trade deterioration in the early 1980s, higher world interest rates and the third oil shock).
- The cost of disinflation was a loss of output.
- An overvalued exchange rate (linked to the point above).
- The poor economic performance occurred because there were not the expected gains in productivity.

How many of these criticisms are valid? Certainly the time lags were much longer than proponents of the reforms forecast, and this possibly meant that adjustment costs were accentuated. The over-valued exchange rate was a major factor in accentuating the impacts of subsidy withdrawals on the farms, as was the agricultural terms of trade deterioration. These factors are discussed in detail later in the chapter. Similarly, disinflation was costly in the short term, and as discussed earlier, the unemployment costs as a result of labour shedding were large. The first and third points above will always remain controversial, but a guarded 'no' to the first and 'yes' to the latter seems appropriate. To both of these questions the acronym 'TINA' was often used – 'there is no alternative'. These macroeconomic issues are revisited in the final of the chapter.

External Factors Influencing Trade Policies

Did external factors and pressures play a role in the reforms? The answer to that is probably 'no', although the role of the Australia–New Zealand Closer Economic Relations Trade Agreement ANZCERTA (CER) was important, especially since it provided a cushion for increasingly exposed manufacturers by way of free entry to the still protected Australian market. The CER was established between these two nations in 1983; all tariff and non-tariff barriers were progressively liberalized and eliminated. In 1988 it was reviewed with the provision to accelerate the time frame for full trade liberalization to 1990, and importantly it was also expanded to include trade in services and investment.

Following the CER the economies came closer together. Both adopted free trade policies with each other and enjoyed relatively free trade with the rest of the world, and capital and labour now move freely between the two countries. The concordance of the CER implementation and the border liberalization adopted by both countries over a similar time frame have been important for two reasons. First, the remaining high but dropping tariffs against third countries gave a 'window of opportunity' for exporters on both sides of the Tasman to exploit. Second, the lower overall tariffs have been reducing the dangers of so-called trade diversion (where goods are imported from a source just because they are cheaper through tariff preferences and not because they are benchmarked to best international prices). There is, however, a major difference between New Zealand and Australia in the importance of the CER in maintaining tariff reforms. In Australia, the influence of New Zealand duty-free imports is low, while in New Zealand the 20 per cent of imports coming from Australia was high enough to put real pressure on the entire tariff structure and hasten wider liberalization.

The GATT/WTO was not a factor in mandating changes to trade policies. It was important for locking them in once in place. Such was the zeal of New Zealand trade officials that (a) they bound tariff at rates as low as possible, among other commitments, and (b), they used the review process of the CER and the newly formed Asia-Pacific Economic Cooperation process (APEC) and the global search for new FTA partners as opportunities to do the same. New Zealanders subsequently held several high positions in the WTO during the 1990s and 2000s, with Mike Moore as Director General and Crawford Falconer succeeding Tim Groser as Chairman of the WTO Agricultural negotiations in the early 2000s. Moore was a crucial Minister in the reform process, while Groser and Falconer were both influential Ministry of Foreign Affairs officers during the 1990s.

On the FTA front despite a lot of effort the harvest has proven to be a general disappointment to date.[11] During the 1990s and through the early part of the 2000s FTAs were mooted and discussed with China, Chile, Korea, Hong Kong, Singapore, China, Malaysia, Thailand, the ASEAN block as a whole, and more recently Egypt, Japan and the Gulf States. Agreements were signed first with Singapore (a duty-free county/zone and non-agriculture producer), and this was extended to a so-called P4 (Pacific Four) that extended the Singapore FTA to include Chile and Brunei. The P4 contained an extended phasing-in period (18 years) for dairy exports from New Zealand to Chile, to ensure comprehensiveness of the FTA. The Hong Kong FTA negotiations came close to fruition but fell at the last hurdle, while the Thailand FTA is operational and comprehensive, albeit with lengthy phase-in periods. The others, except Korea which never got off the ground at that time but has since re-emerged, remain in the negotiations stage.

In addition New Zealand has vigorously pursued the possibility of an FTA with the US, but the political dimensions are complicated. New Zealand's anti-nuclear policy of the late 1980s, which refused entry to nuclear powered ships to New Zealand harbours, has not been forgiven in Washington DC. However, given the partial and rigid 'template nature' of US 'FTAs', it remains a moot point as to whether New Zealand would accept one.

On the regional front, despite the much hyped 'free trade by 2010' of the Bogor Declaration, APEC has become a political talkfest and photo opportunity as members blithely disregard their earlier declaration. Unilateral concessions made by New Zealand such as the duty and quota free access to imports from least developed countries sounded impressive,[12] but as the imports from these countries are minimal their trade policy impacts have mimicked these levels.

The salient point about the multilateral, regional and bilateral policies is that despite a lot of political activity, only the CER has significantly influenced New Zealand's import trade policies and regimes, and its actual trade. The only change to New Zealand's tariff schedule mandated by the Uruguay Round of the GATT was to decrease the duty on light beer to zero (hence the 'small beer' jibe for the agreement). However, while New Zealand was not obliged to make any policy changes as a result of the GATT agreement, agriculture did benefit a lot from the liberalization of many global food markets of direct interest to New Zealand farmers. This (and other more detailed aspects of the New Zealand agricultural reforms) is discussed in Sandrey and Vink (2006).

Electoral Reforms

The ramifications of New Zealand's trade and broader economic liberalization spread into every area of New Zealand life, not least its politics. Of course many events contributed to the growing support for and eventual introduction of the 'Mixed Member Proportional' (MMP) electoral system, which sought to democratize parliament more effectively. But there is no doubt that this important political reform was in a sizable part due to the way in which the left elements of the Labour party felt betrayed by the 1984 election that saw policies move sharply to the right and away from the traditional worker support base.

Until the first MMP election in 1996 the vote was for members of parliament chosen on a 'winner takes all' basis, both at the electorate and national levels. This meant that a large element of the voters who did not vote for either of the main parties was disenfranchised. The first 'M' of MMP means that half of the members were elected as before, with the second half based upon the percentage share of the overall popular vote for each party (with a minimum 5 per cent threshold) awarded from the party lists.

The 1996 election was won by the governing National Party, which won around a third of the vote. However, the smaller New Zealand First party, which won 17 seats, was placed in the position of 'kingmaker', and able to provide the necessary majority to whichever side it chose. They eventually chose to form a coalition with the National Party. The Alliance (left of centre) and the new ACT New Zealand (right of centre and led by a disgruntled Roger Douglas) also benefited.

The net result is that parliament in New Zealand had become much more democratic, and now it is doubtful that a programme such as the 1984–87 reforms could be pushed through with such ease. This is true in spite of the fact that New Zealand only has one House, so there is no 'second level' to potentially block legislation. A more diverse parliament is what the aggrieved Labour Party supporters of the late 1980s wanted. While this constituency may have applauded several of the moves such as elimination of farm supports and the reductions of tariffs that brought lower prices to consumers, they resented the same suite of policies when unemployment continued at high levels, welfare policies were not addressed as they would have liked, and the interest rates on their homes increased.

THE CONSEQUENCES

Border Trade Policy

The basic economic principle underlying the reduction of border tariffs in New Zealand was to reduce the cost excess imposed by these tariffs on the exporting sector. It was generally considered that as the supports were removed from agriculture the reduction of this cost excess plus the conversion to a floating exchange rate would broadly act to compensate farmers, given the overwhelming profile of agriculture in exports. On the second part this supposition was wrong, as the exchange rate appreciated rather than depreciated. On the first the issue became one of timing more than anything; the tariffs on inputs were removed but over a much more leisurely time path than agricultural subsidies were removed.

From 1990 most tariffs were gradually reduced through a series of tariff reviews, and in September 1998 the government announced a phasing plan to remove most tariffs by July 2001 and all tariffs by 2006. This was subsequently rescinded and replaced by a freeze by the labour-led government; instead the tariff book became the subject of another review in 2003.

Table 4.1 New Zealand's current tariff reform path

2003 tariff	July 2006	July 2007	July 2008	July 2009
17–19%	17%	15%	12.50%	10%
10–12.5%	10%	7.50%	5%	5%
5–7.5%	5–7.5%	5–7.5%	5%	5%

Source: Ministry of Economic Development.

By 2003 95 per cent of global imports by value entered New Zealand duty free, either because the Most Favoured Nation (MFN) tariff is set at zero; because of preferential tariff arrangements with Australia and other FTA partners, Pacific Island countries and Less Developed Countries; or because they fall under the tariff concession system in Part II of the New Zealand Tariff.[13] The actual applied tariff rates on protected sectors in New Zealand are typically in the region of 5–7 per cent. Certain sectors, however, receive higher protection; for example, most clothing and footwear items at 2003 faced a 19 per cent tariff (or more when specific tariffs, expressed in dollar terms per garment, are applied to low-cost clothing).

The outcome of the New Zealand Government's review of tariffs for post-2005 was announced on 30 September 2003. Under the review's decisions, New Zealand's few remaining applied tariff rates will reduce according to the programme set out in Table 4.1.Not shown in the table is that at 2003 around two-thirds of the entire tariff collection was from the sensitive textile-clothing-footwear (TCF) sectors, and around 75 per cent of this TCF sector import was from China. Thus, over half of the entire tariff take was from Chinese TCF imports, and any FTA agreement with China on TCF will effectively dictate the future of the entire tariff policy. As concessions made to China may then be made available to a wider import source, complete duty-free access is only a short step away.

Agriculture: Bearing the Brunt Of Adjustment

Since agriculture is such a large contributor to New Zealand's output and exports, special attention must be given to the changes this sector went through during and after the reform period. The brief euphoria of a devalued currency lasted for a year or so from late 1984, and was followed by the pain of a sharply appreciating dollar for the next three or four years. To appreciate the impacts fully it is necessary to analyse the real exchange rate (RER) over the period. The RER had been remarkably stable from 1976 to 1984 (even though the currency was managed, domestic and international price movements influence the RER), then improved (from farmers' perspectives) in 1985 as the nominal dollar depreciated sharply, deteriorated (from farmers' perspectives) from 1986 to 1988, and then recovered again in 1989 as the inflation rate finally came under control and the New Zealand dollar stabilized. Subsidies were rapidly being removed during the early part of this period.

As world commodity prices were volatile immediately following the initial reforms, the lower farm prices placed stress on onshore processing industries. These processors were, in turn, forced to reduce their margins. Labour market reforms, such as the abolition of compulsory union membership and greater flexibility in the labour negotiation process, saw a shift from the traditional large and inflexible agri-processing plants to newer more flexible ones that were able to adjust much faster to seasonality and other changes. Freedom to exit from the industry, which had not been a feature of the previously regulated environment, took place concurrently with the new-found freedom of entry. However, the consequences for farmers as shareholders in some of these plants were rather mixed as the adjustment process worked its way through.[14]

Sheep meat producers were the most protected sector, and the worst year for lamb producers was 1985/86 when all the contributions to farm gate returns were negative and the farm gate price fell to under half of that of the previous year. The next year farmers were partially rescued by increasing international prices of meat and skins, as well as the reprieve of the end of the subsidy withdrawals (but only in so far as the withdrawal process had come to an end when there were no more subsidies left to take away from farmers). The patterns for mutton (older sheep meat) were somewhat similar, while dairy, not being as highly supported, did not suffer the same subsidy withdrawal symptoms. Both wool and beef were intermediate between the two extremes of sheep meat and dairy, although wool was more heavily supported and that support was withdrawn more quickly.

There are three main areas where it is useful to track the consequences for agriculture. These are farm incomes, land prices and the composition of farm production, although all three have complex and often lagged interrelationships. By 1987 nominal farmland values had reduced to below 1981–82 boom prices, and in real terms were only about 40 per cent of their peak values. Prices increased in subsequent years, and by 1995 the price of most categories of farmland had recovered to around 86 per cent of their 1982 value in real terms. The price of most categories of farmland is now higher than the pre-reform peak.

These initial declines in farm values, coupled with higher interest rates and lower incomes, placed stress upon farmer equity and debt levels. Despite these adverse conditions few farmers were forced to exit the land, as most confounded expectations and stayed on by a combination of tightening spending, drawing on reserves and seeking outside employment (along with spousal support on all three, and especially the final one). Although accurate figures are not available, it is thought that perhaps only 1 per cent of farmers were forced off the land rather than the predicted 10 per cent. The data shows clearly the split emerging between the heavily supported sheep and beef farmers and the lightly supported dairy farmers as the subsidies were withdrawn.

Initially the reforms had little effect on farm size. However, over time some of the most fertile farmland was converted into horticulture and there has been a growth in the number of farms producing horticultural products, which typically are smaller in size than other land uses. Additionally, areas of marginal land were converted to forestry and the most marginal of land was retired into native bush. The distribution of farms has become more bimodal, with sheep and beef farms becoming fewer but larger, and a number of smaller, diversified farms emerging.

Perhaps the real story is in stock numbers. While a relative comparison between livestock numbers has become more complex as the productivity from a breeding ewe or dairy cow 30 years ago has changed through technology, it does appear that rather than a major reduction in overall livestock equivalents over time there has been a movement around the composition of these units. The most striking feature was the reduction in sheep numbers as the move away from that highly subsidized sector took place. The deer sector is a fascinating case study,[15] while the mohair goat industry came and largely went.

Overall, total aggregate agricultural production did not decline that much following the reforms in the decade following 1984, as dairy, deer and fruit production replaced the traditional sheep and beef sectors. Part of this was due to production lags, in particular in the fruit sector, which had been stimulated by export incentives through the early 1980s. Production since the reforms has been driven by market prices, although the role of production lags and the inter-linkages between dairy and beef output that comes from around half of the beef output being cull dairy cows cannot be ignored.

The Role of Agricultural Marketing Changes as a Component of Trade Policy Reform[16]

This is an important and usually overlooked component of New Zealand's trade reforms. Until the reforms the critical link between farm gate and the final marketplace for the major agricultural products was largely controlled by producer marketing boards. For dairy products, apples and kiwi fruit, these boards had exclusive export powers, while meat exporters were licensed and their activities regulated by the Meat Board (from October 1982 to December 1985 the Meat Producers Board took exclusive control of meat exporting). Town milk and eggs were subject to supply controls under the umbrella of their respective boards. In most sectors the marketing boards either directly or indirectly operated price-smoothing mechanisms. The only real exception was wool exports, as most of the product was auctioned.

Given the large percentage of agricultural produce that is exported, this relationship is pivotal, and arguments ranged freely on the extent that the marketing boards were able to enhance returns through single desk selling or market coordination, on the one hand, versus adding a burden through bureaucratic inefficiencies on the other. The crucial question, therefore, is the extent to which these marketing arrangements were reformed, and their consequential impact upon the sector's performance.

Interestingly, some members of the WTO have targeted the New Zealand Dairy Board (and its successor, Fonterra), as a State Trading Enterprise (STE) that must have its powers reduced. This suggests that at least in the eyes of many international observers Fonterra is able to enhance market returns through powers vested in it by the government, and that therefore some market power does exist.

The dairy sector has faced the fewest adjustments, partly because fewer subsidies were directed to this sector and partly because the vexing question of economic rents associated with international quota markets has been difficult to resolve. The processing industry has been almost exclusively a cooperative-based one,[17] with a steady process of mergers and amalgamations from the 168 dairy companies in 1961 through to 42 in 1981, 9 in 1998 and only 4 in 2001. At this latter date the two major companies and the Dairy Board merged into Fonterra, a cooperative company that processes around 95 per cent of New Zealand's milk supply and controls at least one-third of the world trade in dairy products. The statutory powers of export monopoly were removed, although a mechanism for domestically allocating New Zealand's butter and to a lesser extent cheese quota to the lucrative EU and other markets remains, and the almost-complete dominance of cooperatives in the New Zealand dairy sector remains a feature of the market, along with the strong international processing and marketing linkages of Fonterra.

The meat sector went through dramatic changes. At the time of the reforms the New Zealand Meat Board had complete control of the beef and sheep meat (but not venison) export market (but not processing), and the changing profitability of the sector that led to declining sheep numbers also led to a significant industry restructuring that left considerable animal and corporate 'blood on the floor'.

Cooperatives were relatively new to this sector, which was traditionally dominated by overseas interests, but Evans and Meade (2005) report that cooperatives now account for around half or more of the current processing. The once-mighty Meat Board now operates as two shells: the Meat Industry Association to allocate and monitor the lamb supply for the EU quota, and the combined body Meat and Wool New Zealand to coordinate the industry (but without any powers of enforcement), and collect and disburse the compulsory industry levies for functions that include research and development. Otherwise, the market, where New Zealand holds a 50 per cent and 8 per cent global share of the sheep meat and beef trade, respectively, remains an open and competitive one. Around two-thirds of both New Zealand's lamb and beef are exported under quota to the EU and the US respectively.

Since accounting for one-third of total exports in 1960, the importance of wool has steadily declined in tandem with its relative prices to become largely a by-product to the meat sector. Marketing has traditionally been through the auction floor, and this has remained important, as around 80 per cent of the clip is sent overseas with limited further processing.

Exports of apples and kiwi fruit dominate the horticulture sector, with New Zealand holding a global trade share of around 5 and 25 per cent respectively. Around 55 and 95 per cent of the domestic production respectively is exported. Wine should also be included in this category, a horticultural product that is riding and creating the so-called new world wine industry wave along with, *inter alia*, South Africa, Chile, Australia and Argentina. The 'glamorous and high-flying' kiwi fruit sector[18] benefited from marketing and input subsidies, and particularly taxation subsidies, during the 1978–82 period that fostered the growing boom and led to high returns to early entrants, while, except for a grape pull-out scheme in the mid-1980s, wine has 'gone it alone'. The marketing structures for these three sectors have varied, and the comment must be made that in the case of both wine and kiwi fruit, product differentiation and astute marketing in the face of increased global supplies have been major factors in the success of these two sectors.

In summary, there is a large diversity in the marketing structures and their evolution in response to deregulation. The successful evolvers have been the dairy and kiwi fruit sectors; the disasters have been the meat and apple sectors; while the wool and wine sectors have really stood on the sidelines. Is it a coincidence that the dairy sector in particular has the successful industries following deregulation?[19] Perhaps, but then wine has been very successful as well, and, conversely, the sheep meat industry went through the largest structural changes at both the farm and off-farm levels.

The New Zealand Agricultural Experience: Overall Conclusions

New Zealand's export profile has changed since 1960. How much of this can be attributed to the reforms of the mid-1980s is of course a moot question, as many of the changes were already in movement at that time. Dairy has not regained ground since the 1960s, but of course this is partly due to the increase in non-traditional exports. Wool has been on a steady decline to obscurity as the world price has declined, but otherwise there has been little change from 1992 in the meat, fruit and vegetables, fish, forestry and aluminium export shares. This reaffirms that much of the response to the reforms had been completed by 1992, and more recent changes (notwithstanding lag responses) have been from global market returns as agriculture has actually maintained its overall share in New Zealand's exports.

I would agree with the New Zealand Institute of Economic Research (NZIER, 2004) in that a number of lessons can be learnt from the New Zealand experience. Crucially, farmers have the scope and ability to make changes in reaction to the reduction in assistance, therefore raising business profitability above what it would have been had such a reaction not occurred. Importantly, they do not bear all the adjustment costs, as they do not face perfectly inelastic supply or demand curves, with the result that the burden of adjustment is shared across the markets. Given time, profits recover from the initial shock as asset prices adjust to lower product prices, outputs change and demand grows: resources will be redirected towards those products with comparative advantage. Macroeconomic stability plays an important role in re-establishing agricultural profitability, but adoption and innovation in the sector are by far the most important factors in re-invigorating the sector post-reform.

In a speech to Federated Farmers, Alan Bollard, the Governor of the Reserve Bank of New Zealand,[20] examined the new relationships between agriculture, monetary policy and the New Zealand economy. Against expectations, the role of the agricultural sector has increased in recent years, with much of this being due to the enhanced technological change that a market approach has brought to the sector, and global 'shocks' in recent years that have been benign to New Zealand. These shocks have included the foot-and-mouth outbreak in Europe, increasing sheep meat prices, and North American mad cow disease outbreaks, which increased demand for Australasian beef in Japan at a time when Australian droughts reduced beef exports from that country. In particular, farmers have learned to become more sophisticated in handling volatility, and this has in turn increased the demand for farmland to the extent that agricultural lending now represents around one-third of all registered bank lending to the corporate sector in New Zealand. In a true central banker fashion, the

Governor warns against the downside of this exposure for both bankers and their clients, but he does temper this by concluding that the sector is in a much better position to handle the looming 'rebalancing' than it was 'in the turbulent 1980s'.

But perhaps we should give the final word to farmers themselves. The Federated Farmers of New Zealand (2005) report on 'Life after subsidies' is a glowing testament to an agricultural sector operating in the absence of subsidies and urges international reform with a missionary zeal. They glorify the better life after subsidies, stress the productivity growth that exposure to market forces has dictated and relish being 'more in charge of their own destiny'.

THE LESSONS AND THE FUTURE

New Zealand today is a different place from the early 1980s, but whether it is a better place is still hotly debated. That something had to be done is generally accepted by most (but again not all). The adjustment costs cannot be ignored, although impossible to calculate. Did the means justify the ends? There is no question that the recent improvements to the economy detailed below were achieved at a cost during the late 1980s and early 1990s period. But of course the counterfactual remains conjecture.

Export composition and destinations have changed. For destinations the reliance upon the United Kingdom has gone, but the EU is still the destination for 15.5 per cent of the exports. Australia has been stable at around 20 per cent, up from 12.6 per cent during 1980, while the US has been consistent at around 13 per cent in 1980, 1990 and 2006. Asia remains important, although there have been some destination switches around the region with China in particular becoming more important (5.7 per cent in 2006).

By product, agriculture still accounts for around 53 per cent of the exports, but there have been product switches in the sector. Wool, at 18.1 per cent in 1980 and a lower 8.7 per cent in 1990 has continued this slide to 2.5 per cent in 2006. Dairy has gained from 15.9 per cent in 1980 to 20.6 per cent in 2006, while meat declined from its 1980 level of 23 per cent to a more stable 15 per cent for 1990 and 2006. Despite its early promise forestry has stabilized at a consistent 9 per cent for the periods examined, and fisheries products have run into supply constraints at around 4 per cent of the exports. When one considers the rise of tourism, if tourism exports or foreigners coming to New Zealand are exports of natural scenery, then the dependence upon the land-based natural resources for exports remains paramount.

Nearly a quarter of a century after New Zealand's trade reforms, designed in part to shift dependence away from agricultural exports, there is a certain irony in seeing the Secretary of the Treasury recently considering that

> Meeting the challenges of globalisation will require a greater transformation of New Zealand's primary commodities to create new higher value-added goods and services that are branded and marketed in more complex and sophisticated ways. The primary sector is the only one in New Zealand that has all of the crucial attributes required to do this – including cost and quality competitiveness, international scale, an extensive science base and established channels to market.[21]

Quite, and such a pity that dairy products, New Zealand's real competitively produced export, faces one of the most highly protected global markets. However, having said that, the aggregate export data on dairy above hides the significant diversification to over 1000 products derived from milk and being exported to 26 countries that import at least 1 per cent of the total and another 11 countries importing between 0.5 per cent and 1 per cent. This is a remarkable achievement and probably a diversification equalled by few from a single simple product.

The Economy of New Zealand: an Overview[22]

After a period of weak growth during the late 1980s, New Zealand's economic performance improved significantly during the 1990s. From mid-1991, the economy grew strongly with particularly strong output from 1993 to 1996, with annual average growth in real GDP peaking at 6.8 per cent in June 1994. Growth slowed during 1997 and 1998, performed strongly again post this period. Over 2002 to 2004 growth in GDP was generally in the 3.5 per cent to 4.5 per cent range, but recent rates have dropped below 2 per cent.

The main sources of recent growth have been household spending and business investment, because the demand for imports associated with a strong domestic economy, together with relatively weak export growth, has resulted in net exports subtracting from aggregate growth. Given the balance of domestically-oriented spending and export revenue, as well as strong profits by foreign-owned companies, the annual current account deficit is expected to increase from its September 2005 level of 8.5 per cent of GDP. The combined influences of New Zealand's strong banking system, sound fiscal position and floating exchange rate, together with the role of foreign direct investment in building up external liabilities, mean that concerns about the size of the current account deficit need to be kept in perspective.

Following a prolonged period of fiscal deficits, New Zealand achieved surpluses in 1993/94 and has remained in surplus since. Net debt has fallen from 49 per cent of GDP in 1992/93 to 7.1 per cent in 2004/05.

New Zealand experienced a substantial improvement in inflation performance during the 1990s relative to previous decades. Annual inflation as measured by the CPI remained below 3 per cent from the September 1991 quarter through to the June 2000 quarter, but declined to 1.5 per cent on an annual basis in the year to June 2003 and remained close to that rate until June 2004 when it increased to 2.4 per cent. It has been marginally over 3 per cent for most of the period since then. The unemployment rate has also continued to decline, from around the 6 per cent to 8 per cent range in the late 1990s, to 3.4 per cent in September 2005, the lowest level in 17 years.

Final Comment

The introduction to this chapter briefly mentioned that the reform process included reforms to the welfare system itself. While the basic concept of a welfare state remained, many of these reforms were quite important and resulted from a fundamental first-principles look at what was required from a modern welfare system rather than adopting a piecemeal approach to reforms. The availability of a strong welfare 'safety net' did much to mitigate the financial pain for those suffering things such as a job loss during the reforms, but of course other aspects such as the financial costs and social stigma of accepting a lessened life-style remained.

The point in raising this issue is not to get into discussing the details but rather to emphasize that this is very much a difference between New Zealand and many other developing countries that have attempted similar reform processes. Those losing a job in New Zealand were largely able to get on with their lives, albeit a different and perhaps less rewarding life, which may have entailed living on a social grant for an extended period. Conversely, in many developing countries there is really no safety net, at least not of the same depth and coverage as is taken for grated in New Zealand and other OECD countries. Therefore the human cost can be much more severe. Finally, it is honest to acknowledge that, possibly, the reform process may have hurt the lower income persons disproportionately, the majority of which are indigenous Maori and Pacific Island persons. But of course the counterfactual is impossible to know. It is entirely possible that lower income groups would be even worse off now had the economy been left to stagnate indefinitely.

NOTES

1. With reference to the seminal book (Sandrey and Reynolds, 1990) which describes in detail the background, the policy shifts and the consequences of New Zealand's agricultural reforms.
2. The loss of unfettered access to the UK market was a dramatic blow to New Zealand given both its reliance on that market and the nature of the export basket in dairy in particular. Sheep meats were less affected as a special access deal was negotiated, while with wool the problem was not one of access but rather steadily declining prices from around that same time.
3. The total public debt as a percentage of GDP gradually declined from nearly 70 per cent in 1960 to a low of around 40 per cent in 1974 before climbing dramatically again to around 70 per cent in 1985 and 1986 before peaking at around 77 per cent in 1987. Prior to 1974 most of the debt was domestic debt, but from that time through to 1984 overseas borrowings became much more important. From around 1984 a conscious decision was made to retire most of the overseas debt.
4. It is said that at one stage the Minister of Labour knew the names of all the 27 registered unemployed persons in New Zealand.
5. This 'cost excess' describes the situation whereby protection to the domestic (generally non-tradable) sectors increases the costs of the exporting sector, eroding its efficiency. This is discussed in more detail later in the chapter in the context of the arguments made that showed the economic justification for the reduction/removal of these 'cost excesses'.
6. One surprising result was that working days lost due to strikes declined sharply, and by 1995 only 17 per cent of workers were in effect unionized.
7. For example, railways cut freight rates by 50 per cent in real terms between 1983 and 1990, reduced staff by 60 per cent and made its first operating profit in six years in 1989/90 (Brash, 1996). It does however remain a moot point as to how successful the later privatization of the railways was. Several years later the government was effectively forced to retake a degree of control as the new ownerships 'asset stripped' the system and ran it down. A similar fate awaited Air New Zealand, the national flag carrier, and enterprises such as New Zealand Steel that imploded in spectacular fashion.
8. The unemployment story is fascinating. Levels were minimal through to 1977, when they climbed to around 5.5 per cent in 1983, before retreating again to around 4 per cent until 1985. From that period they again increased to a peak of 11.1 per cent in March 1992 and they stayed in double figures until June 1993 before retreating again. A decade later unemployment had declined to 4.3 per cent, and has stayed below that level since. The post-reform unemployment shock was somewhat lagged, but was definitely the result of the drive for greater economic efficiency. Labour was shed in many government departments and related institutions. In the short term, efficiency and productivity gains are almost defined by labour shedding.
9. This was the period when the Prime Minister got 'cold feet' and suggested that the reform process pause 'for a cup of tea'.
10. There is a celebrated cartoon whereby the despairing Minister says something to the effect of 'I have followed your advice and every action has led to disaster', with the official replying with 'just think how much worse it would have been had you not followed our advice'.
11. This statement should be nuanced now that a break-through on the Chinese FTA negotiations has occurred. New Zealand is the first OECD country to negotiate a comprehensive FTA with China.
12. Since 1 July 2001 New Zealand has offered duty-free and quota-free access to all imports from LDCs. This was the first comprehensive scheme of this nature in the world.
13. Part Two of the New Zealand Tariff Schedule is a very thick and imposing document that lists at the extremely detailed level exemptions to the general tariff (Part One of the Schedule) whereby goods can be imported duty free. Initially it was a way of reducing

import costs for export-oriented sectors but over time it moved increasingly into providing duty-free access for products not made in New Zealand and therefore accentuating the basic (Part One) schedule as a means of protecting domestic industries. Reformers saw it as a means of slowly gnawing away at tariff protection.

14. This highlighted a major difference between dairy farmers who were and continued to be loyal to their own farmer-cooperatives and sheep farmers who tended more towards chasing short-term higher prices that may have been on offer from rivals to their own cooperatives.
15. Deer were introduced into New Zealand by the white settlers, and by the early to middle part of the twentieth century they had become both a recreational hunting facility but, more importantly, a pest in the bush lands. In the late 1960s commercial hunters started harvesting the feral animals for venison to supply the European market and velvet for the lucrative Asian market. In the 1970s this evolved into capturing the feral breeding stock for commercial farm production as the animals were domesticated, and by the early 1980s the industry was generating economic rents to owners of female animals, who were able to take advantage of disequilibrium prices as new entrants clamoured to get in. At this stage the by-product velvet was supplying returns to owners of stock, as few animals were being slaughtered for venison. Around the end of the 1980s the high prices for female animals collapsed and the herd began an orderly transition to a new domestic livestock industry. This saw the end of feral capture and the start of the marketing of venison globally as premium meat. Breeding numbers have stabilized at around 1.5 million head in recent years as the industry has matured (Sandrey and Vink, 2006).
16. This section draws heavily from Sandrey and Reynolds (1990), Harrington (2005), and Evans and Meade (2005).
17. Dairy processing plants are cooperative in the sense that farmers completely own the company through shares that entitle them both to present milk for processing and then partake in any profit distribution at the end of the season. Meat processing plants were generally closer to a normal commercial ownership in that complete farmer ownership was rarer.
18. Like the domestication and marketing of the red deer, the kiwi fruit industry is an outstanding global example of a highly successful fruit export that developed from very humble beginnings.
19. The dairy sector really benefited from several factors. The first was that as it had few, if any, direct production supports prior to the reform process, it consequently had fewer adjustment pains. The second is that new entrants into dairy were able to benefit from lower overall land prices on former sheep farms that facilitated the conversion process to dairy farms, while the third is that dairy products benefited from better market access to global markets secured as a result of the GATT/WTO Uruguay Round Agreement on Agriculture outcome.
20. See Bollard (2006).
21. 26 July 2006, John Whitehead, Secretary to the Treasury, Simpson Grierson Policy Maker Seminar Series, Wellington. http://www.treasury.govt.nz/speeches/beyond2010/.
22. This section is based on information found on the New Zealand Treasury website: www.treasury.govt.nz.

REFERENCES

Bale, M. and T Dale (1998), 'Public sector reform in New Zealand and its relevance to developing countries', *The World Bank Research Observer*, **13**(1), February.

Bollard, A. (2006), 'Agriculture, monetary policy and the economy', available at http://www.rbnz.govt.nz/speeches/2682999.html, 18 July.

Brash, D.T. (1996), 'New Zealand's remarkable reforms', Occasional paper no. 100 London: The Institute of Economic Affairs.
Duncan, I., R. Lattimore and A. Bollard (1992), 'Dismantling the barriers: tariff policy in New Zealand', Research Monograph no. 57, Wellington: NZIER.
Easton, B.H. (1994), 'Economic and other ideas behind the New Zealand reforms', *Oxford Review of Economic Policy*, **10**(3), 78–94.
Easton, B.H (1998), 'Microeconomic reform and productivity growth: workshop proceedings', proceedings of a conference 'Microeconomic reform and productivity growth': 26–27 February, (Productivity Commission and ANU, 1998) pp. 155–81.
Evans, L. and R. Meade (2005), 'The role and significance of cooperatives in New Zealand agriculture: a comparative institutional analysis', available at http://www.maf.govt.nz/mafnet/rural-nz/profitability-and-economics/trends/index.htm.
Federated Farmers of New Zealand (2005), 'Life after subsidies', continuously updated from 1994, Wellington, New Zealand.
Harrington, A. (2005), 'The contribution of the primary sector to New Zealand's economic growth', New Zealand Treasury Policy Perspectives Paper 05/04, November Wellington, New Zealand.
Hazledine, T. (2002), 'Agency theory meets social capital: the failure of the New Zealand economic revolution of 1984–91', seminar paper presented at the University of Auckland and elsewhere.
NZIER (2004), 'Adjustment to agricultural policy reform – issues and lessons from the New Zealand Experience', NZ Trade Consortium Working Paper no. 35, February.
NZIER (2006), 'Structural reform: Action and reaction in a small country case: the case of New Zealand', presented to a meeting of the National Economic Research Organisations, OECD Headquarters, Paris, 12 June.
Sandrey, R. and H. Smith (2003), 'An assessment of the gains to New Zealand from the Uruguay Round of trade negotiations', available at: http://www.mfat.govt.nz/foreign/eco/uruguayround/uruguayindex.html, June.
Sandrey, R. and R. Reynolds (eds) (1990), *Farming without Subsidies*, Wellington, New Zealand: MAF Publications.
Sandrey, R. and N. Vink (2006), 'How can South Africa exploit new opportunities in agricultural export markets? Lessons from the New Zealand experience', TRALAC Working Paper no. 19, Stellenbosch: US Printers.
SYNTEC (1984), 'The structure of industry assistance in New Zealand', report for New Zealand Treasury and others.
SYNTEC (1988), 'Industry assistance reform in New Zealand', report for the Ministry of Agriculture and Fisheries and others.

PART II

THE PARTIAL REFORMERS

5. Malaysia

Mohamed Ariff and Gregore Pio Lopez

BACKGROUND

Malaya gained independence from the British in 1957 with a nascent democracy, framed by the Federal Constitution, which provided for a constitutional Supreme Head of State, bicameral Parliament and a federal government structure.[1] On 13 September 1963, Sarawak and Sabah on the Borneo Island together with Singapore joined the Federation of Malaya to form Malaysia. Singapore was expelled from Malaysia on 9 August 1965.

Malaysia is a pluralist society comprising three major ethnic groups in the Peninsula with a mix of indigenous people on the Borneo Island. At the time of independence, the balance between ethnic Malay and other citizens was equal. In 2005, *Bumiputeras* (ethnic Malays and other indigenous people) accounted for 65 per cent of the population, Chinese 26 per cent and Indians just under 8 per cent. Because of Malaya's economic history, Malays were also predominantly rural. This composition, together with the 'special position'[2] granted to the *Bumiputeras* (sons of the soil) by the British, has had a profound impact on domestic politics, which has in turn strongly influenced trade and broader economic policy reforms.

At Independence in 1957, Malaysia was a dualistic low-income economy reliant on commodities, mostly tin, rubber and palm oil, for its foreign exchange earnings.[3] While palm oil earnings have remained significant, Malaysia has diversified its export earnings into other sectors such as manufacturing and tourism. Table 5.1 illustrates the changes in the structure of the Malaysian economy since 1965.

This economic modernization developed in an ad hoc manner between 1957 and 1970, after which greater policy intent and direction came to be provided through long-term development plans. These were the New Economic Policy (NEP: 1971–1990), National Development Policy (NDP: 1991–2000) and the current National Vision Policy (NVP: 2001–2010). Within these long-term frameworks, specific policies such as the Industrial Master Plans, Malaysia Inc., and the Privatisation Policy were also formulated, usually encompassed by five-year rolling 'Malaysia Plans'.

Table 5.1 Composition of gross domestic product (in percent)

Sector	1965	1975	1985	1995	2005
Agriculture, livestock, forestry & fishing	29.0	29.5	20.8	13.5	8.2
Mining & quarrying	7.9	4.2	10.5	7.5	6.7
Manufacturing	10.5	14.3	19.7	33.1	31.6
Construction	4.7	4.6	4.8	4.5	2.7
Electricity, gas & water	1.9	2.6	1.7	2.3	4.1
Transport, storage & communication	3.7	7.2	6.4	7.4	8.8
Wholesale & retail	15.7	13.7	12.1	12.3	14.7
Finance, insurance, real estate & business services	6.0	7.3	8.9	10.8	15.4
Government services	6.9	7.8	12.2	9.5	5.5
Other services	13.6	8.1	2.3	2.1	4.8

Source: Economic Reports and Malaysia Plans (various years).

The overriding objective of these policies was and still is to cultivate and maintain national unity. This was to be achieved primarily through the eradication of poverty and the restructuring of the Malaysian society – to reduce the identification of race with economic activities and geographical locations. The roots of these core policy objectives can be traced to the 10 May, 1969 general elections – Malaysia's third since independence – in which the ruling Alliance government[4] lost its two-thirds majority in Parliament for the first (until the recent election) time.[5] The elections were accompanied by severe political unrest, culminating in the 13 May, 1969 race riots, and ensuing demands by the radical faction within the United Malay National Organisation (UMNO) that affirmative action policies in favour of the *Bumiputeras* be significantly strengthened. This in turn rested on the observation that Malays remained by some margin the poorest ethnic group in Malaysia (see Table 5.2). The NEP represented a shaken Alliance government's direct response.

In fact, the First and Second Bumiputera Economic Congress in 1965 and 1968 had already reflected the growing demands of the *Bumiputera* elites. Although the economy grew at a stable rate of 5.7 per cent between 1960 and 1969, it was mostly in the modern sector, which bypassed the rural communities where *Bumiputeras* were predominant. Equity and equality objectives were therefore to be achieved through a wide range of direct income and wealth redistribution policies to assist the *Bumiputera*. However, key to the redistribution effort was that it would come from an expanding economy, as argued by non-*Bumiputera* interests, and not

Table 5.2 Poverty rates in Malaysia (in percent)

Sector	1957/58	1970	2005
Total	51.2	64.8	5.7
Rural	59.6	58.7	11.9
Urban	29.7	21.3	2.5
Indian	35.7	39.2	2.9
Chinese	27.4	26.0	0.6
Malays	70.5	64.8	8.3

Source: Abu Bakar and Hassan (2003) and Ninth Malaysia Plan.

through appropriation. The Alliance government, which from 1973 became National Front (Barisan Nasional[6]) governments, has since used the theme 'Growth with Equity' to mobilize support for these development policies.

The NEP comprised seven main elements, and set a 1990 deadline for achieving specific targets:[7]

i. Economic growth at approximately 6 to 7 per cent annually
ii. Economic restructuring to reduce various economic and social imbalances:
    - Reduction of the income gap between *Bumiputeras* and other groups
    - Achieving a wealth target of 30 per cent public quoted shareholdings
    - Creation of a *Bumiputera* commercial and industrial class
    - Employment patterns at all levels in firms to reflect the multiracial composition of the population
iii. Reduction of poverty irrespective of race
iv. Full employment of the labour force, with specific emphasis on absorbing surplus labour from the rural sector
v. An interventionist and proactive government
vi. Social policy for conflict avoidance
vii. Monitoring of the implementation of the NEP

Underpinning the development policies noted above were Malaysia's industrialization policies, which included trade policies. Trade policies in Malaysia are therefore contingent on the objectives of Malaysia's development policies, especially since 1970. While external factors have played an important role in Malaysia's trade reforms, appeasement of the ruling political party (UMNO) in the name of the *Bumiputera* community has always been at the core of industrial and trade policy formulation in Malaysia.

On the international front, Malaysia maintained a policy of neutrality by being a member of the Non-Aligned Movement (NAM) and promoting ASEAN[8] as a Zone of Peace, Neutrality and Freedom. In 1974, Malaysia initiated diplomatic ties with the People's Republic of China, considered a radical move at the time. However, western capital and interests were courted and welcomed as a buffer against perceived threats of Communism and indigenous Chinese capital. Britain, through the granting of independence to the Alliance Party and the continued support given to them after the 1969 race riots, ensured that Malaysia remained a market economy, but one in which state capitalism dominates a range of sectors the government considers strategic.

INDUSTRIAL POLICY AND TRADE REFORMS

Industrial policies are measures taken to develop or enhance the industrial capacity or capability of a nation. Trade policies are often part and parcel of industrial policies. In Malaysia, trade, industrial and development policies are all entwined, with 'National Unity' being the end objective. Trade policy broadly defined encompasses all measures governing international trade such as tariffs, quotas, import and export restrictions, non-trade barriers and ownership restriction for foreign investment and takeovers. In the era of multilateral and preferential trade agreements, trade policy also extends to all the 'trade-related' regulatory issues, especially in the context of trade negotiations.

Industrial Policies

There have been four phases of industrial policies in Malaysia's industrial development:

- Phase I: Import substitution industrialization (1957–1968)
- Phase II: Export oriented industrialization (1968–1986)
- Phase III: Heavy industries import substitution (1981–1985)
- Phase IV: High technology export oriented industrialization (1986 to present)

Phase I – Import substitution industrialization (ISI-1): 1957–1968
Manufacturing was not a significant component of the newly independent Malaya's economy, as reflected in Table 5.1. Post-colonial governments thus promoted industrialization, which began with a low-key phase of import substitution (IS) in the 1960s. The Pioneer Industries Ordinance of

1958 signalled the beginning of this phase by offering tax relief on profits for so-called 'pioneer' firms in the IS sectors. The government also provided infrastructure, credit facilities and tariff protection to these firms.

In the early stages, the new industries concentrated mainly on manufacturing consumer goods for which there was a home market. The growth of manufacturing output was rapid in the initial years, mainly due to low base values. In relatively short order, growth slowed as the small and low average-income domestic market began to saturate.

Import substitution largely failed to realize its objectives: the contribution of the manufacturing sector to the country's GDP increased marginally from 11 per cent in 1957 to 13 per cent in 1968, and manufacturing's share of total employment increased from 6 per cent to just 9 per cent. Alarmingly, total unemployment increased from 6 per cent in 1962 to 6.6 per cent in 1967, due mostly to a slump in the rubber prices, leading to reduction of acreage and production of rubber. It was clear that import substitution could not effectively solve the unemployment problem. As is often the case, the generous investment incentives had favoured capital-intensive projects, resulting in relatively low rates of labour absorption.

Phase II – Export Oriented Industrialization (EOI-I): 1968–1986

Accepting the limitations of its small domestic market, Malaysia began to encourage greater export orientation, initially through the Investment Incentives Act of 1968. Several factors were responsible for this policy shift. The most critical factor was the failure of import substitution to generate growth of manufacturing output and employment, as noted above. Mounting domestic political tensions caused by unemployment forced the government to look for immediate employment creation industries. Other factors that influenced the shift were the spectacular success of export-led industrialization of the Asian NICs[9] and the change in the intellectual climate in Malaysia towards greater emphasis on trade, amidst growing evidence associating exports with efficiency and import substitution with inefficiency.[10]

However, greater export orientation did not entail the complete abandonment of import substitution. EOI-I and ISI-I were pursued together, with stronger emphasis given to EOI. Investment incentives were restructured to encourage manufacturers to export; examples included export allowances, accelerated depreciation of capital equipment and buildings, tax holidays and investment tax credits, and other fiscal incentives. Pre-shipment and post-shipment export credit re-financing facilities at concessionary rates of interest were also introduced.

The establishment of free trade zones (by the Free Trade Zones Act of 1971) was perhaps the most aggressive measure taken by the government to promote manufactured exports. These FTZs operate as 'foreign enclaves' with duty-free access to imported inputs and machinery, while at the same time enjoying a wide range of investment and export incentives, and weaker labour laws, such as prohibiting the formation of trade unions.[11] By focusing on labour-intensive industries, the FTZs absorbed surplus labour, especially from the Malay community. Investment regulations were also liberal – multi-national corporations (MNCs) were granted 100 percent ownership.

To meet the equity objectives of the NEP, the government introduced the Industrial Coordination Act (ICA) in 1975.[12] It stipulated that all new manufacturing projects above a predetermined threshold have at least 30 per cent *Bumiputera* ownership. This unfortunately had a crippling effect of small and medium scale enterprises (SMEs).[13] Nevertheless, growth in the FTZs contributed to a substantial increase in manufacturing value-added as a share of GDP, from 10.4 per cent in 1970 to 19.6 per cent in 1980. Employment increased from 270 000 to 755 000 over the same period, and unemployment fell from 7.8 per cent 5.3 per cent.

Phase III – Heavy Industries Import Substitution Industrialization (ISI-II)

The incorporation of the Heavy Industries Corporation of Malaysia (HICOM) introduced Malaysia to heavy industrialization. With it came extensive public investment and burdensome protectionist measures. Through HICOM, investments were made in the national car project, motorcycle engines, cement plants, petrochemical and gas projects, and steel plants, with active participation from Japanese and South Korean firms. HICOM relied on state funds for these projects, as the private sector was reluctant to take the lead role.

Dr Mahathir, the third Prime Minister, promoted heavy industrialization to deepen the industrial capacity and capabilities of Malaysian firms and develop a more balanced, integrated national economy, as the export oriented sectors were dominated by MNCs with few links to the rest of the economy. Furthermore, the impressive gains made by the Republic of Korea and Japan through heavy industrialization prompted Dr Mahathir to introduce 'The Look East Policy', which promoted 'Picking Winners' through close collaboration between selected corporations in Malaysia, South Korea and Japan in heavy industries.

Phase IV – High Technology Export Oriented Industrialization

ISI-II was a failure on most counts. With the nation facing severe debt crisis due to various unprofitable heavy industrialization projects, and falling foreign direct investment due to a global recession, the government re-emphasized EOI, quietly suspending selected NEP privileges. Critical among these was the liberalization of foreign equity ownership with the introduction of the Promotions of Investment Act (PIA) in 1986. It granted additional tax incentives and pioneer status for periods of five years for export oriented manufacturing, agriculture and tourism enterprises. Amendments were also made to the 1975 Industrial Coordination Act to allow industrialists to invest in new projects or to expand and diversify existing investments with less attention paid to, *inter alia*, equity requirements (number of employees, paid-up capital).

The timing for this liberalization was perfect. It coincided with structural changes in Japan, South Korea, Taiwan and Hong Kong, caused mainly by exchange rate appreciation due to the Plaza Accord, the loss of Generalized System of Preferences (GSP) benefits, and rising wages. These forced many of their manufacturers to seek lower-cost production sites offshore. The Industrial Master Plan 1 (IMP1), launched in 1986, identified 12 industrial sub-sectors that were to be promoted, and gave further impetus to these foreign investors and manufacturers in general.

Flanking Policies

With the implementation of the New Economic Policy between 1970 and 1991 (and related development policies), the role of the state, comprising the public sector and publicly owned or controlled enterprises, increased tremendously. The nature of government intervention also changed from a trusteeship approach and direct intervention in the 1970s to a more business-like, facilitative approach from the mid-1980s onwards.

Government allocation for development expenditure increased from RM4.6 billion in the First Malaysia Plan (1966–1970) to RM11.5 billion in the Second Malaysia Plan (1971–1975) – the first after the race riots. The amount tripled to RM36.7 billion in the Third Malaysia Plan (1976–1980), and the Fourth Malaysia Plan (1981–1985) was allocated RM42.8 billion. This was the period when 'direct' government intervention was highest.

The federal government intervened through four methods:

i. Enlarging the public sector (establishing new government departments and expanding existing ones).
ii. Establishing new statutory bodies, such as the Malaysian Industrial Development Authority (MIDA), and Malaysian External Trade Development Corporation (MATRADE).
iii. Creating new public enterprises, such as HICOM Bhd, Perusahaan Otomobil Nasional (PROTON), amongst others.
iv. Creating 'Trust Agencies', instruments to hold equity on behalf *Bumiputeras* who couldn't themselves, especially in the 1970s. Examples

Table 5.3 State owned enterprise by paid-up capital, 1988

Level	Number of companies	Total capital (RM million)	Govt Equity (RM million)	Govt. Equity as % of total capital	Average capital (RM million)
Federal	556	18,521	12,738	68.78	33.3
State	553	5,048	3,829	75.85	9.1
Regional	49	241	170	70.54	4.9
Total	1,158	23,810	16,737	70.29	20.6

Source: Jomo and Tan Wooi Syn.

Table 5.4 Malaysia: state owned enterprise by sector, 1988

Sector	Federal	State	Regional	Total
Agriculture	5	19	3	27
Construction	8	26	1	35
Extractive	6	27	1	34
Finance	100	33	1	134
Manufacturing	153	155	14	322
Plantation	22	61	12	95
Property	44	53	1	98
Services	162	135	16	313
Logging	0	25	0	25
Transport	56	12	0	68
Others	0	7	0	7
Total	556	553	49	1158

Source: Jomo and Tan Wooi Syn.

include Perbadanan Nasional Bhd (Pernas), and Permodalan Nasional Berhad (PNB).

The state governments were also involved in establishing their own public enterprises under the auspices of the State Economic Development Corporation (SEDC). Table 5.3 and 5.4 illustrate the extent government intervention in the economy had reached before the privatization programme, which gathered momentum after the mid-1980s recession.[14]

Public sector expenditure rose sharply under the NEP, from 29.2 per cent of GNP in 1970 to a peak of 58.4 per cent in 1981. At the time of independence in 1957, there were only 23 public enterprises engaged mainly in the provision of public utilities, transportation, telecommunication, agricultural development and finance. However, during the period 1975–1989, 901 public enterprises were created, drastically increasing the total number of public enterprises operating in Malaysia.[15] The state also took over foreign interests or developed partnerships with existing foreign corporations in Malaysia.[16]

At the same time, however, certain state institutions have been crucial in developing the nation's external economy. The Malaysian Industrial Development Authority (MIDA) and the Malaysian External Trade Development Corporation (MATRADE) were instrumental in attracting FDI and promoting Malaysia as a location for foreign investors.

Although privatization has been implemented since the early 1980s, the government continues to play a leading role in the Malaysian economy through Government-Linked Companies (GLCs) and Government-Linked Investment Companies (GLICs).[17] There are currently 57 GLCs and seven GLICs in operation, and 50 per cent of all GLCs are listed on the *Bursa Malaysia*. They have a collective market capitalization of RM295 billion, accounting for 36 per cent of the *Bursa Malaysia*'s total, and 41 per cent of the benchmark KLCI.[18]

The failure of government strategies to develop *Bumiputera* entrepreneurs through state-owned enterprises (SOEs), and now through GLCs, reflects the overall failure of the NEP. The performance of GLCs relies mainly on the ability to merge, acquire or privatize national assets, rather than create and sustain new economic activities.

Privatization and Deregulation

The early 1980s saw privatization becoming a buzzword, thanks to the policies implemented in the United Kingdom and the USA by Margaret Thatcher and Ronald Reagan, respectively. This was reinforced by the fact that underperforming or failed SOEs were proving a significant burden on Malaysia's fiscal position. The dismal performance of SOEs is reflected in Table 5.5. On average, more than 50 per cent performed only satisfactorily or less than satisfactorily, and almost 40 per cent were loss-making (measured by the utilization of shareholders' funds).

However, most important to the privatization drive was Mahathir's acceptance that *Bumiputera* entrepreneurial development was not being achieved through public companies. Although this policy reversed earlier government policies, the end goal was still the redistribution of resources to the Malay community through the restructuring of employment and ownership of share capital in the corporate sector, aimed at creating a *Bumiputera* Commercial and Industrial Community (BCIC). The privatization policy was a corollary to Mahathir's 'Malaysia Inc.'.

Table 5.5 Malaysia: relative performance of state owned enterprises, 1980–1988 (in percent)

Year	Sick[a]	Weak[b]	Satisfactory[c]	Good[d]
1980	12.53	26.24	10.88	50.35
1981	13.19	26.74	9.63	50.44
1982	15.25	29.15	9.86	45.74
1983	12.12	30.12	10.04	47.72
1984	14.02	26.98	11.80	47.20
1985	16.79	30.20	11.09	41.92
1986	18.95	29.54	13.31	38.20
1987	19.23	27.43	13.87	39.47
1988	16.67	24.15	14.42	44.76

Notes:
a: Companies with negative shareholders' funds
b: Loss-making companies with shareholders' funds < 200% of paid-up capital
c: Shareholders' funds < 100% but currently profitable
d: Shareholders' funds > 100% and profitable.

The Evolution of the Trade Policy Regime

Malaysia's trade regime had always been designed to support Malaysia's industrialization policies, while responding to regional and global pressures. At all times the government has insulated, but never excessively so, sectors of the Malaysian economy considered sensitive or strategically important to achieving the development and NEP objectives. The chronology of Malaysia's trade regime is captured below:[19]

- Phase I (1957–1968): Tariffs were used mostly for protecting infant industries producing consumer goods. Moderate tariff protection was the key instrument used to encourage new investments in manufacturing. However, the protection was mild. The average bound tariff rate in 1965 was estimated at only 13 per cent. Very few quantitative restrictions were used to limit imports.
- Phase II (1968–1980): Free Trade Zones were established. Incentives were granted to encourage manufactured exports, partly linked to export performance.
- Phase III (1981–1985): High protection, in comparison to tariffs in other sectors, was given to the industries targeted for the attempted heavy industrialization drive (automobile, petrochemical, iron and steel, and cement industries). Both import duties and import restrictions for competing goods were used, substantially raising average

levels of protection. The average effective rate of protection (ERP) in the manufacturing sector increased from approximately 25 per cent in the early 1960s to 70 per cent in the early 1980s.

- Phase IV (1985 onwards): The economic crisis of 1985–87 caused by the global recession and deficit spending for heavy industries led to the introduction of a voluntary structural adjustment reform package. This included significant tariff reductions and the removal of quantitative restrictions. The average ERP for manufacturing declined to below 30 per cent by the late 1980s. From the late 1980s, further tariff reductions were introduced as part of the Common Effective Preferential Tariff (CEPT) of the ASEAN Free Trade Agreement (AFTA). With the slow progress of the Doha trade talks at the WTO, launched in 2002, Malaysia has pursued bilateral and regional trade agreements, which has brought about further trade liberalization.

Average ERPs tended to increase for import-competing industries during the 1960s and 1970s, after which they began to fall. In 1962 the average ERP stood at 25 per cent, and rose to 50 per cent by 1972. It then began to fall from 61 per cent in 1974 to 42 per cent in 1980 and to 28 per cent in 1987. Average ERPs for consumer goods in 1969 were 72 per cent, and for intermediate goods 33 per cent. In 1987, the figure for consumer goods had fallen to 9 per cent, but on intermediate goods it had risen to 65 per cent. Although Malaysia has had high ERPs over the years, its average bound tariff rate was generally low throughout.[20]

Despite trade policy being driven by perceived industrial policy imperatives, trade reforms have made Malaysia's one of the most open economies among developing countries. Exports of goods and services grew at 14 per cent per annum during the period 1971–90, and at a higher rate of 17 per cent per annum between 1991 and 2000. As a percentage of GDP, exports of goods and services rose from 46 per cent in 1970 to 123 per cent in 2005 while imports rose from 41.3 per cent of GDP in 1970 to 100 per cent of GDP in 2005. In total, trade accounted for 87 per cent of GDP in 1970 and grew to an astounding 223 per cent of GDP in 2005 (see Table 5.6). It is clear that external demand for Malaysian products dictates the pace at which the economy moves. The external sector is critical to Malaysia's 'growth with equity' policy, as the internal market is small.

Trade policy reform has influenced both the composition of exports and the direction of trade. Most striking is the composition of exports. In the 1970s, rubber, palm oil and forestry products accounted for 55 per cent of total exports. From the mid-1980s, strong diversification into manufactured goods has occurred; the share of manufactures in total exports

Table 5.6 Exports of goods and services

	1970	1980	1990	2000	2005
Exports of goods and services (RM million)	5,389	30,676	88,675	427,004	611,082
Imports of goods and services (RM million)	4,888	29,342	86,241	358,530	494,529
Trade balance	501	1334	2434	68474	116,553
Exports of goods and services (% of GDP)	45.6	57.5	74.5	124.4	123.4
Imports of goods and services (% of GDP)	41.3	55.0	72.4	104.5	99.9
Total (% of GDP)	86.9	112.6	146.9	228.9	223.2

Source: Adapted from UNDP Malaysia (2006).

Table 5.7 Share of exports (per cent), Malaysia, 1970–2005

	1970	1980	1990	2000	2005
Agriculture	52.1	35.5	18.7	6.1	7.7
Minerals	22.8	34.5	17.7	7.2	13.2
Manufacturing	15.8	25.2	58.8	85.2	77.4
Others	9.3	4.8	4.8	1.5	1.7

Source: Malaysia Plans (various years) and MITI Annual Report 2006.

reached 77 per cent in 2005 (see Table 5.7). Within the manufacturing sector, the electrical and electronics sub-sector is the most important. This has also led to intermediate goods accounting for an ever-growing share of total exports, and a concomitant relative decline in the importance of final consumption goods.

Trade policies have also had a significant effect on direction of trade. In line with Malaysia's commitment to 'open regionalism', Malaysia continues to participate actively in ASEAN, the Asia-Pacific Economic Cooperation (APEC) forum, and the Asia-Europe Meeting (ASEM). Malaysia is also active at the sub-regional level within ASEAN, notably the Indonesia–Malaysia–Thailand Growth Triangle and the Brunei–Indonesia–Malaysia–Philippines–East Asian Growth Area.

As the importance of manufacturing sector has grown, the USA has become Malaysia's largest export market, accounting for almost 20 percent by 2005 (see Table 5.8). Exports to China have also increased dramatically, from 1.3 per cent in 1970 to 11.5 per cent in 2005, indicating China's growing importance as a global trading power (or increasing

Table 5.8 Direction of Malaysia's external trade (in per cent)

	1970		1980		1990		2000		2005	
	X	M	X	M	X	M	X	M	X	M
USA	13.0	8.5	16.4	15.0	16.9	16.7	20.5	16.6	19.7	12.9
ASEAN	24.7	15.6	22.4	16.4	28.9	18.9	26.5	24.1	25.8	24.5
Singapore	21.5	7.2	19.1	11.7	22.7	14.9	18.4	14.4	15.6	11.7
EU	19.2	23.0	16.9	15.4	14.9	14.6	13.7	10.8	11.7	11.6
Japan	18.2	17.7	22.8	22.9	15.8	24.0	13.1	21.0	9.4	14.5
China	1.3	5.2	1.7	2.4	2.1	1.9	3.1	4.0	6.6	11.5
India	0.4	1.5	2.2	0.9	1.6	0.7	2.0	0.9	2.8	1.0
Total (RM million)	5,163	4,289	28,172	23,451	79,646	79,119	373,459	311,459	533,790	434,030

Note: X = exports, M = imports.

Source: Adapted from UNDP Malaysia (2006).

links with ASEAN/East Asia). This has meant that the shares of exports destined for the European Union (EU) and Japan are declining, as is their importance as a source of imports. Exports to the EU were 19.2 per cent in 1970 and dropped to 11.7 per cent in 2005. ASEAN is now the largest source of imports.

The key trade policy-making institution is the Ministry of International Trade and Industry (MITI). It is a powerful Ministry, is always led by senior politicians,[21] and works closely with the Economic Planning Unit and the Ministry of Finance. These Ministries are closely linked to business interests, making some aspects of policy-making easier than might be the case in other developing countries. The drawback is that this leads to a relative lack of transparency in high-level decision-making, and widens scope for corruption.

Malaysia is best characterized as a steady liberalizer. Although industrial policies have changed dramatically in response to global situations and domestic political imperatives, since the mid-1980s the Malaysian government has held course on progressive external liberalization, and has maintained a good degree of policy coordination and coherence. Most self-imposed targets and deadlines are met; those missed are often due to pressure from the *Bumiputera* constituency – both business and the public. Examples include sectors such as the national car project (Proton) and its vendor schemes, which were to have been liberalized under the AFTA; government procurement; and the rice sector, which continues to be protected for political reasons. The government argues that these constitute important development policies, required for achieving national unity objectives.

Much of Malaysia's liberalization has been unilateral in nature, but trade negotiations have played an important role. Malaysia acceeded to the GATT in 1957 but did not participate actively in the global trade policy debate. This was reversed during the Uruguay Round. Malaysia, together with four other ASEAN members[22] formed a strong common stance on market access issues, especially in industrial goods. Similarly, on agriculture issues, Malaysia, as a member of the Cairns group, argued against subsidies in developed economies and various other distortions.[23]

At the same time, Malaysia has also pursued various bilateral trade agreements, some of which go beyond market access in goods to include chapters on services, investment, trade facilitation, competition policies, intellectual property rights, standards development, conformity assessments, education and training, research and development and small and medium enterprises development. As at 2006, Malaysia was at various stages of negotiation with its partners (see Table 5.9).

Table 5.9 Malaysia's trade negotiations

Trade Agreement Level	Status
Multilateral	
WTO Doha Development Round	Negotiations ongoing (2001–)
Regional	
ASEAN Free Trade Agreement (AFTA)	Framework agreement completed 1992*
ASEAN–China FTA	Framework agreement concluded (2002–2010/15) Agreement in trade in goods concluded
ASEAN–India CEC	Negotiations ongoing (2004–)
ASEAN–Japan CEP	Negotiations ongoing (2003–12)
ASEAN Economic Community	Negotiations ongoing (2003–2020)
ASEAN–Republic of Korea	Framework agreement concluded (2004)
Bilateral	
Malaysia–Japan Economic Partnership Agreement	Framework agreement concluded (2003–2012)
Malaysia–Australia FTA	Negotiations ongoing (2004–)
Malaysia–New Zealand FTA	Negotiations ongoing (2004–)
Malaysia–United States FTA	Negotiations (2006–)
Others	
Global System of Trade Preferences Among Developing Countries (GSTP)	1989
Trade Preferential System among Organisation of the Islamic Conference	2004
Preferential Trading Arrangement (PTA) among Group of Developing Eight (D8)	2004

Note: * The framework agreement was completed in 1992. The agreement is implemented through various protocols with the most common being the Common Effective Preferential Tariff (CEPT).

Source: UNDP Malaysia 2006.

Related Microeconomic Reforms

Changes in Malaysia's trade policies have induced various different microeconomic policy reforms, and exposed areas where reform of existing policies or the introduction of entirely new ones has become necessary. The guiding principles throughout, however, have been and remain state control of strategic and sensitive sectors, and that *Bumiputera* interest must be safeguarded.

Foreign investment controls In 1974, the government set up a Foreign Investment Committee (FIC), mandated to work according to the 'Guidelines for the Regulation of Acquisition of Assets, Mergers and Take-Overs' of foreign firms with interests in Malaysia. The FIC has far-ranging powers and formulates policies to promote the achievement of NEP objectives in the corporate sector. However, it regulates inward investments in certain non-manufacturing sectors only. MITI/MIDA regulates investment in the manufacturing sector, while the Ministry of Domestic Trade and Consumer Affairs controls investment in the wholesale and retail sectors. There are no restrictions on outward investment except for a blanket ban on trade and investment with Israel, which Malaysia does not recognize.

Beginning in the late 1970s, the government has taken over most foreign-controlled interests established during colonial times. The vehicles used were state-owned investment corporations such as Permodalan Nasional Berhad (PNB) and Perbadanan Nasional (PERNAS). Plantation corporations such as Sime Darby, Guthrie, Harison Crossfield, Highland Lowland, and London Tin, the largest tin mining corporation in Malaysia, along with many British trading houses, were all targeted by these state investment corporations. Other foreign corporations from the colonial period were required to be incorporated locally.

Labour laws Successive governments have argued that Malaysia's rapid growth was achieved mainly through the maintenance of relatively cheap, productive labour. This has resulted in relatively weak labour laws and regulations, and has eroded the role played by trade unions in policy decisions. In 2005, only 9 per cent of labour force was represented by a total of 617 trade unions.[24]

Before the 1969 riots, trade unions were a dominant force in local politics, acting mainly through the Labour Party. One of the responses to the riots included amending Malaysia's labour laws. The changes served two purposes – to curtail labour movements links with politics, and to control labour more effectively in the new, mainly labour-intensive export-oriented industries and especially the free trade zones. Some of the major reforms included strengthening the Registrar of Trade Union's power to prevent electronics factory workers from forming a union, allowing shift work for women, restricting the right to strike, and limiting trade union activities and rights.

The government continues to promote the notion that Malaysia's global comparative advantage is in low-cost manufacturing, determined in large part by relatively low wages. This reinforces the government's desire to maintain labour markets that are flexible, but that do not simultaneously threaten *Bumiputera* interests. However, Malaysia's economic performance, especially since the 1990s, has resulted in strong labour demand and upward pressure on real wages. The government's response has been to liberalize policies on migrant labour, allowing foreign workers to find jobs not just in the free trade zones, but also now in the manufacturing and plantation sectors, construction, selected services such as hotels and restaurants, healthcare, and information technology. Trade union demands for minimum wage laws have routinely been ignored by the government, which argues that such legislation would make Malaysia less attractive to FDI.

Sectoral Reforms Key sectoral reforms have occurred in financial services and some professional services (for example legal and accounting), which were heavily protected until the early 2000s. The pressures to reform and open have been almost exclusively external in source and nature.

The impacts of the 1997/98 financial crisis created the initial pressure to reform the financial sector; indeed the chaotic environment at the time provided much-needed political 'space' to begin a serious discussion on the matter. Before the financial crisis there were 37 locally incorporated banks, of which 23 were domestic and 12 foreign-owned. It was agreed that Malaysia was 'over-banked' and in the light of consolidation globally in the financial sector, there was a need for similar consolidation locally.

However, it is arguable that this restructuring was heavily influenced by politics; the ruling party, and *Bumiputera* elites linked to the ruling party, appear to have been the major beneficiaries. Financial institutions controlled by Malaysian Chinese were forced to merge with or sell out to government-owned or government-backed *Bumiputera* financial institutions, despite the former traditionally performing better. Nevertheless, Malaysia's WTO membership, and ASEAN's drive to become an Economic Community, have forced further opening in these sectors since the post-crisis scramble to restructure. While they remain relatively well protected from international competition, more meaningful external liberalization seems inevitable.

In the agriculture sector, there are limitations on foreign ownership, including ownership of land. The government provides direct support to the rice and tobacco sectors; in 2004 alone, the government expended almost RM813 million to support approximately 350 000 rice farmers. In the mineral sector, except for petroleum, the government allows for 100 per cent foreign ownership for projects involving extraction or mining and processing. However, mergers and acquisitions are subject to FIC approval. The Petroleum Development Act 1974 ensures the upstream oil and gas industry is controlled by the government through PETRONAS.

Competition policies To date Malaysia has no competition policy in place, although the need for it was mentioned in the Eighth Malaysia Plan

(2001–2005).[25] This is most likely informed by Malaysia's experiences with privatization, which have resulted in privately-owned enterprises facing little or no competition in certain sub-sectors. The emergence during the 1990s of so-called 'new generation' issues in trade negotiations further heightened the need to develop competition policies, as these became key issues in the WTO and in some bilateral trade agreements, especially advanced economies such as the US, ASEAN members have also already agreed to devise a regional competition policy, although it is not yet clear precisely what form this might take.

The main challenge to implementing competition policy in Malaysia is the perception that it would undermine NEP objectives, and favour the positions of non-Malays and foreign interests in the economy. An illustrative example is government procurement, a market estimated to have been worth RM92.7 billion or 20.6 per cent of GDP in 2004.

Government procurement is used to support equity and transformation objectives, transferring technology to local industries, and creating opportunities for local service-oriented companies. Procurement processes are opaque, and bidding tends to lack robust competition. Effective competition policy would at least require such activities to be investigated, and findings could potentially prove highly controversial.

THE CONSEQUENCES OF MALAYSIA'S OPENING

Trade reforms in Malaysia have progressed steadily in sectors that are not critical to the ruling party. Large sections of the domestic economy remain within the direct and indirect control of the government, whilst almost all of manufacturing, many primary activities, and some services have been comprehensively opened to international competition.

Protection Levels Today

Tariffs have for some time been the main trade policy instrument used to control imports. Bound tariff rates have decreased steadily; the trade-weighted average bound tariff for all products is now 4.2 per cent. This is significantly lower than most other major Asian economies (see Table 5.10).

The simple average applied MFN tariff is approximately 8.6 per cent. However, duties are higher for tariff lines where there is significant local production, and typical tariff escalation, where tariffs on raw materials are lower than on value-added goods, is detectable. A sales tax of 10 per cent is also levied on most goods, but not on raw materials or machinery used in export production.

Table 5.10 Weighted average bound tariffs, selected Asian countries (percentage)

Country	Year	All Products	Primary Products	Manufactured Products
China	1992	32.1	14.1	35.6
	2004	6.0	5.6	6.0
India	1990	56.1	34.1	70.8
	2004	28.0	36.1	25.3
Indonesia	1989	13.0	5.9	15.1
	2003	5.2	3.1	5.8
Japan	1988	3.6	4.4	2.7
	2004	2.4	3.9	1.6
Korea	1988	14.0	8.3	17.0
	2004	10.0	19.0	5.0
Malaysia	1988	9.7	4.6	10.8
	2003	4.2	2.1	4.6
Pakistan	1995	44.4	36.1	49.2
	2004	13.0	8.9	15.7
Philippines	1988	22.4	18.5	23.4
	2003	2.6	5.0	2.0
Singapore	1989	1.1	2.5	0.6
	2003	0.0	0.0	0.0
Thailand	1989	33.0	24.3	35.0
	2003	8.3	4.4	9.3
Vietnam	1994	20.6	46.7	13.1
	2004	13.7	16.7	12.5

Source: UNDP Malaysia (2006).

Although the tariffs are low in Malaysia, 17 per cent of Malaysia's tariff lines (mainly in the construction equipment, agricultural, minerals, and motor vehicles sectors) are subject to non-automatic import licensing designed to protect import-sensitive or strategic sectors. The tariff structure remains relatively dispersed (at least by industrialized-country standards), as do certain tariff peaks. These are highest in automobiles, where the applied MFN rate can be as high as 300 per cent, due to the government's protection of the national car project.

However, tariffs on automobiles have been reduced drastically under the AFTA and bilateral preferential trade agreements (PTA) in recent times, underscoring the government's inability to continue to protect Proton. After 20 years of protection, Proton has been on most counts a disaster, having failed to penetrate any export markets. Unlike the Japanese and South Korean carmakers (after which the idea of Proton was modelled) which successfully managed to penetrate and dominate the competitive export markets of the US and EU, Proton has survived purely on the basis of government support and a protected domestic market. Realising that Proton is unlikely to ever become profitable, the government is now seeking a strategic partner, which may pave the way for the sector's liberalization.

Economic Impacts: Macroeconomic, Microeconomic and Developmental

On balance, the macroeconomic risks of Malaysia's openness have been managed prudently, albeit not completely problem-free. During the 1960s the government remained fiscally conservative and maintained balanced or surplus budgets. However, to achieve NEP objectives in the 1970s and 1980s, budget deficits were tolerated and were financed mainly through the Employees Provident Fund and newly discovered oil revenues. Budget deficits grew from 3.7 per cent of GDP in 1970 to about 19 per cent of GDP in 1982 and remained around 14 per cent of GDP during 1983–87.[26]

Rising deficits forced the government to borrow externally, causing debt to balloon from RM15.4 billion in 1981 to RM53 billion in 1986. As part of the response to this unsustainable situation, the country maintained budget surpluses for the period 1993–97, but reverted to deficits to bolster economic growth after the financial crisis. However, the external debt position has since been capped at about 40 per cent of GNP.

Malaysia has tended to record surpluses in merchandise trade and deficits in services trade, with the former exceeding the latter in most years since independence. This has translated into a relatively unpredictable current account balance over the years. Since the financial crisis, Malaysia, along with most of east Asia, has consciously maintained large current account surpluses, as the accumulation of foreign reserves is widely viewed as an essential tool for managing the risks of potential future volatility. Strong FDI and portfolio inflows have contributed to overall balance of payments surpluses and gross foreign exchange reserves stood at USD70 billion in 2005.

Malaysia's rapid growth has also been achieved without undue inflationary pressure. Except for the periods during the oil shocks and the financial crisis, inflation has been stable at around 4 per cent. The main reason for the low inflation rate is extensive intervention by the Central Bank (Bank Negara Malaysia: BNM) in the open market. BNM consistently mops liquidity in the financial system and manages the exchange rate to contain inflationary pressures on the economy. It allows the exchange rate to appreciate when the economy is overheating (as in the period before the crisis). However, Malaysia controls the prices of many essential items (for example food, fuel and utilities) and provides subsidies

Table 5.11 TFP contributions to GDP growth, 1976–2000

Period	Rate of Growth (%)				Contribution to Growth (%)		
	GDP	TFP	Capital	Labour	TFP	Capital	Labour
1976–80	8.48	2.64	4.13	1.71	31.1	48.7	20.2
1981–85	5.15	−1.04	4.16	2.03	−20.2	80.8	39.4
1986–90	6.23	1.87	2.17	2.19	30.0	34.8	35.2
1991–95	9.47	3.15	3.84	2.49	33.2	40.5	26.3
1996–00	4.88	0.42	2.67	1.79	8.6	54.7	36.7

Source: Chew and Wong (2004).

in key commodities (for example, rice, fuel), which substantially reduces inflationary risks.

On balance, the government has succeeded in providing a stable macroeconomic environment, which, along with other advantages such as a productive and relatively inexpensive labour force, has enabled Malaysia to attract significant quantities of FDI, especially in manufacturing. This in turn has provided the foundation for Malaysia's post-independence economic development.

Annual FDI inflows have risen from a low of US$94 million in 1970, when Malaysia first began to encourage greater openness and export orientation, to almost US$4 billion in 2005. However, these inflows have declined from the boom years of the mid-1990s, when they peaked at US$7 billion in 1996, just before the financial crisis. The inward FDI stock stood at US$48 billion in 2005, down from US$53 billion in 2000. There are two main reasons for this: the Malaysian government is becoming more selective in approving FDI as it attempts to promote high value-added sectors (for example biotechnology, ICT); and foreign investors are heading to more favoured destinations such as China and Vietnam.

It is unclear how much of Malaysia's impressive aggregate productivity gains can be attributed to trade reforms, since total factor productivity (TFP) growth has been erratic over the various different plan periods. However, during the heavy industrialization period (ISI-II, 1981–85), TFP growth was negative (See Table 5.11). In general, the sectors that were exposed to international competition, such as manufacturing, the large plantations, and selected services, performed better than the sectors that were protected.

The manufacturing sector has for some time been the leading sector of the economy, and generates significant foreign exchange and employment. It is also the only sector (barring automobiles) that has been fully liberalized. Yet, as with Malaysia's productivity gains, it is difficult to argue conclusively that liberalization has driven economic growth, especially considering the extent of state intervention in the economy. Between independence in 1957 and 2005, Malaysia's real GDP grew on average at 6.5 per cent a year. Within the same period, nominal GDP per capita grew by 7 per cent a year, and has increased from USD334 in 1978 to USD5042 in 2005. Poverty has been reduced from 49.3 per cent in 1970 to 5.7 per cent in 2004.

Unemployment has fallen from 8.0 per cent at the beginning of the First Malaysia Plan (1971–1975) to 3.5 per cent in 2005. Population growth has been stable, although the increase in number of migrant workers in the country continuously increases the labour supply. Officially, Malaysia has 1.8 million legal migrant workers. The number of illegal migrant workers is estimated to be at 700 000. Migrant workers are conservatively estimated at 23 per cent of the total labour force.[27] As noted earlier, this maintains downward pressure on wage rates, particularly in low-skilled occupations.

Malaysian policy makers currently face the relatively new problems of jobless growth and graduate unemployment. The former is attributed to increased productivity through the use of technology, while graduate unemployment is attributed to a mismatch between tertiary education outputs and market needs. Policy makers are increasingly hard-pressed to balance the demands of the markets/business with affirmative action policies for the *Bumiputera*, and to resist legitimate demands for greater labour protection. Moreover, these labour market challenges inevitably translate to renewed pressure to address the migrant labour question.

LOOKING AHEAD

Malaysia has generally succeeded in undertaking the so-called first generation reforms, which primarily address border measures only. However, it has yet to address the second generation, behind-the-border regulatory measures comprehensively. There are still many sectors of the economy directly controlled by the state.

An important obstacle to this remaining liberalization is UMNO's *raison d'être* as the 'protector of the Malay race'. UMNO believes this is possible only by controlling parts of the economy considered strategically important, thereby maintaining the legacy of the NEP. To this end, GLCs and GLICs remain critical political tools for UMNO, and the successive governments it controls.

Therefore a key precondition for further liberalization is transparency. Many of Malaysia's regulatory decisions are shrouded in secrecy, and arguably are developed arbitrarily according to specific subjective criteria. However, in order to increase transparency in policy-making, democracy must be improved. Furthermore, the country must grapple the issue of racism, as the government sees any demand for better, more transparent governance as a challenge to the status quo, which is designed to protect and benefit the *Bumiputera*.

Further trade liberalization would also challenge the government's continued attempts at 'picking winners', and continued commitment to protecting sensitive sectors, such as government procurement, services, utilities, energy and automobiles. It now seems clear that these policies are intended to mask successive governments' predilection for favouring business interests closely aligned to the state – to maintain its support base. In short, further regulatory reform will only come when the government rethinks its development policies, including affirmative action, and retreats further from markets that are not essential to the provision of public goods.

CONCLUSION

Malaysia is committed to maintaining an open economy. In the modern developing context, the level of openness achieved is remarkable because it has often been unilaterally driven, and often a major element of Malaysia's responses to changing global scenarios. Malaysia's opening owes very little to pressure from trade partners, the WTO, or donor conditionalities.

However, it must be noted that the trade reforms undertaken by Malaysia to date have suited the ruling party. Put differently, those reforms that do not suit UMNO's goals have been ignored. And, contrary to what one might expect, the market-based growth that has accompanied these reforms has come at the expense of democratic freedom. The state, acting as an 'agent of development', has emasculated important branches of a democracy (for example Parliament the judiciary and the civil service). Trade liberalization has *strengthened* the state; economic growth and *Bumiputera*-friendly policies have ensured Barisan Nasional's control of state organs. Growth and development has also been used as a reason to suppress dissenting views, and to force through reforms.

However, the ever-expanding agendas of modern bilateral and regional trade agreements will force Malaysia to address more regulatory reform. Recent (and ongoing) negotiations towards an FTA with the United States attest to this. The Federation of Malaysian Manufacturers (FMM) support further liberalization in goods trade, but various other Malay chambers of commerce oppose the deal because of their fear of losing certain privileges. These include the requirements placed on foreign companies operating in

Malaysia, and preferential government procurement processes. Similarly, the Malaysian Trade Union supports the FTA only if it includes a strong labour chapter, something the US Congress increasingly promotes, but with which the Malaysian government is uncomfortable. Hence in future it is likely that trade negotiations will play a more pronounced role in Malaysia's trade reforms than has been the case previously.

This may prove challenging to politics in Malaysia. However, one must keep in mind that the NEP is a pragmatic, not ideological policy framework, and can therefore be altered or replaced when it is no longer deemed useful. More broadly speaking, economic policy-making in Malaysia has proven flexible over the years. Furthermore, the NEP will only retain support if it produces economic growth. Further liberalization is likely to bring growth, but it will simultaneously erode the policy space for NEP-type policies, allowing greater scope for market forces to operate.

The key challenge Malaysia faces now is that growth is not 'trickling down' to its intended constituencies, but is being captured at the highest levels. Income disparity in Malaysia is highest in the ethnic group that the NEP is supposed to have benefited (the *Bumiputera*). In addition, the original goal of 'National Unity', which was to have been achieved through policies simultaneously promoting growth and redistribution, has now been tainted by critics arguing that it has resulted in nothing more than 'UMNO/Malay Supremacy' or persistent promotion of 'the UMNO/Malay Agenda'.

From a strictly economic perspective, the NEP's performance is commendable, as growth rates have been large enough to allow for significant redistribution. However, the NEP's implementation has also alienated large swathes of Malaysia citizens, including *Bumiputeras* who have not benefited to any significant degree. This discontent, and the loss of competitiveness attributable to affirmative action policies, is worrying for the future of the Malaysian economy. Malaysia's ranking, both in Transparency International Corruption Index and its competitiveness rankings in the Global Competitiveness Report has been erratic at best and regressive at worst. Malaysia must now reconfigure itself and move away from race-based policies if it wants to continue to prosper.

NOTES

1. Parliament consists of an elected lower house (Dewan Rakyat) and an appointed upper house (Dewan Negara).
2. Article 153 of The Federal Constitution of Malaysia grants the Yang diPertuan Agong (The Supreme Head of State) responsibility for safeguarding the rights and privileges of the Malay (and other indigenous people) of Malaysia, collectively called the *Bumiputeras*.

3. Although Malaya is a resource-rich nation, British imperialism and capital had for 200 years (1874–1957) siphoned Malaya's resources.
4. The Alliance Party is made up of the three major ethnic groups – the United Malay National Organisation (UMNO), the Malayan Chinese Association (MCA) and the Malayan Indian Congress (MIC). In the 1969 elections, the Alliance formed a coalition with the Sarawak United People's Party. But after suffering unprecedented losses in those elections, the UMNO (led by Tun Razak), in order to re-gain a two-thirds majority in Parliament, expanded the number of political parties in the Alliance to include the Peoples Movement Party (GERAKAN), the Pan Islamic Party of Malaysia (PAS) and regional parties from the Borneo states. This new alliance was called The National Front (Barisan Nasional), and UMNO was the dominant party.
5. This restricted the Alliance's ability to amend the Constitution at will. The Alliance was also unable to form state-level governments in four states, especially in the urban West Coast of Peninsular Malaysia – Selangor, Perak and Penang, and the Malay heartland of Kelantan, in the east of Peninsular.
6. Barisan Nasional has 14 component parties as at 2005. UMNO leads the Barisan Nasional.
7. More details on the various targets are provided for in the Outline Perspective Plan 1 (OPP1). Available online at: http://www.epu.jpm.my/new per cent20folder/development per cent20plan/2nd per cent20opp per cent20content/opp2/t2-1.htm
8. ASEAN – Association of South East Asian Nations. The founding nations of ASEAN are known as the ASEAN 5. They are Indonesia, Malaysia, Philippines, Singapore and Thailand. Brunei joined in 1984, Vietnam in 1995, Lao PDR and Myanmar in 1997 and Cambodia in 1999.
9. Asian Newly Industrializing Countries: Republic of Korea, Taiwan, Hong Kong and Singapore.
10. Mohamed Ariff and Muthi Semudram (1987).
11. Historically, industrial relations legislation was deliberately developed to weaken the labour movement (Anantaraman, 1997). The Industrial Relations Act of 1967 governs labour relations in Malaysia, but provides relatively low protection to workers, and was sometimes ignored by other legislation, such as the Free Trade Zones Act. For example, it was only in 1988, after the recession of 1985–87, that workers in the electronic and electrical industries were allowed to form trade unions in FTZs.
12. The main purpose of the ICA was to restructure equity ownership according to the 30:30:40 formula (30-Bumiputera, 30-foreign, 40-Chinese/non-Bumiputera Malaysians) (Gomez and Jomo, 1999).
13. The initial company-size threshold was RM250 000 and 25 employees. This forced many Chinese SMEs to stop expanding their business to avoid giving away 30 per cent of equity. After realizing this negative impact and so as not to deter foreign investment, the government revised the threshold upwards to RM2.5 million and 75 employees.
14. Mahatir launched the Privatization Policy in 1983. However, the Guidelines on Privatization were only released in 1985, while the Privatization Masterplan and the Privatization Action Plan were issued in 1991.
15. Ariff, Mohamed (1994).
16. The 'Dawn Raid' or backdoor nationalization as termed by the British is often quoted as an example where state capitalism or Malay ethnic nationalism used market mechanisms to take control of foreign private sector interests in Malaysia.
17. GLCs are defined as companies that have a primary commercial objective and in which the Malaysian Government has direct controlling stake. GLICs are defined as Federal Government-linked investment companies that allocate some or all of their funds to GLC investment.
18. KLCI: Kuala Lumpur Composite Index.
19. Based on UNDP Malaysia (2006: 25). Note that the phases described here correspond closely to the different periods of industrial policy focus discussed earlier.

20. Alavi (1995).
21. Dr Mahathir Mohamed and Tengku Razaleigh Hamzah – both senior UMNO members – preceded Minister Rafidah Aziz at the helm of MITI. Ms Aziz was until recently Malaysia's longest serving trade minister, having come into this position in 1986. She is also head of UMNO's Women's wing (Wanita UMNO).
22. Singapore, Thailand, Indonesia and Philippines.
23. Athukorala (2005). Malaysia subsidizes its rice industry and is a net importer of rice. Its position in the Cairns group is motivated mainly by its interest in oil palm where it is the largest exporter and competes with other vegetable oils from the US and EU.
24. The Country Report on Human Rights Practises, 2006, by the US State Department (2007) provides an excellent write-up on current labour issues in Malaysia (http://www.state.gov/g/drl/rls/hrrpt/2006/78780.htm).
25. Pro-competition regulation does exist in the telecommunications sector.
26. Wong and Jomo (2005: 58).
27. Kanapathy (2006). The number of illegal immigrant workers is estimated and can vary from 700 000 to 5 million, as noted by the President of the Malaysian Trade Union Congress, www.mfasia.org/mfaStatements/MTUC per cent20statement per cent20on per cent20MWs per cent20in per cent20Malaysia.pdf.

REFERENCES

Abu Bakar, Nor' Aznin and Asan Ali Golam Hussan (2003), 'Globalization and Inequality: The case of Malaysia', Paper presented at the Wider Conference on Sharing Global Prosperity, Marina Congress Centre, Helsinki, Finland, 6–7 September 2003.

Alavi, R. (1995), 'The performance of highly protected industries in Malaysia', presented at a MIER econometrics conference, Kuala Lumpur.

Anantaraman, V. (1997), *Malaysian Industrial Relations: Law & Practice*, Serdarg: Universiti Putra Malaysia

Ariff, Mohamed (1994), 'Structural change, economic development and the role of the state: The malaysian experience', in Vu Tuan Anh (ed.), *The Role of The State in Economic Development: Experience of the Asian Countries*, Hanoi, Vietnam: Social Science Publishing House.

Ariff, Mohamed and Muthi Semudram (1987), 'Trade and financing strategies: a case study of Malaysia', working paper no. 21, London: Overseas Development Institute.

Athukorala, Prema-Chandra (2005), 'Trade policy in Malaysia: liberalisation process, structure of protection and reform agenda', in *ASEAN Economic Bulletin*, **22**(1), April.

Chew, K. and C. Wong (2004), 'Explaining growth: Malaysia', paper presented at the Global Development Network Conference, Tokyo.

Faaland, Just, J.R. Parkinson and Rais Saniman (1990), *Growth and Ethnic Inequality: Malaysia's New Economic Policy*, Norway: Chr. Michelsen Institute.

Gomez, E.T and K.S. Jomo (1999), *Malaysia's Political Economy: Politics Patronage, and Profits*, New York: Cambridge University Press.

Jomo, K.S. (ed.) (1994), *Malaysia's Economy in the Nineties*, Malaysia: Pelanduk Publications.

Jomo, K.S. (2004), 'The new economic policy and interethnic relations in Malaysia', Identities, Conflict and Cohesion Programme Paper No. 7, UNRISD.

Jomo, K.S. and Tan Wooi Syn, 'Privatisation and re-nationalisation in Malaysia: a survey', accessed at http://www.jomo.ws/research/research.htm.
Kanapathy, U. (2006), 'Migrant workers in Malaysia: an overview', Country paper prepared for workshop on East Asian Cooperation Framework for Migrant Labour, Kuala Lumpur, http://www.isis.org. my/files/puts/papers/VIS MIGRATION-NEAT 6 Dec 06.pdf
Lim, David (1982–83), 'Malaysia development planning', *Pacific Affairs*, **55**(4), Winter, 613-39, paper accessed at: http://www.mtuc.org.my/anantharaman per cent20paper.htm.
Milne R.S. (1987), 'Levels of corruption in Malaysia: a comment on the case of Bumiputera Malaysia Finance', *Asian Journal of Public Administration*, **9**(1), 56–73, accessed at http://sunzi1.lib.hku.hk/hkjo/view/50/5000264.pdf.
Tham, Siew-Yean (2004), 'The future of industrialisation in Malaysia under WTO', *Asia Pacific Development Journal*, **11**(1), June, 25–47. 2004.
UNDP, MIER and ISIS (2006), *Malaysia: International Trade, Growth, Poverty Reduction and Human Development*, Malaysia: UNDP Publications.
US Department of State (2007), 'Country report on human rights practices', Bureau of Democracy, Human Rights and Labor.
Wong, Hwa Kiong and K.S. Jomo (2005), 'Before the storm: the impact of foreign capital inflows on the Malaysian economy, 1966–1996', *Journal of the Asian Pacific Economy*, **10**(1), 56–69.
World Trade Organisation (2005), 'Trade policy review Malaysia', report by the Secretariat, WT/TPR/S156, December.

6. Brazil

Mario Marconini

INTRODUCTION

This chapter probes Brazil's trade policy reforms – one of the most crucial areas in Brazil's economic policy framework – with a view to putting them in perspective at a particularly auspicious moment in the country's history. World trade has been bullish for a number of years and Brazil, alongside many of its competitors, has benefited significantly from it. The question remains, however, whether good regulations, intelligent reforms, and relatively young but important institutions can survive changes to these global conditions – a question which itself raises a number of other questions. Has significant reform in fact taken place? If so, how, and to what extent? Is additional reform needed now, and in what respect? Additionally, is Brazil in a position to enact new reforms, or has complacency set in? What are some of the lingering problems and possible solutions?

HISTORICAL PARAMETERS

After decades of industrial policy and protectionism, changes in trade policy began to become inevitable in the late 1970s, as the widespread import substitution system was beginning to break down. The country had gone through two major oil crises, with a consequent substantial reduction in public savings – from close to 8 per cent of GDP in the beginning of the 1970s to close to zero in 1983–85. During the first years of the 1980s, Brazil would go through a major recession, and imports would decline consistently due to the devaluation of the exchange rate and the imposition of import controls. Even in the most internationalized sectors, imports did not top 15.7 per cent of total consumption.

With recession and low public savings, the pressure to cut investments and subsidies increased. With the second oil shock in 1978–79, inflation would spiral, reaching 100 per cent annually as early as 1979 and climbing during the 1980s to the 2000 per cent level by 1990. However, as Abreu (2007) argues, economic stagnation alone could not explain why the 1990s were inaugurated with a new trade policy. At best it could explain why the first democratic election after 30 years would be won by an unknown political figure, from the northeast of the country, whose mark was the delivery of one strong anti-establishment speech, criticizing both the political and economic elite. It was the vision of Mr Collor de Mello himself that would drive the radical changes in trade policy but, ironically, not for trade's sake: Mr de Mello's speech was against governmental intervention *tout court*, of which trade policy was merely a particularity.

Trade liberalization in Brazil took place in three bouts of tariff reductions. The first one was in 1988–89, even before the election of Collor, when the nominal average tariff fell from 57.5 per cent to 32.1 per cent – a large decrease of 44 per cent. The aim here was to do away with redundancies in the tariff structure. The second and most significant bout of liberalization took place in 1991–93, this time under Collor, with an array of pro-trade measures, including a unilateral reduction of barriers to imports (tariff and non-tariff), the extinction of CACEX (*Carteira de Comércio Exterior do Banco do Brasil*) – the iconic trade agency of Brazil's import-substitution period – and the search for a new approach to trade and integration in the Southern Cone of the Americas (the 'Common Market of the South' – Mercosur). Tariffs were reduced in this period to a nominal average of 13.5 per cent – a decrease of approximately 58 per cent. The third bout of liberalization took place in 1994 alongside the launching of the anti-inflation stabilization plan, the 'Real Plan', and as a support towards the plan's aim to keep domestic prices under control. The nominal average tariff would decline to 11.2 per cent, a decrease of 17 per cent.

Plano Real would therefore reinforce in 1994 the liberal orientation of the beginning of the decade. The Plan was, of course, about macroeconomic stabilization and not trade liberalization as such. Yet, another process, also launched in the beginning of the decade, would combine with the Plan to consolidate the move towards free markets – at least in the sub-region. Mercosur's Customs Union come into force in 1994 with the passing of the *Ouro Preto* Protocol. Most of the 11 000 tariffs on trade between the four original members were reduced to zero after a little more than three years; the protocol introduced a Common External Tariff (CET) for the bloc. Both the intra-zone trade rules as well as the CET were launched on 1 January 1995.

This coincidence in time and purpose between the internal priorities of economic policy and the external priorities of trade and integration policy made for rare consistency in this initial phase of liberalization of the Brazilian economy. Brazil's recourse to Mercosur as a tool for addressing internal problems such as controlling inflation would also constitute a major historical rarity as the bloc moved forward in the second half of the decade and beyond. An additional element favouring the initial pro-trade bias of the new Cardoso Administration (in 1995) was the implementation of the results of the recently concluded Uruguay Round of multilateral trade negotiations (the Agreement establishing the World Trade Organization actually came into force on the same day as Mercosur's Customs Union – 1 January 1995).

Interestingly enough, despite the favourable framework of the mid-1990s, not much liberalization effectively took place during the first Cardoso Administration – or, in fact, ever since. The Cardoso government's perceived 'liberal' legacy has little to do with standard trade liberalization. There was market opening in this period, but it was primarily driven by foreign investment needs, not trade. The privatization programme, and not trade policy, was the dramatic market opener towards the end of the decade.[1] Ventura-Dias (2007) also points out that despite having ended the discretionary protectionism of the previous decades, the trade reform of the 1990s ultimately did not result in a very different inter-industrial protection structure, with the two most protected sectors in 1987 maintaining their position into the mid-2000s (transport parts and equipment, and textiles and apparel). In addition, even beyond 1994 with the stabilization plan and the last bout of liberalization, discretionary protection persisted. Ventura-Dias (2007), citing work by Baumann et al. (1997), points to the lack of economic rationality in trade policy immediately following stabilization: between July 1994 and September 1996 eight variations in tariffs were identified, oscillating between zero to 20 per cent.

Indeed, Abreu (2007) identifies a temporary reversal of trade liberalization in the post-1994 period. Starting with the Mexican crisis of 1994, Brazil, along with the rest of the world, had to endure in the second half of the 1990s a series of international financial crises. These demanded policy reforms, amongst which, first and foremost, were trade-related 'adjustments'. In Brazil, the Mexican crisis coincided with Cardoso's first election. Cardoso had served as the previous administration's finance minister, responsible for the implementation of the Real Plan. His main opponent in the election was a candidate from Brazil's industrial powerhouse state, São Paulo. This historical detail would have much to do with the future of trade policy in the country, since for all the differences in political platforms, trade policy was not among them. Both candidates carried with them the weight of the '*paulista*' industry and its 'natural' and historical protectionist tendencies.

The automotive sector is the best example. A special regime was instituted by the new government, raising the level of effective protection from 27.5 per cent to 113.8 per cent within one year, and peaking at 217.5 per cent by 1996. This entailed raising nominal protection for cars from 20 per cent at the end of 1994 to 70 per cent in mid-1995, alongside the imposition of import quotas – supposedly for balance of payments reasons. When WTO members contested Brazil's measures in a historic Balance of Payments consultation in 1995, the country had to devise another means to maintain its controversial regime. It would do so by incentivizing principal trading partners to negotiate tariff quotas and associated measures.[2]

The automotive regime would epitomize the trade policy to come under the Cardoso Administration in the second half of the 1990s – the absence of a strong constituency in favour of free-markets, and discretionary reversals of earlier liberalization. This represented no major change from Brazil's historical trade-policy-making processes, but in this case changes were made in the context of a freer economy.[3]

INSTITUTIONS VERSUS PERSONALITIES

Until its demise, CACEX was the strongest institution in Brazil's trade policy regime. Its strength emanated from the need, dictated by policy at the time, for trade to be centralized, administered and guided by an uncontested import substitution strategy, focused on internal protection from imports and the promotion of exports on the basis of subsidies. CACEX was therefore the institutional expression of the *administration* – and not the *formulation* – of trade policy, in consonance with the objective of congregating all trade-related matters under one umbrella. CACEX's strong hand tracked broadly the preferences of the different dictatorships. Centralized decision-making, a very low degree of transparency, and disregard for accountability vis-à-vis society marked this period in trade policy-making, as well as in other areas of government.

The end of CACEX constituted the beginning of a new institutional era in Brazilian trade – an era which is still far from reaching a definitive conclusion. Collor de Mello (1990–92) closed CACEX and created the all-powerful Ministry of the Economy, Finance and Planning. As its title indicates, the new institution coordinated three vectors of economic policy – trade, finance and economic planning – which until then were often confused in day-to-day dealings (and, as it turns out, after then as well).

In one sweeping move, therefore, Collor would simplify matters and come as close as Brazil ever has to achieving coherence in trade decision-making. The creation of a definitive and clear locus for trade was made possible by Collor's overhaul of all facets of economic policy-making, and the institutional apparatus underpinning it. The Collor Administration would also pursue an innovative foreign trade policy, moving away from the preferential agreements of the past towards a much more ambitious enterprise, one result of which was the common regional market, Mercosur.

Had the experiment (Collor's government) lasted, what appeared as a consistent move towards modernization and opening, both internally and externally, might have supported and been sustained by a strengthening institutional environment. Although still lacking the sophistication necessary to fully capture and translate the evolving nuances of the international trading system in the mid-1990s, Collor's attempt was legitimate, and did move the body politic a few notches in the right direction. Had it not been for his abrasive, arrogant style, combined with contempt for all established powers, trade policy might have prospered.

That chapter in institutional reform would end, however, with the subsequent government. After Mr de Mello's impeachment in 1992, his vice-president, Itamar Franco, became head of state, and reinstated the division amongst the various spheres of economic policy-making by creating the Ministry of Industry, Trade and Tourism, and bringing back the Ministries of Finance and Planning.

The main institutional initiative in trade by the Cardoso Administration (1995–2003) was the creation of the presidency-seated CAMEX (*Câmara de Comércio Exterior*) – the Board of Foreign Trade – with a view to correcting the perceived lack of coordination among ministries and agencies involved in trade policy. The trade and industry ministry was then solely entrusted with most trade policy implementation tasks, except for some customs matters such as tariff revenues, customs valuation, or foreign exchange regulations, where competencies were shared with the Ministry of Finance and the Central Bank. As to the new 'generation' of agreements spearheaded by Mercosur itself, the lead-ministry was to be External Relations. CAMEX would come to handle the complexities of the inter-agency process while, hopefully, giving a clear orientation to trade policy-making.

In addition to the creation of CAMEX, significant outside influences began to force further opening of Brazil's trade regime. Although Mercosur became a Customs Union on Cardoso's inauguration day, the sub-regional experiment had hardly 'scratched the sovereignty surface', since it had mostly dealt with tariffs and related measures only. Issues such as investment, services, competition policy, intellectual property, and government procurement, for example, would only become important by virtue of another international initiative, the Free Trade Area of the Americas Agreement (FTAA), a hemispheric initiative involving 34 countries in the Americas. Cardoso's predecessor had committed Brazil to this process at the 1994 Miami Summit.

With the FTAA deliberations, CAMEX, and the government more broadly, were suddenly faced with more than just managing three bouts of liberalization and the implementation of the then recently concluded Uruguay Round of Multilateral Trade Negotiations. Issues that other countries already considered trade-related by the time Cardoso took office were not yet part of the Brazilian trade policy establishment. The FTAA would force these issues upon the 'trade politic', and the reaction was certainly less than optimal.

While the Ministry of External Relations moved quickly to organize thematic 'national sections' to deal with the immensity of the FTAA negotiations, other ministries were unable to contribute effectively, as they had failed to adopt an equally proactive approach to the new generation issues *outside the realm of the FTAA*. In other words, the new issues of the world trading system, as brought to the sub-region via the hemispheric negotiations, presented Brazil with immense institutional challenges. Inevitably, Brazil became reactive to the given international agenda.

This had a major impact on Brazil's interest in the negotiations, since, in the absence of clearly defined domestic priorities, positions taken could only be defensive; a classic case of fear born of ignorance. Had Brazil really understood the nature of its own market for services or procurement, had it delved into its own approach to foreign direct investment, had it really understood the details of the approach adopted in NAFTA, its adopted positions in these talks might have been different.

The FTAA and later the Mercosur–European Union negotiations were important in forcing the government to attempt to re-organize itself around issues, including those that were traditionally not considered within the realm of foreign trade. However, the interest in doing so was not spread widely enough; the challenges introduced by these negotiations never reached the heart of domestic politics and policy-making. The alarm for institutional reform in the traditional areas of trade policy was thus never sounded, and the new issues never fully addressed.

Up until today, and certainly by the time President Luiz Inacio da Silva ('Lula') took office in 2003, trade in services, for example, has not been effectively integrated with trade policy-making, despite the existence of a multilateral regime since 1995. This is partly because the issue is much more convoluted than trade in goods, and partly because the necessary homework has not yet been undertaken. The FTAA wave has come and gone and the Brazilian trade politic continues to focus primarily on traditional issues. Only recently has the trade and industry ministry created a secretariat devoted to 'trade and services'.

In the meantime, as the country seemed to react only to international calls to negotiate, trade policy and reform, in the hands of CAMEX, drifted. During the second Cardoso Administration, it was moved from the Presidency to the Ministry of Development, Industry and Foreign Trade (MDIC). This represented a clear demotion from its 'royal' position to the weakest ministry in the economic chain. Needless to say, this left the board even fewer instruments with which to coordinate across different levels of government. Brazil had completed a rather tortuous full circle, having gone from the experiment of an all-powerful economic ministry in the beginning of the 1990s to a weakened board of trade by the end of the decade, and an overall lack of vision with respect to some of the most important themes in the international agenda of the New Millennium.

Despite having as many as 34 ministries in his first mandate and 36 in his second, President Lula did not change much in the overall institutional apparatus applying to foreign trade. CAMEX remained within the MDIC and the regime remained reactive, moving from problem to problem without an overarching comprehensive strategy that went beyond a focus on export promotion. Institutionally, therefore, not much was done to improve the trade bureaucracy and its systems – still one of the most burdensome in the world according to various editions of the World Bank's 'Doing Business' studies.[4]

Furthermore, the Lula Administration permitted the consultation mechanisms for trade negotiations to fade away along with the negotiations themselves. No longer do thematic working groups convene in the context of the National Sections – whether to discuss issues in the dead FTAA talks or the lingering Mercosur–European Union negotiations. The only consultative process that takes place is for the WTO Doha Round, and even here there is no formal structure or content. There are no formal meetings with the government, no minutes of such meetings, and no formal representation. Consultations are ad hoc, depending apparently on the need for government to consult according to the government's own definition of priorities and strategies. The private sector and society seek out the government to find out what is being negotiated much more often than the government seeks out interested parties to find out their positions on particular issues.

On the internal trade front, CAMEX continues to operate as in the previous government, dealing with matters of a second or third level of importance. On the external front, diplomats remain not only the main negotiators but also the main decision-makers. Common to both is a lack of a collegial process combined with a decision-making process that favours concentration amongst a small group of key officials. A constant element spanning both Lula mandates has been an unusually strong influence of the Deputy Minister of External Relations and the International

Advisor of the President – both imminently political officials – on issues relating to international trade negotiations.

In the absence of a strong institutional set-up that ensures transparency and predictability in decision-making, trade becomes hostage to matters that go beyond trade itself, and which, in turn, are also decided behind closed doors. Trade-related decisions that are far from trivial, such as the entry of Hugo Chavez's Venezuela into Mercosur, or the granting of market economy status to China, are but two examples of the new approach to trade policy-making in Brasilia and attest to the risk of appropriation of the trade dossier by non-trade authorities.

Clearly, the institutional question in trade policy is particularly difficult when it refers to the area of international negotiations. In many other countries around the world, it is not clear that international trade negotiations should be conducted by diplomats, who have little 'real world' experience in trade (as opposed to officials from the ministries that operate trade agreements, and often have themselves straddled the public–private divide in their own professional experience). In the recent past, there have been proposals from prominent private sector leaders in Brazil suggesting that a new trade ministry should replace MDIC, and take on not only the formulation of trade policy, but also the negotiation of international trade agreements.

Despite Brazil's problems in trade policy-making and in trade negotiations, such a proposal is unnecessary. To begin with, the Brazilian diplomacy is widely recognized within the country as well as overseas as one of the best in the world. During the last 10 to 15 years, the Ministry of External Relations (*Itamaraty*) has consolidated its reputation as one of the best negotiating machines in trade, having achieved various successes at the WTO, including spearheading the G20, the dispute settlement victories against the US on cotton and against the EU on sugar. Successes in other forums include the leadership of Mercosur, the deepening of relations with the Andean Community, and the launching of the IBSA Trilateral initiative, amongst others. Thus, *Itamaraty* has 'naturally' become the lead negotiating institution and 'owner' of the negotiating dossier – both outwardly as well as inwardly.

CAMEX remains a significant part of the solution to all institutional trade-related problems. It needs to be effectively empowered to formulate, coordinate and lead the work on trade so that all bottlenecks and impasses could be resolved – including in the area of international negotiations. The institution should be structured accordingly, possibly starting with its reinstatement within the Presidency headed by a strong personality with Ministerial authority. For now, however, this does not appear likely, as the incentive for institutional reform is dulled by a strong global economy and Brazil's even stronger trade performance.

POLICY VERSUS POLITICAL WILL

Institutions are important but they can never replace clarity of purpose – leadership – in policy-making itself. Countries need to have a clear sense of their needs and goals prior to deciding anything else – perhaps even prior to devising the institutional apparatus itself. Even in the absence of good institutions, a country may do well in trade if it knows what it wants, *and* if it is guided by consistency, predictability and transparency. Giving economic agents, investors and other governments consistent signals may be worth more than liberal signals as such, particularly if the latter can be easily and unpredictably replaced with measures or actions that go in the opposite direction. To be sure, institutions mitigate such risks, but only if they are both strong and well designed.

Most developing countries possess a mixture of institutional and leadership strength. However, whereas institutions are of limited use in the absence of strong leadership, such leadership can overcome flawed policy-making processes and produce beneficial policy outcomes. Whenever governments are unclear about what they want, or lack strong, purposeful leadership, policy formulation and implementation tend to hinge on political games.

This may have been the case with both of Cardoso's mandates, as no single official could claim the lead in trade policy. The strength of Pedro Malan, the Minister of Finance closely associated with the success of the stabilization plan, naturally influenced trade policy, but he could not overrule the Ministry of Industry and Trade on operational issues, or *Itamaraty* on trade negotiations. Matters were complicated by the Minister of Planning at the time, José Serra (future Presidential candidate who lost to Lula in 2002), who had a much less liberal view of trade and investment.

In Brazil, a strong Head of State with a clear view on trade and a leadership style that overrides internal divides is uncommon. In recent times, Collor de Mello has proven to be the only leader that could overcome Brazil's internal policy divides, and did so in a relatively emasculated institutional setting. He had a very clear view on trade and investment policies, considering both a crucial part of his government programme, insofar as through them much of the intended modernization and internationalization agenda could be achieved.

The inevitable corollary of this is that a notable degree of confusion has marked Brazil's trade policy-making during the post-import substitution period. Furthermore, as a country that opened its economy as part of its stabilization strategy, Brazil's trade policy is curiously neglected. Matters relating to inflation and the currency are considered nobler than matters related to trade and trade facilitation. The tensions between the two ministries responsible for these policy areas – the Ministry of Finance, and the Ministry of Development, Industry and Foreign Trade (the current title) – attest to this. Since the 1990s there has been no effective integration, partly due to the institutional make-up, which encourages the perpetuation of fiefdoms.[5] A single Ministry of the Economy could be the solution, particularly if the Minister were to be fully empowered to oversee the whole of the economy, not just parts of it.

The problems this causes are of course not confined to government. Non-governmental actors – primarily business – feel that most administrations have consistently delivered on *macro*economics in the last 15 years, but fallen dangerously short of dealing with *micro*economic problems. The necessary regulatory overhaul – including pension, tax and labour systems – has not taken place. Brazil's tax burden, for example, presently compares with Sweden's, but Brazil's infrastructure and general business costs are far from Swedish standards. Compounding businesses' problems are Brazil's interest rates, consistently the highest in the world; and, more recently, the Real's sharp appreciation vs. the US dollar during 2005–2006.

The separation between foreign and trade policy is equally ill-defined, particularly in recent years. Because *Itamaraty* takes the lead in trade negotiations, policy outcomes are more the result of geopolitics than rational economic analysis. Again, the impacts on the private sector are sub-optimal, and as long as the Lula Administration is willing to pay 'trade prices' for geopolitical interests, the design of agreements with countries such as India and South Africa are unlikely to suit Brazil's economic needs.

Relations with the Andean Community provide another example. Here Brasilia seems prepared to make any concessions necessary to ensure these countries' support for Brazil's foreign policy interests. The private sector sees little benefit in exchanging market access for ethereal geopolitical objectives – particularly in the absence of any consistent consultation process.

Finally, China is now presenting a major challenge to coherence in Brazil's foreign and trade policies. The two countries have enjoyed a formal strategic partnership since the mid-1990s, dating back to the first Cardoso government. This has been elevated in recent years and Beijing has obtained from Brasilia, among other things, the recognition of China as a market economy for trade remedy purposes. Brazil has also hesitated to make use of the special safeguards in China's Protocol of Accession to the WTO. This has caused Brazilian business considerable stress, and epitomizes the complaint that geopolitical priorities taking precedence over concrete trading interests, and that Brasilia is too lenient with Beijing on trade matters.

NEGOTIATION VS. INITIATIVE

The importance of international trade negotiations to Brazil's trade policy outcomes, as seen so far, cannot be understated, especially since the 1990s. During the CACEX period agreements were unambitious. This changed with the launching of a fully-fledged programme for a sub-regional common market (Mercosur) in the beginning of the decade, alongside Brazil's participation, as part of Mercosur, in the FTAA talks from the mid-1990s. Together these put Brazil on a different path altogether. Mercosur called for the free movement of goods, services and factors of production, while the FTAA challenged Brazil with a broad NAFTA-like free trade agreement, involving 33 other countries, and covering goods, services, investment, procurement and intellectual property markets, amongst other commitments.

In addition, 1995 saw the WTO Agreement and the Mercosur Customs Union come into force. Along with the just-commenced FTAA talks, these posed a considerable challenge to the ability of the government to reconcile its own stabilization, market opening and privatization agendas with these external demands. The Cardoso government would come to resist many demands in the FTAA negotiations, just as the thorny issues in the Mercosur customs union programme – such as tax harmonization, competition policy, and government procurement – would come to the fore.

A new urgency had thus been introduced into Brazil's trade policy outlook. In order to manage the overlapping agendas in the sub-regional, hemispheric and, with the Mercosur–EU deliberations, transatlantic spheres, progress had to be made in developing common policies and positions within Mercosur. This was reinforced by a perceived need to deepen Mercosur's integration to a degree sufficient to avoid dilution by competing trade negotiations initiatives.

In negotiations with the US and the EU, it would be imprecise to characterize the Cardoso government as having been more liberal than the subsequent Lula governments. Cardoso resisted US demands in the FTAA talks. While Lula traditionally opposed an FTAA in any form, during his fourth presidential bid in 2003 he indicated for the first time a conditional willingness to negotiate – thus making his candidacy less radical in the eyes of moderate voters.

Lula's first cabinet thus sought to strike a balance between ministers traditionally amenable to the hemispheric pact, such as those in charge of finance, development/industry/trade and agriculture, and those traditionally opposed to it, such as the Deputy Minister of External Relations, and his International Adviser.[6] The stage was set for a divided government on matters relating to the country's integration into the world economy in general, and on ambitious trade agreements in particular (especially the FTAA). The first evidence of that occurred in November 2003, during the run-up to the Miami Ministerial of the Summit of the Americas process. Lula had to call a meeting with all ministers involved in the FTAA negotiations to inform them that the ultimate 'boss' in that process was the Ministry of External Relations. In so doing Lula was pointing to a possible hardening of Brazil's position, given that Ministry's top officials' resistance to trade liberalization, in particular a free trade agreement of any sort with the US.

The FTAA, the Mercosur–EU and the WTO Doha Round of negotiations were all supposed to be finalized by the end of 2004. None of that happened, and Brazil, along with its Mercosur partners, has been 'let off the hook' as far as external demands are concerned. In the case of the FTAA, Brazil may have accomplished more than just postponing negotiations. With the help of the US itself, who would never have been able to meet Brazil's demands in agriculture, the negotiations faded in 2003 – some nine years after the negotiations were launched.[7] However, the Mercosur–EU negotiations, which had all along been partly FTAA-driven, technically remain still in progress. Negotiators on both sides are waiting to see what happens in the Doha Round talks before resuming the transatlantic process.

Brazil has not stopped negotiating international pacts, but has certainly avoided ambitious agreements. As the Doha Round, the FTAA and the Mercosur–EU negotiations fail or falter, Brazil has been reasonably successful in pushing forward a number of *initiatives*, both on its own and as part of Mercosur. These have been at most narrow preferential trade deals accompanied by various cooperation agreements, as opposed to being modern, ambitious free trade agreements. Often fewer than 1000 tariff lines out of 11 000 possibilities are identified, and only preferential access, not fully free access, is granted.

Initiatives of this sort have been undertaken with the Andean Countries, India and South Africa, and a South American Community of Nations has been established.[8] The India–Brazil–South Africa (IBSA) Initiative, established in 2003, has grown in stature, and ministers are discussing the potential for trilateral trade liberalization. While IBSA is rapidly developing into a viable south–south cooperation initiative, any ambitious trilateral trade liberalization is unlikely. Indeed, there is no doubt that in all these instances foreign policy trumps economic and trade interests.

The current state of affairs may be ideal for the Lula administration. There is no overbearing obligation to negotiate with demanding trade partners, and therefore no need in the near future to make difficult decisions. In addition, Brazil's trade performance is currently strong (see analysis below), encouraging the view that nothing requires reforming at this time – whether in institutional, policy or negotiating terms.

Of concern, however, is that in the absence of ambitious 'imported' negotiating agendas (such as the FTAA), Brazil can easily slip deeper into its 'natural' state of complacency, pretending (or perhaps believing) that bullish conditions are here to stay. This is navel-gazing Brazil of old – a developing country that still moves relatively slowly towards a reasonable degree of integration with the world economy.

Responsibility for this is not Lula's alone. The attitude towards globalization prevalent across his two mandates was evident in those of his predecessor too; together they have been the main protagonists of the post-import substitution period. When it comes to trade policy, Brazil, despite the considerable progress of the last 15 years, continues to function best only under the threat of external pressure. This is highly undesirable, as no country's trade policy regime should be driven by international trade negotiations. Rather, domestic priorities need to be well defined, and must inform positions taken in negotiations, or indeed the decision to negotiate at all.

IMPACT OF POLICY AND REFORM

The opening of the Brazilian economy in the 1990s constituted the primary driving force behind the economy's impressive productivity growth – the foundation of today's competitiveness in a number of important sectors. In comparative terms, the growth of productivity levels in Brazil in the post-liberalization period (1997–2000) were almost as high as those observed in south east Asian countries such as Korea and Taiwan during their corresponding post-liberalization periods. The contrast with the period previous to liberalization in Brazil was stark indeed: 0.35 per cent vs. 2.7 per cent[9] (see Figure 6.1).

Firm-level evidence shows that those involved in foreign trade made the largest productivity gains. Overall, tradable manufacturing sectors registered the highest productivity growth rates, nearing 4 per cent. Non-traded industry, by contrast, increased productivity at only about 1.5 per cent on average. Sectors that were open to world trade have consolidated these gains, in turn becoming more competitive and ever-better positioned to benefit further from world markets.[10]

Brazil has transformed its external sector and trade performance in a remarkably short period of time. A trade deficit of USD7 billion has turned into a surplus of more than USD46 billion inside a decade. In addition, despite the strength of the Real in the last few years, the trade surplus grew by 3.1 per cent in 2006.[11] According to MDIC and WTO data, Brazilian

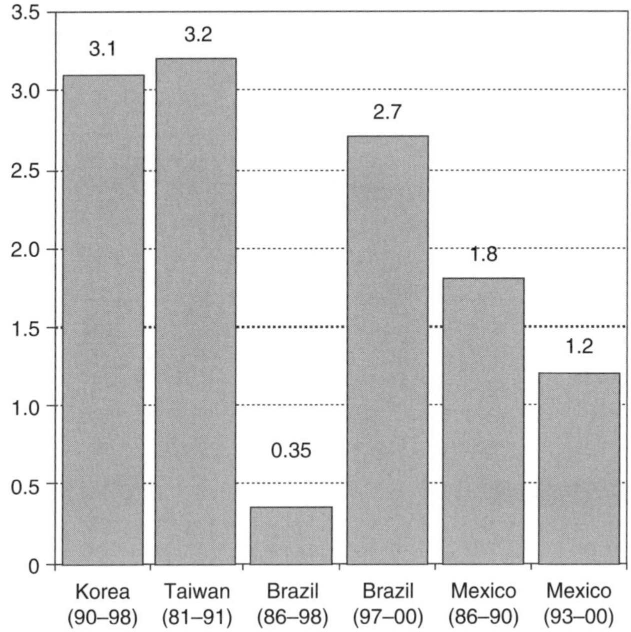

Source: Moreira (2004).

Figure 6.1 Liberalization and annual productivity growth, various countries and years (%)

exports have grown by almost 17 per cent on average annually since 2000; the corresponding figure for total world export growth was only 11 per cent. The performance difference is greater if looking only at the period from 2004–2007: 24 per cent average annual growth for Brazilian exports vs. 17 per cent for world exports.

Further goods news relates to the competitive position of many of Brazil's industrial sectors – traditionally the most risk- and competition-averse in the country. As Figure 6.2 shows, between 1999 and 2003 most of Brazil's industries may be considered 'champions' (gained global market share in a sector of world trade growing more rapidly than the average for total world trade) or 'winners in adversity' (gained market share in sectors experiencing relative decline in importance to total world trade). Even sectors that normally take defensive positions in trade negotiations, such as the chemicals or electrical/electronic sectors, have gained market share amidst highly dynamic global growth. Other defensive sectors, such as automotives and textiles and apparel, have made larger market share gains, but in more subdued, slower-growing global conditions.

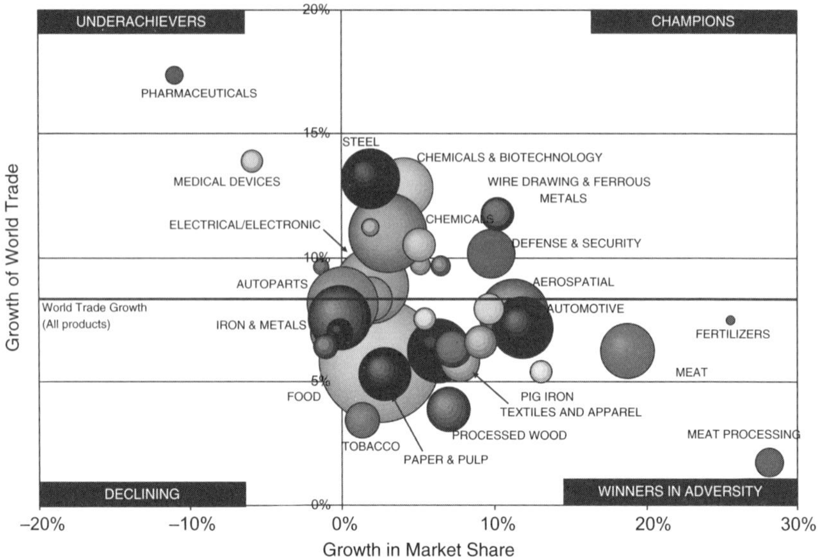

Note: Size of the sphere indicates value of sector's exports in 2003.

Source: Aliceweb (SECEX/MDIC) and UNCTAD.

Figure 6.2 Brazil's changing global positioning in manufactured exports, 1999–2003

Brazil's market openness – as measured by the share of total trade in gross domestic product (GDP) – is now significant. As Figure 6.3 shows, it took Brazil almost 50 years to reach levels comparable to those achieved in the 1950s. In this half-century a historical low of just more than 5 per cent was reached in 1965, while strong, consistent growth in trade's share in GDP began only after the early 1990s' liberalization. According to MDIC data, total trade grew 340 per cent since 1990, 137 per cent since 1995 and 106 per cent since 2000.

However, in relative terms Brazil's openness is unremarkable (Figure 6.4). India, normally seen as a fairly closed economy, is now more open by this measure. The figure for Russia is twice as large as Brazil's, while China's is 2.7 times larger. Brazil in fact more closely resembles the US and Japan, which both possess far larger domestic economies; the overall world average itself is almost twice (1.95) as big as Brazil's. Additionally, Brazil is one of the few prominent countries that did not see its market openness increase during the recent boom in the world economy.

Brazil also now enjoys a high degree of geographic diversification in its

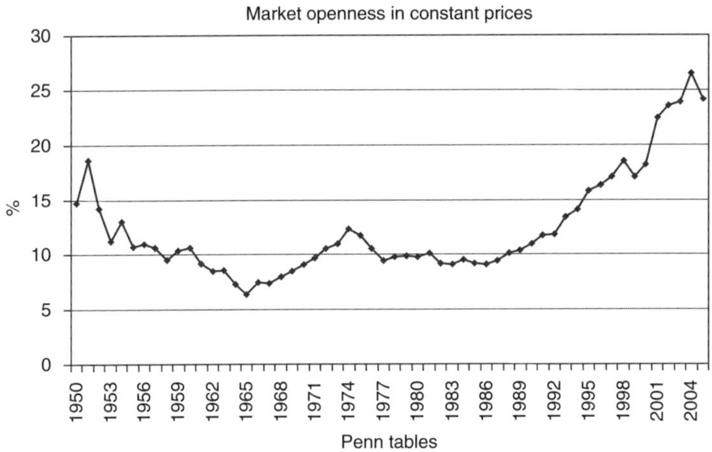

Note: Openness is measured as the share of total trade (imports plus exports) in GDP.

Source: Penn World Tables.

Figure 6.3 Brazil's openness to trade, 1950–2005 (%)

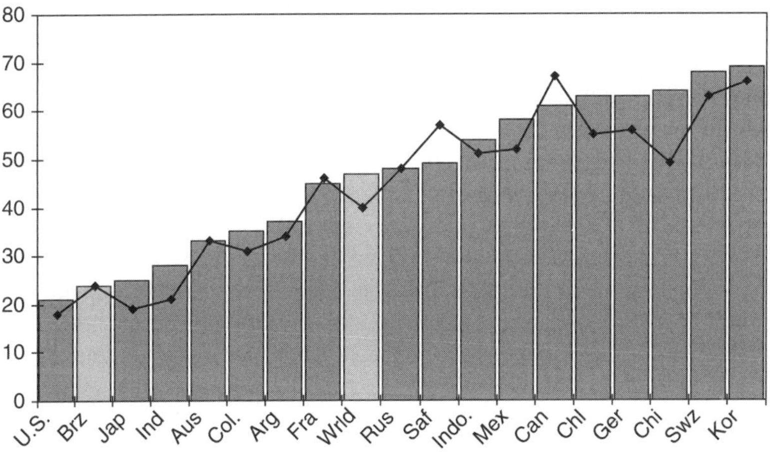

Source: The World Bank, WDI Data Query.

Figure 6.4 Comparative trade openness figures, 2002 and 2005 (%, current prices)

Source: Aliceweb (SECEX/MDIC) and UNCTAD.

Figure 6.5 Brazil's share of world trade, 1950–2004 (%)

trade with the world. MDIC data show that while the US continues to be the most important individual trade partner, accounting for over 17 per cent of overall trade, the European Union, as a bloc, accounts for almost one quarter (22 per cent). Latin America accounts for another 21 per cent and Asia 19 per cent. Brazil's trade is almost evenly divided amongst the world's major economies. Mercosur, supposedly the country's main foreign policy priority, has seen its share slip from around 16 per cent in 1997 to 10 per cent presently. Only Argentina has featured strongly in recent years, regaining its second place in the country rankings (with almost 9 per cent of Brazil's trade). China's stellar growth has seen it rising back to being Brazil's third most important national-level trade partner, with 7.2 per cent.

Nevertheless, despite these encouraging recent developments, Brazil's share in international trade, particularly exports, is declining (see Figure 6.5). Brazil accounts for less than 1 per cent of world trade, a number that hasn't significantly changed in forty years. Given that Brazil accounted for over 2 per cent of world trade in the 1950s, this should be of concern. For an economy among the top ten biggest in the world, 1 per cent of world trade is low.

What of the links between a stronger trade performance and Brazil's broader growth and development? Theory suggests that one of the most important linkages between trade and development, particularly industrial development, is between cheaper imported inputs (especially capital goods) and improved national productivity levels. With greater market openness, capital goods prices tend to drop, encouraging local producers to adopt more modern production techniques, thereby increasing efficiency levels (De Negri, 2006). In Brazil, the prices of capital goods did indeed fall, by about 47 per cent overall between 1990 and 2001. This represents a substantial reduction in an important component of investment costs. However, studies have revealed that the fall in the relative price of investment was only 3 per cent–much lower than the fall in the relative price of capital goods during the 1990s. This implies that other major components of investment costs in Brazil, such as construction, have not improved, or may have worsened.

This in turn has limited the impacts on output and income growth of Brazil's opening. With growing productivity levels for the internationalized sectors and cheaper capital goods, one would expect greater economic growth to follow. Brazil is catching up with its main competitors, but only slowly; its growth performance remains relatively poor.

CONCLUSION: TEN ELEMENTS TO CONSIDER

Brazilian politicians' satisfaction with Brazil's much-improved trade performance brings with it the risk of inaction on the part of the public sector. This is worrying, because the positive results one observes nowadays have much to do with reforms undertaken in the mid-1990s, and the unusually lengthy upswing in the world economy, and owe little to any of the policies or strategies undertaken by the current government. Sluggish decision-making, the confusing regulatory environment in FDI-led sectors, and the lack of crucial reforms in the tax, labour and pension systems, could yet derail Brazil's progress, particularly in the context of a global recession. Presently Asia's demand for many of Brazil's exports offsets some of these risks, but a general downturn, especially a tightening of global liquidity, will present Brazil with serious challenges.

There is no doubt that the Brazilian trade regime has evolved since the initial round of liberalization. However, with the possible exception of the Collor de Mello government, there has been no consistent strategic plan for trade policy, and changes seem to be little more than reactions to developments in the world trading system. It would thus be false to argue that Brazil's improved trade performance is due to well designed policy backed by efficient institutions. Rather, the significant changes have been Brazil's liberalization, which coincided with rapidly improving global economic conditions. Most other aspects of Brazil's trade policy-making regime remain unchanged. The following ten elements of Brazil's trade regime capture its essence in the present day, and point out areas in need of reform.

Bureaucracy

According to the World Bank studies on the costs of doing business, Brazil compares poorly with its fellow large developing countries in a number of trade-related categories. The ease of exporting or importing, measured in the number of days required per transaction, is the worst amongst the BRICSAM,[12] with more than 22 days needed for an import transaction and almost 18 for an export transaction (versus 9.8 and 10.4 for OECD countries). Between 2007 and 2008, Brazil fell 23 positions in the overall ranking for 'trading across borders' items, from 70th to 93rd place. India moved in the opposite direction, climbing 63 positions in the period, from 142nd to 79th. These numbers indicate serious inefficiencies and a lack of urgency to reform basic elements of the trade regime. This is in turn due to institutional inertia, which continues to prevail over pragmatism and transparency.

Personalities

Brazil's trade-policy-making system still relies too much on personalities. When former Minister Furlan left MDIC no one was sure who the next minister might be. To some extent this happens in any country – even in the most mature democracies around the world. The problem in Brazil is one of degree. In other words, fear of the unknown in trade policy should be mitigated by strong institutions. Institutions should ensure a degree of predictability *regardless* of ministerial changes. Additionally, although under a presidential regime, Brazil's cabinet is determined according to 'Parliamentarian' standards – via government coalitions – which further raises levels of uncertainty and unpredictability.

Organization

Trade policy in Brazil continues to be spread all over the 'Esplanada dos Ministérios' (The Plaza of the Ministries). Many ministries have a say in trade policy and more than one is involved in final decision-making. This is to some extent natural, but makes coordination important, and coherence more difficult to achieve. High-level struggles for ultimate control of trade policy are also a problem.

Brazil has a Board of Foreign Trade, which is tasked with coordinating policy processes and ultimately taking decisions. This requires refinement, however, as ministries at times decide for themselves how to proceed on particular issues. Trade negotiations in particular give rise to a great deal of conflicting signals and policies. Decisions on positions to take in negotiations can and often are 'unilaterally' decided by the Ministry of External Relations, regardless of the Ministry of Development, Industry and Foreign Trade's arguments. Since the negotiators are career diplomats and not functionaries from the Ministry formally in charge of trade, conflicts are bound to arise. Relieving the Brazilian diplomacy of trade negotiating duties was debated prior to the election of President Lula, but the status quo was maintained. Given this, the government must attempt better coordination across ministries, and must establish clear lines of command over the various subjects under negotiation.

Consultation

Governments need to consult when it comes to trade policy. The interested parties, increasingly, are not just business groups but also representatives from various segments of civil society. Consultations should occur under a formal, predictable and accountable regime, via consultative groups comprised of representative persons or institutions. In Brazil, this system is still ad hoc, and has arguably worsened under the current government. The private sector and interested segments of society need to have a *locus* where they express their views – and that should not be limited to individual meetings with ministers and officials.

Strategy

Much of what is happening in Brazil's foreign trade is the result of helpful developments beyond the direct control of policy-makers, not planning. This is often the case with relatively open developing economies, but strategic, proactive planning is nevertheless imperative. In addition, strategies should be made known to interested parties. Brazil has no green or white papers whereby policies are presented in a concise, structured fashion for comments by the various interest groups. Strategy therefore goes hand in hand with the need to have quality consultation.

Policy-making

Trade continues to be a residual of Brazil's so-called 'proper economic policies'. Given the severity of the debt and broader macroeconomic crises this is perhaps understandable – the need for continued stabilization has taken precedence, and the Ministry of Finance leads in this regard. Hence trade is viewed as one piece of a macroeconomic puzzle. Brazil's trade performance is 'good' if it supports a strong external position, and 'bad' if not. This leads to inappropriate trade policy design, and institutional tension. The Ministry of Finance often favours liberalization but often lacks much-needed nuance, while the Ministry of Development, Industry, and Foreign Trade is best described as the operational arm of bureaucratic protectionism.

Orientation

Brazil, with a large domestic economy, is not naturally inclined to open its market to foreign competitors. Brazil has done so in spite of this tendency, but further significant efforts in this regard are difficult to imagine. The country opened its markets when governed by a visionary President, Collor de Mello, who was very quickly impeached for irregularities in his short-lived government. Had it not been for his personality and personable style, Brazil might not have opened its economy to any significant degree. Recall that neither the Cardoso nor the current Lula government pursued any substantive liberalization. Since 1995 Brazil has in fact seen a backlash against the processes Collor put in motion – albeit as a result of various global financial crises that forced the country to look more closely at its balance of payments fundamentals.

Fundamentally, there remains no real consensus on trade policy, but 'developmentalists' do agree with 'neoliberals' on one thing: that Brazil should not undergo any further unilateral opening. All seem to agree that Brazil has not received sufficient reward – defined as better access to foreign markets – in exchange for its efforts to liberalize.

Geopolitics

In Brazil as in most countries trade policy is closely related to – if not a subset of – foreign policy. International agreements, starting with the WTO, aim to sterilize the politics of trade by setting rules, principles, and establishing a dispute settlement system. Yet countries' decisions to seek certain agreements or to pursue what they perceive as trade policy are often still based on political objectives. In Brazil, this is becoming particularly problematic. The country is confusing trade with geopolitics, as attested by the types of agreements it has been negotiating, agreements with very little commercial ambition but involving partners that somehow serve a political interest. Agreements such as the ones negotiated between Mercosur and India or South Africa, to take two examples, are good examples thereof.

Evaluation

The trade policy regime of a country must be constantly evaluated as to its functioning and the attainment of set objectives. This evaluation should be unbiased, empirical and involve interested parties who should be able to contribute with their views and experiences. A regular system of reporting the results of such evaluations should also be in place to provide predictability in the way governments handle trade policy. The parameters of the evaluation should be clear from the outset with a view to securing legitimacy in the exercise. Brazil has no such system in place yet. Evaluations are done in an irregular fashion, much at the whims of the authorities who pick what and when to evaluate, and which results to reveal. A predictable, regular and transparent system of evaluation would do much to improve the Brazilian trade policy regime.

Bias

Brazil is often guilty of stasis and inaction, most often due to prolonged periods of 'navel-gazing'. In the absence of an external stimulus, Brazil will not seek to liberalize, since the value in doing so is seemingly lost amongst other priorities. Hence without ambitious trade negotiations Brazil is likely to continue on its path of adaptive commercial diplomacy, seeking out shallow, politically-driven trade agreements or simply withdrawing when ambitious proposals such as the FTAA emerge. Given the very different approach taken by many of Brazil's competitors, mainly in Asia, this seems misplaced. The present government needs to be convinced of the merit of anything beyond greater access to developed-country agriculture markets. In so doing, it must develop a more fully-fledged world view, and a proactive appreciation of risks and opportunities in the not-so-distant future.

NOTES

1. Additionally, the debate within the Cardoso government itself would ultimately put a damper on further liberalization efforts. 'Developmentalists' would pit themselves against 'stabilizers' and neutralize any unilateral impetus to further open the economy to foreign competition. The basic premise of the divergence in outlook was that those that were in favour of the stabilization of the economy were somehow against 'development' while those that were in favour of development were somehow against a stable economy – a curious and self-defeating dichotomy. The debate centred on levels of exchange and interest rates, as well as the trade-off between macroeconomic (read, further liberalization) and microeconomic (read, industrial interventionism) policies.
2. As a 'formal' position at the WTO, Brazil would argue that as a member of the then recently created Mercosur Customs Union, it had the right to maintain its regime according to the (equally recently introduced) Trade-Related Investment Measures Agreement (TRIMs) – particularly since Argentina had a similar regime in place, was negotiating a bilateral agreement within Mercosur with Brazil, and had managed to exempt its regime from TRIMs obligations. However, Brazil, unlike Argentina, had failed to notify its regime 180 days before the entry into force of the WTO, as required by the TRIMs Agreement. Brasilia therefore devised an alternative, and 'bought' its legality by offering countries willing to forgo legal action a 50 per cent reduction in automotive tariff rates, in addition to other benefits. This measure encouraged the European Union, Japan and Korea into a tacit acceptance of Brazil's regime. The US would later complain, but further negotiations, particularly in relation to automotive parts, would result in 'peace' at the WTO as well.

3. Other sectors that experienced a reversal in policy orientation at this time included sugar, steel, chemical and pharmaceutical products, wood and pulp products, and textiles.
4. World Bank (2008).
5. For example, within the Ministry of Finance, the Receita Federal (Brazil's Internal Revenue Service) constitutes a virtually autonomous agency controlling customs valuations and tariffs. There is little cooperation with the MDIC, nominally in charge of implementing and overseeing Brazil's trade policy.
6. 'Amorim indica secretário avesso à Alca' in Folha de São Paulo, 2 January 2003.
7. The co-chairs of the negotiations – the US and Brazil at the time – had worked hard to develop a draft agreement they could both support. However, at the November 2003 summit meeting the proposed text met with great opposition from Canada, Mexico and Chile, all citing its obvious lack of ambition.
8. The agreements between Mercosur and India and South Africa have been signed but are not yet in force.
9. Moreira (2004).
10. Moreira (2004).
11. The impacts of exchange rate strength were nevertheless evident in 2006 – it was the first year since 1997 that exports grew more slowly than imports.
12. Commonly understood as referring to Brazil, Russia, India, China, South Africa, and Mexico.

REFERENCES

Abreu, M.P. (2007), *Comércio Exterior: Interesses do Brasil*, Rio de Janeiro: Elsevier.

Baumann, Renato, Josefina Rivera and Yohana Zavattieo (1997), 'As Tanfas de Importação no Plano Real', *Pesquisa e Planjamento Econômics*, **27**(3).

De Negin, J.A. (2006), *Tecnologia, Exportação e Emprego*, Rio de Janeiro: Institute of Applied Economic Research.

Lopez-Cordova, E. and Moreira, M.M. (2003), 'Regional integration and productivity: the experiences of Brazil and Mexico', in *INTAL-ITD Working Paper n. 14*, Buenos Aires: Inter-American Development Bank (IADB), INTAL.

Marconini, M. (2005), 'Trade-policy making in Brazil', in *Trade-Policy Formulation in Latin America*, A Project by the Inter-American Development Bank, the University of Toronto and the Inter-American Dialogue, Washington DC: IADB.

Marconini, M. (2007), 'The FTAA–WTO Divide: the political economy of low ambition', in J.A. McKinney and H.S. Gardner (eds), *Economic Integration in the Americas*, New York: Routledge.

Ministry of Development, Industry and Foreign Trade (various years), Trade Balance.

Moreira, M.M. (2004), 'Abertura e Crescimento: Passado e Futuro', in F. Giambiagi, J.G. Reis A. Urani (eds), *Reformas no Brasil: Balanço e Agenda*, Rio de Janeiro: Editora Nova Fronteira.

Motta Veiga, P. (2004), 'Trade policy-making in Brazil: changing patterns in State: civil society relationship', mimeo.

Motta Veiga, P. (2007),'Política comercial no Brasil: características, condicionantes domésticos e policy-making', in Brazilian Institute for International Trade Negotiations (ICONE), Economic Research Foundation of the University of

São Paulo (FIPE), United Kingdom Department for International Development (DFID) (eds), *Políticas Comerciais Comparadas: Desempenho e Modelos Organizacionais*, São Paulo: Singular.
Penn Tables (various years), Center for International Comparisons of Production, Income and Prices, University of Pennsylvania.
Soares De Lima, M.R. (2005), 'Aspiração Internacional e Política Externa', *Revista Brasileira de Comércio Exterior*, **19**(82), Rio de Janeiro: FUNCEX.
Ventura-Dias, V. (2007), 'Aspectos distributivos do comercio e da politica comercial: questões conceituais e a experiencia Brasileira', in P. Motta Veiga, (ed.), *Comércio e Política Comercial no Brasil: Desempenho, Interesses e Estratégia*, Latin American Trade Network & Centro de Estudos de Integração e Desenvolvimento (CINDES), São Paulo: Singular.
World Bank (2008), 'Doing Business Report', Washington.
World Bank (various years), 'WDI data query', http://genderstats.worldbank.org/data-query/.
World Economic Forum (2006), *Global Competitiveness Report 2006–2007*, New York: Palgrave Macmillan.

7. India

S. Narayan

INTRODUCTION

After several decades of controls and restrictions on imports and exports, comprehensive reforms to open the Indian economy were initiated in the early 1990s. Trade reforms were accompanied by reforms in the industrial sector, lifting of exchange controls, liberalization of foreign investment policy, removal of restrictions on the current account, opening up of financial markets, and other measures.

The changes in policy were triggered by the serious balance of payments crisis in 1991. Earlier coalition governments did not have the mandate to take difficult economic decisions, but in 1991, after a gap of three years, a new political leadership came into power that could address these issues. Further, the Uruguay round of global trade negotiations had been going on for some time, and was nearing completion, and would necessitate the unravelling of several restrictive measures in trade policy.

The changed political environment was conducive to this initiative. The former Prime Minister Mr Rajiv Gandhi had been assassinated, and though the Congress Government that came to power in 1991 did not have an absolute majority, they had the sympathy and support of the public. The new Prime Minister Mr Narasimha Rao brought in Dr Manmohan Singh, an eminent economist, as Finance Minister, and Mr Pranab Mukherjee, a veteran at negotiations, as Commerce Minister. India lost an important ally in the collapse of the Soviet Union, and had to find fresh trading partners urgently. The new government realized the importance of making friends with the United States and of globalizing trade. The reforms that led to the opening up of the Indian economy from 1991 were thus both a political as well as an economic necessity.

Trade reforms implemented since 1991 have done away with import licensing on all but a few goods that are disallowed on environmental, health or safety grounds, and a few which are 'canalized' (imported by Government agencies only). In the case of agricultural goods, all border measures have been replaced by tariffs, as required under the Uruguay

Round Agreement on Agriculture. Procedures have been simplified to reduce transaction costs. The top tariff rate on non-agricultural goods is being brought down to 10 per cent, which is comparable with that of East Asian nations. Most of the export controls have also been removed. Export prohibition now applies only to a small number of items on health, environment or moral grounds. Similarly export restrictions apply only to cattle, camels, fertilizers, cereals, groundnut oil and pulses.

Several foreign exchange restrictions were removed so that the rupee is officially convertible on current account. Many capital account transactions were also freed from restrictions.

Liberalization of trade in services has also taken place. Insurance, banking, telecommunications, e-commerce and other infrastructure sectors have been thrown open for foreign direct investment. Rules for foreign institutional investments into financial markets have been liberalized.

Both exports and imports of goods and services have increased substantially in the last 15 years. India's share in world exports of goods and services which was 0.8 per cent in 2002 is targeted to rise to 1.5 per cent by 2009.

Before we discuss in detail the reforms in the last 15 years, it is necessary to look at what happened in the preceding four decades. There were efforts, from time to time, to liberalize imports even from the First Five Year Plan in the 1950s, though they were ad hoc and on a smaller scale. However, events of economic and political importance intervened often, which made it difficult to adopt initiatives that would substantially liberalize India's international trade.

BACKGROUND

After attaining independence in 1947, India adopted a democratic political system based on universal franchise and a federal structure. The Indian National Congress was the dominant political party, which ruled without interruption for about three decades after independence. When planning for economic development was launched in 1951, the stated objective was to establish a 'socialistic pattern of society' that envisaged, among other things, a dominant role for the public sector in industrial development, and a strategy based on import substitution necessitated by scarce foreign exchange resources. The Congress party, which had a clear mandate from the people, could implement the public sector-dominated and import substitution-based policy without much resistance from other parties.

In the years preceding India's independence, import controls were in force mainly to conserve foreign exchange and prioritize shipping during

World War II. In the post-war years, the scope of Open General Licenses was widened considerably, but following the adverse balance of payments position of 1947, trade restrictions were revived and exchange control was extended to cover all activities. The main objective of import controls was conservation and regulation of scarce foreign exchange. The following years alternately witnessed periods of liberalization and tighter controls, always in response to balance of payments positions.

The national leadership, to whom the British handed over power in 1947, had to cope with recurring foreign exchange shortages. When planning for development commenced, the strategy for industrialization came to be based on import substitution. The policy of industrial licensing that was adopted was sensitive to political issues such as the relatively high degree of concentration of economic power and wealth. The leftist parties and many economists kept this issue in the forefront of parliamentary debates, and influenced the licensing system towards greater reliance on the public sector.

During the five-year period (1951–56) of India's First Plan, certain progressive measures for liberalization of imports were introduced, particularly the India Tariff (Second Amendment) Act of 1954 which changed the tariff rates for 32 items, permitting the Government to increase import quotas and issue additional licences over and above normal entitlements. However, this modest attempt to ease import controls was halted by yet another exchange crisis at the beginning of India's Second Five Year Plan (1956–57). The import control regime tightened in response. Conservation of foreign exchange and its allocation for various activities became the central objective of trade and foreign exchange policy.

Allocation of scarce foreign exchange to a large number of industries – large and small enterprises – for importing capital and intermediate goods, all of them vying for priority consideration, was a difficult job, and the bureaucracy charged with this job had to rely on ad hoc rules based on indicators such as installed capacity, employment, and so on. The government, at the same time, denied foreign exchange to import a product if domestic substitutes were available in sufficient quantity. The application of this 'indigenous availability' principle was not, however, done in an efficient way since the quality of the domestic substitute, the price at which it was supplied, and delays in delivery were often ignored. These administrative controls were in place until 1965–66.

The import control regime must also be seen in the context of India's industrial policy during this period. Industrial development was closely regulated from 1956. Investments in public sector enterprises were, in any case, subject to direct planning. Physical capacity controls extended to private sector investments as well. This was achieved through an exhaustive licensing system along with a detailed setting of targets by the Planning Commission while formulating the Five Year Plans. Industrial targets were relatively few in the First Plan and were largely a projection of industrial capacities based on rough estimates of demand and supply possibilities. In the Second Five Year Plan, the system of targets and licensing of investment was continued, but with the Second Plan's emphasis on expanding the capital goods sector, target-setting assumed greater importance.

However, neither the extent of the shift to capital goods industries nor the overall levels of investment in consumer goods industries was based on any sound empirical knowledge. Consequently investments in public sector enterprises for heavy industry were based on estimates of demand and supply that, at the very least, were inefficient. Private sector investments were constrained and regulated. In the Third Five Year Plan (1961–66) the strategy of sizeable investments in heavy industries and the licensing system for the private sector continued, but greater attention was given to inter-industry balances and phasing of investment.

Despite regulation and investment controls, industrial production recorded a growth rate of 5.75 per cent per annum in the period 1951–56, and nearly 7.5 per cent from the beginning of the Second Plan. In the first three years of the Third Plan (1961–64), the rate of growth was about 8 per cent per annum. Growth of output of the organized industrial sector accelerated through the three Plans and the share of investment, output and value-added shifted decidedly in favour of metals, machinery and chemicals. Thus the shift in investment strategy in the Second Plan resulted in rapid growth of output and value-added in these 'basic' industries during this period.

Export performance during the first decade of planning shows stagnation in both average prices and volumes. Economic policy during this period was rather indifferent to the need for promoting exports. As a result, India's share in world exports came down from 2.1 per cent in 1951 to 1.2 per cent in 1960. Steps to remedy the situation were taken only towards the beginning of the Third Plan (1961–66), with some limited success.

Notwithstanding the tight import control regime, import of goods and services in the decade 1951–61 and thereafter showed a generally increasing trend while exports more or less stagnated, as shown in Table 7.1. Imports of capital goods, machinery and equipment for the developing heavy industry base accounted for the increases in total imports.

The 1960s and 1970s was a period beset with tumultuous political and economic events. The political scene in India changed radically after the death of Prime Minister LB Shastri in January 1966. The Congress party was engulfed by an internal struggle, and after a few weeks, during which time an acting Prime Minister was in office, Mrs Indira Gandhi came to lead the government. Mrs Gandhi had an uneasy relationship with some

Table 7.1 India's trade performance during the first three Plans: 1951–1966 (US$ millions)

Year	Imports		Exports		Year	Imports		Exports	
	Goods	Services	Goods	Services		Goods	Services	Goods	Services
1951	1852	185	1574	270	1959	1969	188	1325	302
1952	1622	153	1363	295	1960	2259	294	1315	357
1953	1241	146	1126	282	1961	2139	358	1388	317
1954	1343	145	1150	285	1962	2288	406	1412	337
1955	1566	169	1370	267	1963	2493	424	1623	404
1956	2124	152	1323	278	1964	2946	462	1714	430
1957	2625	156	1463	287	1965	2932	516	1678	352
1958	2219	178	1185	279	1966	2600	501	1531	423

Note: Goods are valued at market prices, imports and exports are valued f.o.b. Freight and insurance entered as service payments.

Source: Little et al. (1970: 395).

senior leaders of the Congress Party, which ultimately led to its split. The later part of 1960s also witnessed non-Congress governments coming into power in several states.

Moreover, Mrs Gandhi came to power at a time when the economy was in distress. She was initially persuaded by liberal economists to move towards a freer system of exchange controls, and to depreciate the rupee closer to its value; this resulted in a 37 per cent devaluation in 1966. The government also took steps toward liberalization of import licensing, tariffs and export subsidies. These measures were extended to 59 industries covering 80 per cent of the organized sector's output. The industries were given freedom to import their raw materials and components. However, since the necessity to obtain licences remained due to continued application of the principle of indigenous availability, the scope of import liberalization was limited.

Unfortunately, the devaluation of the rupee coincided with a second consecutive drought in the country, which led to an industrial recession. At the same time, much of the aid package of $900 million promised by the World Bank, who had urged the Government of India to devalue, could not be utilized in 1966–67 due to the recession. It was not possible to consider dismantling protective barriers while there was a lack of effective demand for output in several industries.

The continuation of the principle of indigenous availability was partly because of the recession. Food shortages, high prices and shrinking employment opportunities contributed to a negative public perception of the devaluation of the rupee. The widely held belief was that the devaluation was forced by the World Bank and was not the correct prescription. Severe domestic criticism, a political leadership that was keen to distribute export subsidies, and an industrial sector that had learned to profit from protection came together to reverse the import liberalization measures in less than two years after 1966–67. For Mrs Gandhi, this was a political setback, and she remained wedded to the end of her days to the principles and advantages of a closed economy, tightly controlled by the state. She was persuaded that direct public expenditure was the only means of alleviating poverty, and that, for this, means of production should be tightly regulated by the state, or remain in the hands of the state.

Thus the late 1960s and early 1970s saw a further tightening of import controls. At the same time, Mrs Gandhi had to face political challenges that made it imperative to project a new pro-poor socialist image. She sought to identify with the poor and underprivileged with new schemes to help them. Nationalization of banks, removal of privileges of erstwhile rulers of princely states, and nationalization of coal and oil followed in rapid succession. But it was the war with Pakistan in 1971 – which led to the creation of Bangladesh – that paid the highest political dividends, leading to a resounding victory in the elections which followed.

A revitalized Mrs Gandhi was convinced that state controls over the economy were the right path for the nation. But opposition was growing. A combination of splinter groups of Congress (known as Congress-O), the Bharatiya Janata Party (BJP, formerly named Jan Sangh) and other parties were agitating against the policies (economic as well as political) of Mrs Gandhi. By mid-1975, the combined work of opposition parties reached a climax, leading to the imposition of an internal emergency by the President on the advice of Mrs Gandhi.

The US was not favourably inclined towards the political leadership in India under Prime Minister Indira Gandhi. Hostile US policy immediately before and after the Bangladesh war in 1971 was partly responsible for the kind of economic isolationism India experienced in the early 1970s. Also, the World Bank's failure to deliver the $900 million in promised annual aid was partly due to pressure from the United States, which further strengthened the hands of isolationists. By 1975–76, the import control regime had become so restrictive that the share of non-oil, non-cereals imports in GDP fell from an already low 7 per cent in 1957–58 to 3 per cent in 1975–76.

The tight import restrictions adversely affected the profitability of industrial units since essential raw materials and machinery could not be imported in required quantities or on time. Industrialists therefore started lobbying for liberalization of import of raw materials and machinery for which there were no domestically produced substitutes. At the same time, an improvement in export performance and remittances from overseas workers in the Middle East led to an accumulation of a healthy foreign exchange reserve. Policy-makers were ready to consider some liberalization of trade controls.

The trade liberalization measures initiated in 1976 progressed gradually (as discussed in the following section), more or less unaffected by political developments and regime changes in the next fifteen years. In 1977, when the emergency was lifted and elections were held, Mrs Gandhi's party lost to a coalition of opposition parties (except communists and other leftists) but this government could last only about three years due to internal dissensions in the coalition. In the elections held in 1980, Mrs Gandhi came back to power.

After her death in October 1984, her son Rajiv Gandhi was elected leader of the party, sworn in as Prime Minister, won the general elections, and was in office until 1989. His government initially attempted several measures to liberalize trade and to free the economy from controls, but later became embroiled in several controversies that weakened the decision-making process, and eventually led to the Congress party's defeat in the ensuing elections. In the next eighteen months, two minority governments, with support from BJP in the first case and from Congress in the second case, were in office, until elections were called again in May 1991. However, as mentioned earlier, the trade reform measures initiated earlier were not halted or hampered by these political developments. In fact, the Congress regime during the 1980s was favourably inclined to continue with trade reform measures, but the circumstances were not conducive to introducing these in a comprehensive fashion.

REFORMS: 1976–91

With the reintroduction of the Open General License (OGL) list in 1976 a new phase of liberalization commenced. The OGL was in existence since pre-independence days but had become defunct after import controls were tightened in the late 1960s. The new OGL system operated on a positive list basis. Items included in the list could be imported without licence if the importer was the actual user (AU). In the case of machinery imports, clearance from the licensing authority may have been required if the sector in which the machinery was to be employed was subject to industrial licensing.

In 1976, the OGL list contained only 79 capital goods items. By April 1990 the number of items in the list increased to 1170 capital goods and 949 intermediate inputs. OGL imports accounted for 30 per cent of total

Table 7.2 Foreign trade of India: 1980–81 to 1990–91 (Rs. billion, current prices)

Year	Imports	Exports	Balance of Trade
1980–81	125	67	−58
1981–82	136	78	−58
1982–93	143	88	−55
1983–84	158	98	−61
1984–85	171	117	−54
1985–86	197	109	−87
1986–87	201	125	−76
1987–88	222	157	−66
1988–89	282	202	−80
1989–90	354	277	−77
1990–91	432	326	−106

Source: Ministry of Information & Broadcasting (1993).

imports by 1990. While the tariff rates were raised substantially during this period, items on the OGL list were given large concessions on those rates, so that the tariffs did not significantly add to the restrictive effect of licensing. By 1990, 31 sectors had been freed from industrial licensing, which had a trade liberalizing effect as it freed machinery from industrial licensing clearance. Improved agricultural performance and the discovery of oil also helped increase imports of machinery and intermediate products. The government also introduced several export incentives, especially after 1985.

Between 1980–81 and 1990–91, while imports increased by 344 per cent, exports recorded an increase of 485 per cent in value terms at current prices, though the trade balance was always negative during this period since the imports were at a much higher level to begin with (Table 7.2). Even when the figures are converted into values at constant prices, the annual rate of growth in both imports and exports would appear to be quite substantial.

THE SETTING FOR COMPREHENSIVE TRADE LIBERALIZATION

The substantial growth in imports and exports (though with a persistent negative trade balance) in the 1980s is at least partly attributable to liberalization measures that were complemented by an expansionary fiscal policy. Though the rate of growth of the economy increased to 7.6 per cent during 1988–91, this was at the cost of a growing fiscal deficit. The fiscal deficit of central and state governments together, as a percentage of GDP, rose from an already high of 9 per cent in 1980–81 to 12.7 per cent in 1990–91 and that of Central Government alone increased from 6.1 per cent to 8.4 per cent.

Correspondingly, the government's debt (internal and external borrowings) accumulated rapidly. Interest payments amounted to 2 per cent of GDP and 10 per cent of Central Government's expenditure in 1980–81, which had increased to 4 per cent and 20 per cent respectively by 1990–91. The situation became critical in 1991 when the government had to face the prospect of defaulting on external commitments for the first time. The government was forced into taking emergency measures, including, amongst others, selling stocks of gold to obtain foreign exchange, using special facilities of the IMF/World Bank, and bilateral assistance from some developed countries. This balance of payments crisis, unlike previous iterations, left a deep impression on policy-makers and forced them to think seriously about lasting reforms in the domestic and external sectors of the economy.

Two major changes in the international environment – the then-recent collapse of the Soviet Union and opening of the Chinese economy – encouraged those in the government to be in favour of a pro-market and pro-free trade approach to economic policy. A new Congress Party government came to power just after the 1991 balance of payments crisis, led by one of the party's veterans (Narasimha Rao) and incorporating as Finance Minister the well-known career economist Manmohan Singh (currently Prime Minister). The new team lost no time in announcing a series of measures, the main focus of which was on trade reforms, fiscal discipline, structural reforms and industrial policy reforms.

The economic reforms initiated by the government generated debate among academics, different interest groups and generally among the educated public. In the beginning there was scepticism all around. Even industrialists were somewhat wary about the effectiveness of the reform measures and the government's commitment to carry them further. Admittedly, the pace of reforms in the 1990s was not fast enough, as there are many constraints in a democracy. However, as the process of reforms continued and results were visible towards the late 1990s and later, apprehensions about opening up the economy to international competition more or less disappeared, notwithstanding the continued harangue of leftist ideologues against the 'evils' of globalization. In the initial years major changes were possible, but the reforms process lost steam after 1993. This was partly due to political pressures on the government, exacerbated by a scam in the stock market that was (incorrectly) attributed to market liberalization.

The Uruguay Round of global trade negotiations was reaching its latter phases during this time. India's participation was conducted by groups of officials in the Commerce Ministry who tended to act in isolation, with inadequate degrees of transparency. As there was little coordination and no consensus-seeking on various important issues, India's negotiators often did not have a clear political brief, and hence were often unwilling signatories to several agreements, including the controversial agreement on Trade-Related Aspects of Intellectual Property Rights (TRIPS). These events caused political difficulties; the Congress government lost power in 1996.

Over the next three years several different and unstable minority-coalition governments would come to power, further slowing the pace at which reforms could be undertaken. Only in 1999 did the BJP and its allies formed a stable government, which remained in power until mid-2004. This period saw the reforms process taken forward on all fronts. The government understood the advantages of opening up the economy to trade and investment, and initiated a succession of measures that liberalized controls. Most importantly, the integration in foreign policy between diplomacy and trade occurred at this time.

It is interesting to note in retrospect that since 1991, no ruling party opposed the reforms. Four different governments were in office during the 1990s, the Congress government which initiated the reforms in 1991; the United Front coalition (1996–98) which continued the process, albeit more slowly; the Bharatiya Janatha Party-led coalition (the National Democratic Alliance), which took office in 1998 and then again in October 1999, and implemented further reforms. Although there is broad consensus among political parties on the need for and direction of reforms, certain specific measures are often subjected to heated debate, and sometimes bitterly opposed by the opposition parties. Presently, a Congress-led coalition of political parties is in power with outside support from leftist parties. Despite the constraints imposed by coalition politics, the wide-ranging economic reforms have come to stay and are likely to move forward in the coming years.

At each stage of the process, there was the triangle of public perception, electoral politics, and sound economic policy to be managed in tandem. Looking back, there were successes as well as mistakes. The Uruguay Round trade negotiations were by and large carried out by the executive, with little political backing, and the fact that even after a decade not all the elements of multilateral free trade have been fully absorbed by all sections of the economy is perhaps a consequence of this elitist approach. That India is not able to present liberal alternatives in the current Doha Round is at least in part due to the fact that the different parties in power in the last decade have not been able to generate a national consensus on the full range and minutiae of these issues.

The political leadership in charge of reforms, Mr Manmohan Singh, and later Mr Chidambaram, lacked the political credibility base to push through a comprehensive agenda. It was only during the BJP-led NDA regime that political leadership was able to implement measures that were both politically feasible and economically correct; but they failed to accommodate the inevitable losers created by these policies, and lost power during the next election. The important feature throughout, however, is that notwithstanding these, the agenda is on track, sometimes fast, sometimes halting, but without taking a step backwards.

PROGRESS OF TRADE REFORMS

First, it is clear that India's trade liberalization was as much due to problems in the domestic economy as it was due to ongoing multilateral negotiations. There is sufficient evidence to conclude that the approach to the Uruguay Round negotiations did not follow a comprehensive strategy, that the negotiators were often left with incremental choices, and that New Delhi was more concerned with trade reforms as an addendum to its overall reform agenda rather than as a separate strategic agenda to be pursued.

Within the country, there was little widespread debate on trade liberalization issues until the WTO agreements were signed. In subsequent years this lack of consensus and participation resulted in WTO negotiations being viewed with some apprehension and concern by the public and the polity, constraining the negotiators, both executive and politic, from moving further ahead.

Second, foreign policy concerns were and remain ever-present in decisions taken on trade policy and strategy. The collapse of the Soviet Union had removed an important trade partner and ally. Relations with the United States continued to be cautious and in fact deteriorated after India's nuclear tests in 1998. The early 1990s found foreign policy looking eastwards to Asia. Political and economic ties with Southeast Asia were strengthened, with much of ASEAN reciprocating India's interest. However, the Asian financial crisis of 1997 adversely affected the growth of Asian trade, and India had to adopt a cautious approach to interactions in this region.

As such, there was a feeling that India was becoming somewhat 'friendless', and consensus grew around the need to reorient foreign policy in the context of economic developments. The NDA government led this process between 1998 and 2004, a policy that has been followed since then by the Congress-led government. On one hand, there was a need to build strategic relationship with the USA, the dominant world power, and many reforms undertaken after 1998 were designed with this in mind. This has been balanced by re-engagement with Asia, with China and Japan in particular, and with ASEAN. Singapore has emerged as an important trading partner, with the first comprehensive economic and trade agreement being signed between the two countries in 2005. Trade with Asia has boomed, and several regional and preferential trade agreements are under negotiation.

Third, with the growth of the economy, there has been a need to ensure a steady supply of raw materials, most importantly oil and coal, to meet the growing needs of the economy. There has been a greater focus on integrating trade and foreign policy objectives, and some results are already visible. The private sector has played an important role in this process, driven by its search for overseas business opportunities.

Fourth, the reality of coalition politics, coupled will the concerns of many import-competing domestic industries, has narrowed the flexibility available to the government for further trade liberalization. In multilateral negotiations, India is considered a free-rider, taking advantage of concessions available, but reluctant to give much in return. The stalled round of negotiations has as much to do with the lean brief that Indian negotiators bring to the table as it has with the reluctance of the US and EU to reduce protection in agriculture.

Finally, the trend towards bilateral and regional free trade agreements is in part due to the inability to offer MFN concessions to all, and in part to participate in the global trend towards such agreements. It is clear that though these RTAs and FTAs are often WTO-plus in some respects, cherry picking does take place, leading to rather limited market access lists. Politically this represents a win–win situation for the countries involved.

What has been the collective impact of these processes on the types and levels of India's trade protection and broader economic policies? The initial package of reforms had done away with import licensing on all but a few intermediate products and capital goods. Consumer goods, then accounting for about 30 per cent tariff lines, remained under licensing restrictions. At present, all goods except for a few disallowed on environmental or health and safety considerations and a few that are imported only by state agencies, may be imported without a licence or restrictions. Under the Uruguay Round Agreement on Agriculture, all border measures on agricultural goods have been replaced by tariffs. And across the board, tariff reforms have been fairly impressive.

Tariff Rates

In 1990–91, the highest tariff rate for non-agricultural (industrial) goods stood at 355 per cent, the simple average rate at 113 per cent and the import-weighted average at 87 per cent. A major task of reforms was therefore to lower tariffs. This was accomplished by a gradual compression of peak rates and a reduction in the number of tariff bands. The top rate fell to 85 per cent in 1993–94, to 55 per cent in 1995–96, to 25 per cent by 2004 and to 12.5 per cent in the following two years. In the 2009 budget, the peak rate is expected to be brought down to 10 per cent, comparable to that of East Asian nations.

In agricultural products, India's approach has been similar to that of most OECD countries, choosing very high tariff bindings (ranging from 100 per cent to 300 per cent) to replace alternative border measures as agreed under the Uruguay Round Agreement on Agriculture. Traditionally India had very low bound rates on some agricultural products such as skimmed milk powder, rice, corn, wheat and millet. These were renegotiated under the provisions of GATT in December 1999 in return for concessions in other products. India's average bound rate in agriculture, according to the WTO, was 115.3 per cent in 2001–02, as compared to the MFN tariff rate of 41.7 per cent.

Export Controls

There were restrictions on export of a number of commodities before the reform process began in the 1990s. Along with liberalization of imports in the reform process, the government reduced the number of items subject to export control from 439 in 1991 to 296 in 1992 with prohibited items reduced to 16. This process of removing export control continued thereafter and export prohibitions currently apply only to a smaller number of items on health, environmental or moral grounds. Export restrictions now apply only to cattle, camels, fertilizers, cereals, groundnut oil and pulses.

Exchange Controls

Exchange controls and overvaluation of the rupee represented additional barriers in the traded goods sector. The government took steps to remove them as part of the liberalization programme. The rupee was devalued in 1991 from 21.2 to 25.8 rupees to the dollar. A dual exchange system was introduced in February 1992. Under this system importers were allowed to sell 60 per cent of their foreign exchange earnings in the open market at higher prices. The balance was to be sold to the government at a lower official price. At the same time, importers were authorized to purchase foreign exchange in the open market at higher prices, effectively ending the exchange control regime. Within a year the official exchange rate was unified with the market exchange rate. In February 1994, many current account transactions including all current business transactions, education, medical expenses and foreign travel were also permitted at the market exchange rate. These steps propelled India to accept the IMF's Article VIII obligations, which made the rupee officially convertible on the current account. In the context of surging foreign exchange reserves, many capital transactions were also freed from restrictions. For example, firms can borrow freely abroad as long as the maturity period of the loan is five years or more. Residents can also remit up to $100 000 abroad every year.

Trade in Services

There has been considerable progress in liberalizing trade in the services sector. The government had a monopoly or near monopoly in insurance, banking and telecommunications. With the establishment of an Insurance Regulatory and Development Authority (IRDA) in December 1999, the insurance sector opened up for private entry, including foreign investors. Foreign ownership up to 49 per cent is now permitted provided a licence is obtained from the IRDA.

In the banking sector, private sector banks (including foreign banks) were already operating in the country. Foreign direct investment (FDI) in private sector banks is permitted up to 74 per cent of ownership under the automatic route. Foreign banks are also allowed to open a specified number of new branches every year. More than 25 foreign banks with full banking licences and about 150 foreign bank branches are operating in India now. Under the 1997 WTO Financial Services Agreement, India has committed itself to permitting 12 foreign bank branches to be established every year. Under the Comprehensive Economic Cooperation Agreement (CECA) with Singapore, selected Singapore banks have been given national treatment, that is, they would be allowed to operate in India under Reserve Bank of India regulations.

Like the insurance sector, the telecommunications sector was also a state monopoly until the early 1990s. The 1994 National Telecommunications Policy allowed the private sector, including foreign investors, to provide basic, cellular and value-added telephone services. With rapid changes in technology, a new Telecom Policy was adopted in 1999. Foreign ownership was increased to 49 per cent permitted in basic, cellular mobile, paging and value-added services and in global mobile communications by satellites, subject to licensing by the Department of Telecommunications. The FDI limit was later raised to 74 per cent. FDI up to 100 per cent of ownership is allowed, with some conditions, for Internet service providers not providing gateways (for both satellite and submarine calls), infrastructure providers providing dark fibre, electronic mail and voice mail. For Internet service providers with gateways, radio-paging and end-to-end width, up to 74 per cent foreign investment is permitted subject to licensing and security requirements.

In e-commerce, FDI is permitted up to 100 per cent. Automatic approval is given for foreign equity in software and almost all areas of electronics. In order to encourage exports and to provide employment of skilled workers, full foreign ownership is permitted in information technology units set up exclusively for exports. Such units can be set up under several schemes including export-oriented units, export processing zones, special economic zones, software technology parks, and electronic hardware technology parks.

The IT industry has been the most significant beneficiary of the opening up of the economy. Between 1995 and 2000 the Indian IT industry recorded a CAGR (compound annual growth rate) of more than 42 per cent. India's exports of computer software beat the global recession of 2001–02 and grew by a healthy 31.4 per cent. In absolute terms software and services exports rose to $7.875 billion in 2001–02 from $5.978 billion in 2000–01. Latest reports from the National Association of Software and Services Companies (NASSCOM) indicate that exports of IT services and products during 2006–07 were $31.3 billion, up from $23.3 billion in 2005–06.

The transport infrastructure sector is another area that has been opened to foreign investment. Full ownership under the automatic route is permitted for projects for construction and maintenance of roads, highways, vehicular bridges, toll roads, vehicular tunnels, ports and harbours. For construction of ports and harbours, automatic approval for foreign equity up to 100 per cent is available. No approval is required for foreign equity up to 51 per cent in projects providing support services for water transport. FDI up to 100 per cent is permitted in airports, though FDI above 74 per cent requires prior approval. Foreign equity up to 40 per cent and investment by non-resident Indians up to 100 per cent is permitted in domestic air transport services.

Attempts to bring private investment including FDI into the power sector have started yielding results. The Electricity Act of 2003 offers a comprehensive framework for restructuring the power sector. It attempts to introduce competition through private sector participation along with the public sector entities in generation, transmission and distribution. The Act completely eliminates licensing requirements in generation and freely permits captive generation. Only hydro-electric projects now require clearance from Central Electricity Authority. Distribution licensees are free to undertake generation, and generating companies are free to do distribution business. Trading has been recognized as a distinct activity, with regulatory

Commissions authorized to fix ceilings on trading margins, if necessary. FDI is permitted in all three activities.

Foreign Investment Policy

India has continued to liberalize its foreign investment regime since 1991. India also continues to streamline foreign investment regulations and reduce or remove equity restrictions. In a recent move to rationalize policy further, in February 2006 equity restrictions were lifted in several activities subject to industrial licensing within 25km of large cities, and in sensitive sectors such as the manufacture of explosives and hazardous chemicals, and 'Greenfield' airports, where investment has been permitted under an automatic route subject to sectoral regulations. Total FDI during 2006–07 was provisionally estimated by the Reserve Bank of India at $8.44 billion. Portfolio investment by Foreign Institutional Investors (FIIs) has sharply increased in the last few years, and is of the order of $14 billion.

Domestic Economic Policy

There have been trade and investment facilitating reforms in the domestic economy as well. Industrial licensing requirements have been removed in all but five industries. Only three industries are now reserved for the public sector. The number of products reserved for the small scale sector has also been reduced.

India had experienced the negative consequences of an expansionary fiscal policy based on ever-increasing borrowings (internal and external) during the years preceding 1991. In order to ensure that such a scenario is not repeated, the government has enacted the Fiscal Responsibility and Budget Management Act (FRBMA) in 2003 which calls upon the central government to take appropriate measures to reduce the fiscal deficit and revenue deficit so as to eliminate the latter by 31 March 2009. The central government's fiscal and revenue deficits have declined as a result of measures taken to achieve this objective. The fiscal deficit as a percentage of GDP fell to 4 per cent in 2004–05 from the high level of 6.2 per cent in 2001–02. It is now estimated to have come down to 3.7 per cent in 2006–07.

Monetary policy is the responsibility of the Reserve Bank of India (RBI). Of late, considerations regarding financial stability have assumed greater importance in view of the increasing openness of the Indian economy and financial sector reforms. The RBI has from time to time taken steps to contain inflation and at the same time provided sufficient liquidity to support investment demand in the economy. It continues to monitor liquidity and inflation closely and also intervenes to sterilize inward flows.

Financial Sector and Capital Markets

The focus of financial sector reform is on the banking sector and is aimed at providing publicly-owned banks with greater autonomy so as to increase their efficiency. Foreign banks have been allowed to establish wholly owned subsidiaries in India as well as offshore banking units in Special Economic Zones. Amendments to the Banking Act, which are under consideration, would raise the current limit on FDI in domestic banks from the present limit of 49 per cent to 74 per cent before the scheduled date of 2009 and lift the 10 per cent limit on voting rights. As a result of reforms undertaken, non-performing loans continued to decline, and the aggregate capital adequacy ratio has risen.

Efforts to create a well functioning capital market are being pursued by the Securities and Exchange Board of India (SEBI), the security market regulator. The security exchanges have been corporatized and are in the process of being demutualized. All listed companies are also required to adopt corporate governance requirements specified in the listing agreement.

IMPACT OF REFORMS

The reforms discussed above have brought about important changes in the growth, composition and direction of India's trade in the last fifteen years. Broader economic impacts, including improvements in productivity, have also occurred.

Growth and Composition of Trade

India's share in world exports of goods and services had declined from 2 per cent at independence to 0.5 per cent by the mid-1980s. By 2002 it had revived to 0.8 per cent and was expected to achieve the level of 1 per cent of world exports in 2006–07 and to 1.5 per cent by 2009. This is because India's exports of goods and services have grown faster than world averages since at least the beginning of the 1990s. Although India's trade performance has been less spectacular than China's, there is no doubt that there has been a remarkable improvement in exports and imports in the 1990s and later, as shown in Table 7.3.

Merchandise trade as a percentage of GDP increased from roughly 21 per cent in 2001–02 to about 33 per cent in 2005–06 reflecting greater openness of India's goods markets. Imports have grown faster than exports, leading to a widening trade deficit. The services trade surplus as a

Table 7.3 Import and export performance, 1986–87 to 2006–07 (Rs. billion, current prices)

Year	Imports	% change	Exports	% change	Trade balance
1986–87	201	1.8	125	14.2	−76
1994–95	900	23.1	8267	22.2	−73
1995–96	1227	36.4	1064	28.6	−163
1996–97	1389	13.2	1188	11.7	−201
1997–98	1542	11	1293	8.8	−249
1998–99	1783	15.7	1398	8.1	−386
1999–00	2153	20.9	1596	14.2	−560
2000–01	2309	10.7	2036	27.6	−273
2001–02	2452	6.2	2090	2.7	−362
2002–03	2972	21.2	2551	22.1	−421
2003–04	3591	20.8	2934	15	−657
2004–05	5011	39.5	3753	27.9	−1257
2005–06	6604	31.8	4564	21.6	−2040
2006–07*	6135		4167		−1969

Note: * = April–December 2006.

Source: DGCI&S, Kolkata, Department of Commerce, Government of India.

percentage of GDP increased from 0.7 per cent to 2.8 per cent in 2005–06 as software and IT exports surged.

The composition of merchandise trade in 2005–06 as compared to 2000–01 is shown in Table 7.4.

The share of goods such as electrical and non-electrical machinery, transport equipment and chemicals in total manufacturing exports has increased, while that of clothing and textiles and agricultural commodities has declined substantially. The share of capital goods (machinery and transport equipment) increased from 7.9 per cent in 2000–01 to 10.9 per cent in 2005–06. There has been good growth in labour-intensive special skill manufactures like jewellery, whose share rose from 2.1 per cent to 3.4 per cent over the period.

Overall, however, the share of manufactures (excluding petroleum products) as a group in total exports declined from 76.4 per cent in 2000–01 to 69.8 per cent in 2005–06. The share of agricultural products in India's exports, which was 26 per cent in 1987–88, has been gradually declining during the 1990s, reaching 14.1 per cent in 2000–01 and 10.4 per cent in 2005–06. Fuels accounted for 34–35 per cent of imports in 2000–01 as well as in 2005–06. The share of manufactures in India's imports has also

Table 7.4 Composition of India's merchandise trade, 2000–01 to 2005–06 (% and US$ billion)

Commodity group	Exports		Imports	
	2001–02	2005–06	2001–02	2005–06
Clothing & textiles	27	17.1	..	..
Fuels	4.3	11.5	34.7	33.7
Electrical & non-electrical machinery	5.1	6.3	12.8	16.4
Transport equipment	2.8	4.6	2.4	6.4
Chemicals	10.5	11.6	9	9.3
Other semi-manufactures	21.1	17.5	12.1	8.4
Iron & steel	2.9	4.8	1.5	3
Other mining	2.9	7.2	4.7	4.7
Agricultural commodities	14.1	10.4	7.6	4.9
Other consumer goods	7.2	7.9	5.1	4.9
Others	2.2	1	1.8	0.9
Gold	..	..	8.3	7.3
Total trade value (US$ billion)	44.3	103.4	51.9	149.8

Source: World Trade Organization (2006).

increased appreciably. The significant point is that the role of agriculture is declining in both exports and imports while that of manufactured goods, as a whole, has been increasing in recent years.

The share of services in total exports rose from 19.6 per cent in 1990 to about 24 per cent in 2001. The main items in India's 'invisible' receipts have been non-factor services, which include travel, transportation, and miscellaneous (in which software services are included); and transfers, official and private (remittances by individuals from abroad). The share of transfers (mostly remittances) and software services in invisible receipts was 35.4 per cent and 22.3 per cent respectively in 2002–03. The current account, which was in deficit till 2000–01, generated a surplus in the next two years, mainly due to a sharp rise in receipts on account of remittances from abroad and software services exports. As discussed earlier, India's software and service exports registered annual growth rates of well over 30 per cent in the last few years.

Direction of Trade

Significant changes have also occurred in the direction of trade during the period of trade reforms, as shown in Table 7.5.

Overall the direction of trade has shifted decidedly in favour of Asian

Table 7.5 Changes in India's geographical trading patterns, 1992–93 to 2005–06 (% and US$ billion)

Region/countries	1992–93		2000–01		2005–06	
	Export	Import	Export	Import	Export	Import
Europe – total	33.8	34.4	25.9	27.6	24.2	22.2
EC countries	28.3	30.2	24	21.1	22.5	17.2
Switzerland	1.1	1.7	..	6.3	..	4.4
Other Europe	4.4	2.5	2	0.3	1.7	0.5
America	21	13.2	24.7	8.2	20.8	8.8
US	19	9.8	20.9	6.0	16.9	6.3
Other America	2	3.4	3.8	2.2	3.9	2.4
Asia	26.5	21.1	26.2	22.2	32.2	27.4
Japan	7.7	6.5	4	3.6	2.4	2.7
Singapore	3.2	2.9	2	2.9	5.3	2.2
China	..	..	1.9	3	6.6	7.3
Hong Kong	4.1	0.8	5.9	..	4.3	..
Other Asia	11.4	10.9	12.4	13.1	13.6	15.2
Africa	3.1	3.5	5.3	4.1	6.8	3.3
UAE	4.4	5.1	5.8	*5.2	8.3	*6.7
Other Middle East	..	..	5.5	..	6.4	..
Others	11.3	22.7	6.5	32.4	1.4	31.7
Total trade value (US $ billion)	18.5	21.9	45.2	51.4	103.4	149.8

Notes:
* = import shares are for the entire Middle East region.
'Other Asia' in 2000–01 and 2005–06 includes Australia.

Source: WTO (2007) and Panagaria (2004).

countries (including China but excluding Japan). Their share in India's exports and imports has risen sharply, by 11 percentage points in respect of exports and by 10.1 percentage points in respect of imports between 1992–93 and 2005–06. Japan's share has, over the years, declined. China has emerged as an important trading partner, accounting for 6.6 per cent of India's exports and 7.3 per cent of India's imports in 2005–06. The share of Middle East countries in India's exports has also increased; in particular, the share of the UAE has almost doubled between 1992–93 and 2005–06. Similarly, Africa accounted for nearly 7 per cent of India's exports in 2005–06 as against 3.1 per cent in 1992–93.

The share of EC countries as well as other European countries showed significant decline during this period. Nevertheless, the EC remains an important trade partner, accounting for over 20 per cent of India's exports and over 17 per cent of India's imports. Special mention may be made of Switzerland, which had a share of 6.3 per cent in 2000–01 and 4.4 per cent in 2005–06 in India's imports. The US's share has remained more stable, albeit declining slightly since the early 2000s. The US represented 21 per cent of India's exports in 2000–01, up from 19 per cent in 1992–93, but by 2005–06 this had declined to about 17 per cent. The US, however, retains the position as India's largest single-country trading partner.

The diversification of India's markets for exports and imports reflects, to some extent, the changing composition of India's trade. For example, India's exports to China increasingly consist of medium-to high-technology products; in 2002–03, three product groups, viz: iron ore, engineering goods and chemicals accounted for more than 70 per cent. Electronic goods, chemicals, and textiles, yarn, fabric and made-up articles together accounted for about half of the total value of India's imports from China.

Asian countries (including Middle East countries) accounted for nearly half (47 per cent) of India's total exports in 2005, while the share of Asia in total world exports was only about one-quarter (26 per cent). In contrast, Europe accounted for only 24 per cent of India's total exports in 2005 though its share in total world export was as high as 40 per cent.

Growth and Productivity

Trade liberalization measures have enabled the Indian economy to achieve growth, increased productivity and greater efficiency. Table 7.6 shows the growth in GDP, per capita GDP and sectoral shares since 2000–01.

The Indian economy has achieved impressive growth rates in the last few years, second only to that of China (amongst the large economies). Per capita GDP has also recorded substantial increases. Table 7.6 also shows that more than half of GDP is accounted for by the services sector. None of this would have been possible without the comprehensive reforms undertaken in the last sixteen years.

In assessing the contribution of liberalization to growth, it is useful to see whether liberalization was accompanied by growth in total factor productivity (TFP). Total factor productivity reflects the efficiency with which factors of production are used and is therefore a key determinant of an economy's performance, especially its international competitiveness. One of the most important sources of TFP growth in the long run is technological progress, something often induced by market-oriented reforms. Growth of TFP in the three main sectors of the economy is given in Table 7.7.

As shown above, average annual output growth in India increased from

Table 7.6 Growth and composition of output, 2000–01 to 2006–07, Rs, US$ and %

Output measures (Rs. and US$)	2000-01	2001-02	2002-03	2003-04	2004-05	2005-06	2006-07
Real GDP at factor cost (Rs. billion, 1999–2000 prices)	18,648	19,729	20,477	22,226	23,897	26,045	28,440*
Percentage change		(+5.5)	(+3.8)	(+8.5)	(+7.5)	(+9.0)	(+9.2)
Current GDP at factor cost (Rs. billion)	19,254	21,002	22,653	25,494	28,559	32,509	37,175*
Percentage change		(+9.1)	(+7.9)	(+12.5)	(+12)	(+13.8)	(+14.4)
Current GDP at factor cost (US$ billion)	422	440	468	555	636	734	..
Percentage change		(+4.5)	(-6.3)	(+18.5)	(+17.6)	(+15.5)	..
Current GDP at market prices (Rs. billion)	21,024	22,811	24,581	27,655	31,266	35,672	41,006*
Percentage change		(+8.5)	(+11.0)	(+12.5)	(+13.0)	(+14.1)	(+15)
Current GDP at market prices (US$ billion)	460	478	508	602	696	806	..
Percentage change		(+3.9)	(+6.2)	(+18.5)	(+15.6)	(+15.8)	..
Current GDP per capita at market prices (Rs)	20,632	21,975	23,299	25,773	28,684	32,224	..
Percentage change		(+6.5)	(+6.0)	(+10.4)	(+11.3)	(+12.3)	..
Current GDP per capita at market prices (US$)	452	461	481	561	638	728	..
Percentage change		(+2.0)	(+4.5)	(+16. 5)	(+13.8)	(+14.0)	..
Sector shares							
Agriculture, forestry & fishing	23.4	23.2	20.9	20.9	18.8	18.3	..
Mining & quarrying	2.4	2.3	2.8	2. 5	3.0	2.8	..
Manufacturing	15.6	15.0	15.3	15.2	15.9	16.0	..
Electricity, gas & water	2.4	2.3	2.4	2.2	2.1	2.0	..
Construction	5.8	5.8	6.0	6.2	6.5	6.8	..
Services	50.5	51.5	52.7	52.9	53.7	54.1	..

Notes:
* = advance estimate. GDP figures for 2005-06 are provisional.
Figures in brackets are year-to-year growth rates.

Source: WTO (2007); Economic Survey 2006–07, Govt. of India.

Table 7.7 Total factor productivity growth in India, 1978–2004 (average annual % change)

	1978–93				1993–2004			
	Overall	Agriculture	Industry	Services	Overall	Agriculture	Industry	Services
Output	4.5	2.7	5.4	5.9	6.5	2.2	6.7	9.1
Employment	2.1	1.4	3.3	3.8	1.9	0.7	3.6	3.7
Capital	1	0.2	1.4	0.3	1.8	0.7	1.7	1.1
Land	-0.1	-0.1	n.a.	n.a.	0	-0.1	n.a.	n.a.
Education	0.3	0.2	0.4	0.4	0.4	0.3	0.3	0.4
TFP	1.2	1	0.3	1.4	2.3	0.5	1.1	3.9
Labour productivity	2.4	1.3	2.1	2.1	4.6	1.5	3.1	5.4
Capital productivity	1.8	1.7	1.4	3.5	2.4	0.5	2.2	5.5

Note: n.a. = not applicable

Source: WTO (2007), quoting Bosworth and Collins (2007).

4.5 per cent during the period preceding the reforms of 1991 to 6.5 per cent during 1993–2004. Of this 2 percentage point increase, 1.1 percentage points were attributable to improved TFP, which almost doubled from an average annual rate of 1.2 per cent during 1978–93 to 2.3 per cent during the period 1993–04. The rest of the rise was largely due to increased investment. Similar is the case in respect of labour productivity and capital productivity. Thus, there has been an overall and substantial increase in productivity during the post-reform period. Growth in both output and TFP has been much faster in the services sector than in industry where performance seems to have been hampered by, *inter alia*, rigid labour laws and inadequate infrastructure. By contrast, growth in output and TFP in agriculture has slowed down, possibly owing to weather and other natural factors.

TRADE NEGOTIATIONS

India's foreign trade policy aims to double India's share of global merchandise trade by 2009 over the 2004 level and to use trade to generate employment. While exports are a key goal, the policy acknowledges the importance of facilitating imports required to stimulate the economy and calls for a simplification of import procedures and reduction of import barriers, and coherence and consistency between trade and other economic policies. While unilateral measures have been implemented in the past, as the process of reforms is continuing, it is natural that the country should take a more active role in international (multilateral and bilateral) trade negotiations to achieve a fair and equitable share of trade benefits.

India is an active member of the WTO. In the current negotiations it has submitted proposals relating to, *inter alia*, agriculture, non-agricultural market access (NAMA), services, disputes, competition policy, trade facilities, rules, TRIPS, and special and differential treatment. A number of these proposals were made jointly with other members and in many cases with developing countries, including the G-20, G-33 and NAMA-11 groups.

India's position prior to the Doha Round of negotiations placed emphasis on securing the objectives outlined in the mandated negotiations and the remaining Uruguay Round implementation issues raised by a number of developing countries. After the failures at Doha, at the Ministerial Conference in Cancun in September 2003, and in Hong Kong in December 2005, India stressed the need to address the question of agricultural subsidies in rich countries and tariff and non-tariff barriers maintained by these countries on products of export interest to developing countries.

India believes that the interests of its 650 million rural poor, who are dependent on agriculture for their livelihoods, cannot be ignored. India is therefore also arguing in favour of special and differential treatment through proportionately lower overall bound tariff reduction commitments by developing countries, coupled with a special safeguard mechanism and a list of special products vital to ensuring livelihood and food security of farmers in developing countries.

However, on agriculture India has difficult questions to ask of itself. First, would small and marginal farmers suffer today because of cheap imports or because of extensive state intervention that has prevented the emergence of an integrated domestic market, distorted resource allocation and cropping patterns because of extensive subsidies, seen a near breakdown of technology generation and dissemination systems in agriculture, and prevented the entry of modern trading and logistics? It is difficult to argue that the external world alone is responsible for the woes of India farmers.

Second, will India be a net importer of cereals and food grains in the coming years? Indian farmers are already shifting to more value-added crops. Given the adverse land–man ratio and the difficulties in establishing a land market, India cannot expect to emerge as a net exporter of wheat, rice, corn and edible oils, which are land-intensive crops.

In respect of non-agriculture market access (NAMA), India and its coalition partners believe that progress must be made towards achieving a fair, balanced and development oriented set of modalities based on the mandated principles of placing development concerns at the heart of the negotiations. India and other developing countries also believe that the developed countries should concede less than full reciprocity in reduction commitments on the part of developing countries, and commit to a comparable level of agricultural market access and appropriate flexibilities to manage adjustment costs and address development needs. On services, India seeks increased market access especially through liberalization of professional services trade in Mode 1 (cross-border supplies) and Mode 4 (movement of natural persons), while securing a balance in the outcome of commitments across all modes.

Regional Trade Arrangements

Multilateral negotiations, especially in sensitive areas like agriculture, involving countries at various stages of development with different resource endowments and political structures, are a protracted and time-consuming process. While the main focus has been on multilateral trade negotiations, India has found it expedient to enter into agreements with other developing countries, including India's neighbours. This was considered necessary to sustain India's exports growth and the unilateral liberalization measures implemented since 1991. Current negotiations have resulted in regional agreements like the South Asian Free Trade Area (SAFTA) and the Bay of Bengal Initiative for Multi-Sectoral Technical and Economic Cooperation (BIMSTEC). Bilateral agreements were entered into in recent years with Singapore, Sri Lanka, Thailand, MERCOSUR and Chile. The Comprehensive Economic Cooperation Agreement was signed between India and Singapore in 2005, and goes beyond trade in goods to include services and investment; the agreements with MERCOSUR and Chile are less ambitious.

India is also seeking to deepen ties with other regional groupings such as ASEAN, the Gulf Cooperation Council, and the Southern African Customs Union, and with the Republic of Korea and Mauritius. Joint Study Groups have also been set up to explore the feasibility of comprehensive economic cooperation agreements with China, Japan, Indonesia, Malaysia, Australia and the Russian Federation. Finally, closer trade and investment ties are also sought with the European Union and the United States through India–EU Strategic Partnership, signed in September 2005, and the US–India Trade Policy Forum. Discussions and consultations are continuing.

LOOKING AHEAD: PROSPECTS AND PROBLEMS

> Twenty years ago the rest of the world saw India as a pauper. Now it is just as famous for its software engineers, Bollywood movie actors, literary giants and steel magnates (Simon Robinson, 'A young giant awakens', TIME magazine, 2 August, 2007)

India has certainly succeeded in achieving greater integration of its economy with the world system through the reform measures implemented in the last fifteen years. As discussed above, the economic growth rate has risen to over 9 per cent, exports have increased substantially, foreign exchange reserves have swelled to a comfortable level, industrial production has recorded healthy growth, inflation has been contained and fiscal discipline has been maintained.

However, the agriculture sector, with low growth and a shrinking share in GDP, is a cause for concern. In 2006–07 the share of agriculture in GDP declined to 18.5 per cent while the share of services sector improved to 55.1 per cent. As agriculture provides a livelihood to around 650 million people, it is imperative that efforts are made to improve this sector's performance, and that of allied activities. Low productivity and 'marginal farmers' present the two greatest challenges. The current trade policy places emphasis on agro-exports, and in order to encourage value addition in traded agro-products, several import concessions are given to exporters. It is also important to have increased access to international markets to provide a stimulus for higher production of agricultural products generally, and products such as mangoes and value-added mango preparations for which there is good demand abroad, in particular.

Although industrial production has improved with a growth rate of 8 per cent to 10 per cent in recent years, its share in GDP is only 26.4 per cent, a small improvement over the last two decades. This is in sharp contrast to the situation in China and other developing countries. There is a need to expand the manufacturing base, in order to provide for greater employment.

Infrastructure bottlenecks continue to constrain growth. Transport and power are the two sectors requiring the most urgent attention. The Eleventh Five Year Plan, unveiled recently, places emphasis on Public Private Partnerships in infrastructure. Indian businessmen have recently come forward to take up large infrastructure projects in transport and power sectors, but a great deal of work remains.

On the trade front, the persistent trade deficit has been a cause for concern. Between 2003–04 and 2005–06, the deficit has more than tripled. Liberalization of trade has led to a sharp rise in imports which could not be matched by exports. India's current account balance, however, showed a surplus in 2002–03 and 2003–04 because of increased remittances by Indian workers abroad, earnings from trade in services (including software services) and, to some extent, portfolio investment by Foreign Institutional Investors (FIIs). But services exports and remittances may not be able to compensate for the burgeoning trade deficit over the longer term, and depending on portfolio investments by foreign institutions there are, at best, risky. It is therefore necessary to expand India's exports in all possible ways. This requires new markets and better access in the existing markets for India's products, combined with greater productivity at home.

Given the persistent difficulties in the Doha Round of WTO negotiations, and in line with the universal trend to forge regional and bilateral trade arrangements, India has embarked upon regional and bilateral trade agreements, as already discussed in this chapter. India needs to concentrate on such agreements with other Asian countries and countries of Africa and Latin America, in order to boost exports on mutually beneficial terms. India should not shy away from the possibility of an Asian Free Trade Area including China and Japan.

Most important, however, is the problem of building political consensus for further reforms. Though there was a broad consensus on the basic direction of reforms, their implementation during the 1990s was not altogether smooth. There have been several instances of political parties supporting reforms when in power and trying to block them when in opposition. For example, the Bharatiya Janata Party (BJP) opposed the liberalization of the insurance sector when the ruling Congress Party wanted to do so, and later the Congress party did the same when the ruling BJP wanted to. The Congress Party agreed eventually and the insurance reforms went through.

At present, certain important measures are pending implementation due to strong opposition by some political parties, mainly leftist parties. The interaction of party politics with economic reforms is a fact of life in India as in other democratic countries. An important aspect of the unfinished agenda should therefore be wide dissemination of information and debate about the necessity of reforms, which should include a frank discussion about some of its temporary negative consequences, if any, and ways of minimizing their impact.

Finally and perhaps most importantly, several steps need to be taken by the government to improve efficiency in policy-making and implementation. Better inter-ministerial coordination and regular review of policy and procedures is important. The Commerce Ministry has to work in close coordination with the Ministries of External Affairs and Finance at every stage of policy formulation as well as implementation. Existing institutional arrangements have to be strengthened for this purpose.

CONCLUSION

In the first two and half decades of planning, India's trade policy was heavily influenced by the socialist policy of its leaders, allowing for import of only essential machinery and raw materials for industries conforming to the prevailing industrial licensing policy of the government. Import substitution was the key word of development strategy. This period was marked by tight import controls and restrictions, though ad hoc attempts were made to relax them at various different stages. Growth in exports was poor, resulting in repeated adverse balances of trade and payments. Poor economic conditions and political developments (especially since the mid-1960s) also contributed to a restrictive trade policy.

The situation changed somewhat after 1976, when it was realized that industrial growth depended on more liberal import policies for machinery and raw materials. Lobbying by industrialists, increasing remittances from abroad, political stability, and a regime during the 1980s comparatively receptive to the idea of trade reforms contributed to a progressive but incremental relaxing of trade controls and restrictions. However, this period also witnessed an unprecedented expansion in fiscal deficits (financed by borrowings, internal and external) leading to a balance of payments crisis by early 1991.

It was the balance of payments crisis in early 1991 which triggered a series of reform measures by the new Congress government, which came to power at that time. Emergency measures included, among other things, assistance from the IMF and World Bank. Despite criticisms and apprehensions from various quarters, a package of comprehensive reforms aimed at ending licensing and controls in industry and trade was introduced. The impact of these reforms is reflected in the substantial increase in growth and productivity, especially in the last five years.

The industrial licensing system has been almost completely abolished, more and more sectors have been thrown open for foreign investment, tariffs on non-agricultural goods have been drastically reduced, non-tariff barriers progressively brought down, and significant efforts are made to promote exports. The Indian rupee is now officially convertible on the current account.

Most significant is that the post-1991 reforms have survived political developments and regime changes, indicating that there has come into existence a broad consensus in the development perspective among major political parties in the country. This does not, however, mean total unanimity of views; on specific issues there are bitter arguments for and against, but the overall direction of reforms is not in dispute.

India has succeeded, to a large extent, in integrating with the global economy. While playing an active role in the ongoing multilateral trade negotiations under the auspices of the WTO, India has been reaching out to many countries, especially in Asia, Africa and Latin America for expanding bilateral trade and promoting joint ventures.

Admittedly, the reform process has to be continued, and the problem areas in the domestic economy such as infrastructure (mainly transport and power) have to be strengthened. The present economic and political conditions indicate that this will happen.

REFERENCES

Bajpai, N. (2002), 'A decade of economic reforms in India: the unfinished agenda', CID working paper no. 89, April, Harvard Institute of International Development.

Bhagwati, J.N. and P. Desai (1970), *India Planning for Industrialization: Industrialization and Policies Since 1951*, London: Oxford University Press.

Bosworth, B. and S.M.M. Collins (2007), 'Accounting for growth', NBER working paper no. W12943.
Business India (2007), July 15.
Economy Today (2007), Budget Special, April.
Little, I., T. Scitovsky and M. Scott (1970), *Industry and Trade in some Developing Countries*, London: Oxford University Press.
Ministry of Finance (2007), *Economic Survey 2006–2007*, New Delhi, Government of India, available at http://indiabudget.nic.in/both-index.html.
Ministry of Finance (2007), *Union Budget 2007–08*, New Delhi, Government of India, available at http://indiabudget.nic.in/u62007-08/u6main.htm.
Ministry of Information and Broadcasting (1993), 'India: a reference annual', New Delhi: Ministry of Information and Broadcasting.
Paragariya, A. (2004), 'India's trade reform: progress, import and future strategy', Paper presented at the Indian Policy Forum Conference, New Delhi, March.
Reserve Bank of India (2006), *Reserve Bank of India Bulletin*, New Delhi, Department of Economic Analysis and Policy, Reserve Bank of India, July, available at http://www.bulletin.rbi.org.in.
World Trade Organisation (2006), International Trade Statistics 2006, Geneva, World Trade Organisation.
World Trade Organisation (2007), 'Trade policy review: India, report by the Secretariat', WTO document No.WT/TPR/S/182, Geneva: World Trade Organisation.

8. South Africa

Philip Alves and Lawrence Edwards

INTRODUCTION

South Africa's trade policy reform is still very much a work-in-progress. The efficacy of reforms undertaken thus far is disputed, and the most likely direction reforms will take in future is increasingly difficult to predict. The changes in economic policy in the 1990s – towards stabilization and liberalization – depended on the confluence of three forces. First, an intellectual battle within the ANC itself, and among its alliance partners – the Congress of South African Trade Unions (COSATU) and the South African Communist Party (SACP) – had to be won.[1] This in turn required key members of the ANC leadership and the first post-1994 cabinet to understand and promote arguments in favour of a liberal economic policy regime in South Africa.

Second, the global policy thrust had to have been in favour, broadly, of more liberalization rather than less. This was guaranteed by widespread adherence to the principles embodied in the so-called Washington Consensus, which reached its zenith in the early to mid-1990s, just when South Africa embarked on its path to economic opening. As such, pro-reform arguments within South Africa would receive international support and backing.

Third, events had to play a role. The peaceful transition from apartheid to democracy is the single most important event in modern South African history. Since every aspect of South African life was in such flux during this period, there was something of a blank canvas for incoming policy-makers to work with – the country was going to be rebuilt, law by law. However, because by 1994 the economy was in a severely weakened state a good degree of concurrence existed on the short-term stabilization efforts the incoming government should undertake. On other issues things were less well settled, and it was only after a currency crisis in 1996 that arguments in favour of strong liberalization began to be included in government policy documents.

Unilateral border liberalization continued until 2000, after which bilateral and regional trade agreements began to play a greater role. Despite trade reform, pockets of high protection remain in manufacturing, and key service sectors remain insulated from domestic and international competition. Regulatory reform in other sectors of the economy, such as the labour market, also remain untouched. Thus the South African trade reform story is incomplete – there is significant scope for more and better quality 'at the border' liberalization, and even more work to be done 'behind the border'.

Whether or not this will materialize cannot be certain, as many powerful interest groups dispute the benefits of the reforms undertaken in the 1990s. To be sure, the economy is more open and healthy than it was under apartheid. But the two biggest problems immediately after 1994 – poverty and unemployment – remain huge challenges today. Hence the South African debate over economic liberalization remains unresolved. The important difference between today and 1994 is that the country now has in place a relatively liberal, market-based economy, and there is no serious attempt to pursue a fundamentally different system.

South Africa finds itself now with little clear direction on whether or not deeper and broader liberalization should be pursued. The drifting Doha Round and piecemeal bilateral negotiations agenda compound the problem. The South African government now speaks of the need for a stronger developmental state, a more interventionist industrial policy, and the need to make better use of state-owned companies (and to create new ones). This has ensured, for now, trade policy's slide down the list of government priorities. It remains to be seen where this thinking goes after 2009's general election.

SOUTH AFRICA'S POLITICAL TRANSITION AND THE ECONOMIC LEGACY OF APARTHEID

South Africa's transition from apartheid to democracy is still in its infancy and its commitment to an open economy barely fourteen years old. Before and during apartheid, which lasted from 1948–1994, trade openness was never seriously considered as a means of growth and employment creation, with the important exception of the export-oriented mining sector. South Africa's trade and industrial policy history before 1994 is primarily one of protectionism and import-substitution, although some trade reforms were implemented (see later). The National Party government also perceived mounting economic isolation – especially in the form of economic sanctions from 1986 – and potential regional insurgencies as national security threats.[2] This 'siege mentality' was fuelled by decolonization in the region and the associated emergence of 'hostile' states on the frontier. This drove ever-greater state involvement in the economy, especially strategic industries.

Amid intensifying political unrest and international pressure during the 1980s the South African economy began to flounder. By 1994 the African National Congress (ANC) inherited an economy that was

> literally on its knees. The short term issues it faced were the after-effects of a severe drought in 1992, a global economic recession ... a large budget deficit,[3] almost no foreign exchange reserves (less than a week of import cover), a private sector creaking under high interest rates, inflation of about 15 percent and massive outflows of currency. [South Africa's] longest downward phase ... since 1945 lasted from March 1989 to May 1993.' (Naidoo, 2006: 110)

Naidoo (2006: 110) continues:

> While these short term issues suggested crisis mode, the longer-term structural weaknesses in the economy, going back to the early 1980s, were even more serious. Investment and employment were in a long-term structural decline ... Large monopolies developed behind high tariff walls.[4] Capital became concentrated in relatively few hands. The education system was churning out people totally inappropriately equipped for an industrialising economy.[5] A large portion of the industrial sector was built on the back of military and armaments requirements for the Angolan/Namibian war or energy self sufficiency.[6] The mining sector was in decline due to diminishing gold reserves and delayed investment, the financial services sector was well developed but with very high cost structures, and manufacturing was being decimated.

The country also suffered severe racially- and geographically-defined income and wealth inequalities, and a significant proportion of the population lived in poverty.[7] These sentiments are echoed in Gelb (1991), Joffe et al. (1993), MERG (1993), Herbst (1994), Price (1994), and Michie and Padayachee (1997), among many others.

Nevertheless, South Africa was not without strengths in 1994. The peaceful transition to democracy itself generated immense international goodwill, which the eminent Nelson Mandela, South Africa's new president, built upon. South Africa's capital markets were well developed thanks to the financial needs of the mining houses, and its manufacturing base was both substantial and relatively diversified (having developed behind prohibitive tariff barriers). Indeed, in certain niches South African manufacturers were global leaders. Physical economic infrastructure was well developed by middle-income country standards (although unevenly provided), and many essential institutions such as the rule of law and the protection of property rights functioned well. And, the marginalized majority of the population notwithstanding, South Africa possessed a sizeable stock of technology and skills.

Table 8.1 South Africa's apartheid balance sheet

Assets	Liabilities
Good transport and communications infrastructure for business and white residential areas.	Inferior transport and communications infrastructure for black residential areas and farms.
	Poor, unsafe public transport for workers.
Good financial sector and regulation.	Minimal black private savings and no black ownership of banks.
	Declining national savings rate.
	Ten consecutive years of government dis-saving.
Well developed capital market.	No black asset-owning class.
Pockets of skilled labour and management.	Most labour poorly educated and trained.
	Severe 'middle management' skills shortage.
Monetary discipline and declining inflation.	High real interest rates.
	Fiscal recklessness.
Some good universities and science councils.	Poor quality of general education for black students.
	Institutional weaknesses in mathematics, science and engineering.
Moderate levels of research and development spending and patent applications.	Very large proportion of this in the defence industry.
Strong exports of primary products.	Uncompetitive, protected manufacturing sector.

Source: Hirsch (2005: 27).

Hirsch (2005) summarizes the situation with an 'apartheid balance sheet' at the time of the political transition (see Table 8.1). The relevant comparators for each asset and liability are other developing countries and those that were transforming their economies into market-based ones at the same time.

Apartheid's economic legacy was compounded by an uncertain environment in the lead up to and during the transition. Naidoo (2006) points out that there was significant uncertainty over the direction economic policy would take under the ANC, an organization with no experience in economic management, and no credibility with international stakeholders. The white capital owning class, accustomed to extracting rents from a malleable apartheid government, was now faced with a potentially unsympathetic, potentially predatory state. An insecure ANC also struggled to trust 'white capital', but accepted that its own success as South Africa's new leader was to a great extent dependent on these business interests.

Part of the problem in the late 1980s and early 1990s was that the ANC was understood by outsiders as being first and foremost a liberation movement steeped in the traditions of Marxism–Leninism, and a firm believer in the power of 'revolutionary agency'. Many returning senior ANC leaders had been exiled for long periods in former Eastern bloc countries and in newly-liberated African countries experimenting with state-socialism. For them, Cold War ideology, defined by anti-imperialism and rejecting the 'Western way', were important political values, and during the 1960s and 1970s ANC economics had veered explicitly to the left, along with most of the developing world (Gumede, 2005).

Thus the voices of 'the left' within the party were prominent. They were well supported by the ANC's alliance partners, the SACP and COSATU, which both benefited, along with the ANC and a range of other organizations, from the new political freedoms of the early 1990s. Initially President Mandela counted himself among them (Gevisser, 2007).

But by the late 1980s, thinking within the ANC was already 'gradually diluting the revolutionary socialist spice' (Hirsch, 2005: 38). This was most probably influenced by the collapse of the Soviet-style socialism; the woeful track record of state-led development in Africa; the success of East and South East Asia;[8] the prospect of full negotiations with the National Party government and private business interests over the shape of a new, democratic South Africa; and ever-quickening economic and financial globalization under the aegis of globally dominant Washington Consensus-based thinking.

Over a very short period, from before until soon after 1994, Mandela went from openly considering nationalizing key sectors (such as mining) after the ANC attained power, to prioritizing the concerns of international investors, international financial bureaucrats, western governments, and private South African business. The ANC was keen to stress its understanding of the importance of macroeconomic stability in South Africa, and of the rights of asset owners.

Nelson Mandela and Thabo Mbeki in particular realized that international financial markets were important sources of macroeconomic instability in South Africa, and that they would expect an ANC-led government to make mistakes. This engendered a remarkable degree of conservatism; the commitment to managing expectations, especially after 1994, was strong.[9] And so by the time the ANC's assumption of power was imminent Mandela had begun to speak of a 'mixed economy' built on a strong private sector but possessing also a large, active public sector. The implied underlying model was continental Europe's social democracies (Hirsch, 2005).

Now the major question seemed to be whether ANC policy would seek growth *through* redistribution (classic Keynesian demand stimulation, led by the state) or growth *with* distribution (taken to imply a more orthodox approach).

Ready to Govern?

The ANC's first major policy conference after its 1990 un-banning took place in 1992, and produced the document 'Ready to Govern' (ANC, 1992). This set the parameters for the ANC's policy agenda once in government. It was also a marketing tool designed to improve the ANC's credibility with international stakeholders. It was based on seven basic principles, which remain the foundation of the ANC's approach:

- Redistribution to meet basic needs, including housing, water, electricity, land, education, health and social security. The short term means for beginning to address this would be budget re-prioritization (away from defence spending); over the longer term a growing economy and budget would allow for up-scaling.
- A stable macroeconomic environment, including monetary and fiscal discipline, to foster growth. An important part of this thinking was informed by the ANC's fear of dependence on the World Bank and the International Monetary Fund (IMF). On monetary policy, the ANC committed to entrenching the South African Reserve Bank's independence.
- Integration into the global economy.
- A collective bargaining system over wages and employment conditions.
- Anti-monopoly policies to address South Africa's high degree of industrial concentration.
- Rural development.
- A restructuring of state-owned finance towards more productive activities.

In combination these were expected to create an environment in which declining domestic savings and investment (public and private) would turn around and international investors would be encouraged to enter the economy. This would raise growth, create new private and public resources, and enable the comprehensive economic transformation the country's majority yearned for.

The document's views on trade and foreign investment were perceived to be liberal. Trade policy was to be designed to raise the economy's productivity and competitiveness, and the government was to commit to participation in the General Agreement on Trade and Tariffs (GATT). 'Any economist, especially in highly protected South Africa, would interpret this as a commitment to a trade policy reform programme' (Hirsch, 2005: 53). The document also committed the ANC to the principle of national treatment of foreign investors, which was eventually enshrined in the country's democratic constitution. This represented a significant departure for the ANC. Overall, 'Ready to Govern' made it clear that the ANC was steering away from its Keynesian–nationalism ideas – the slogan 'growth though redistribution' began to fall out of use (Hirsch, 2005).

However, this does not mean trade liberalization would be prioritized after 1994. Much regarding the right mix of policies remained unresolved within the alliance, and the battle to influence the approach adopted by the new ANC government would be keenly fought. But before exploring this history, we need a better sense of how trade policy changed, before and after 1994.

TRADE POLICY UNDER APARTHEID[10]

It is true that protection levels in 1994 were high, but South Africa under apartheid had been slowly moving from an import substitution industrialization (ISI) model to one focused more explicitly on export promotion (but not necessarily import liberalization). That is, trade policy reform of sorts had been taking place.

Trade liberalization, as defined by the World Bank and used by Bell (1997: 71) includes any act that reduces the bias towards production for the domestic market and against exports. This can be achieved through a variety of measures such as the relaxation of quantitative restrictions (QRs), tariff reduction, devaluation and direct export promotion (subsidies and other instruments).

Using these criteria the progress of trade liberalization since the 1970s has not been uniform, but has been characterized by shifts in trade strategies, and reversals of gains made. Underlying this volatility has been a lack of a consistent trade strategy, as well as a number of external and political shocks such as the collapse in the gold price and the debt crisis of 1985. Nevertheless, reasons why certain changes were made may be discerned, especially towards the end of the 1980s.

During the 1920s, South Africa was one of the first countries to explicitly adopt import substitution as a vehicle for industrialisation, focusing initially on consumer goods sectors (Belli et al., 1993; Jenkins et al., 1997). Once this 'easy phase' had been completed the focus shifted towards import replacement in upstream industries, particularly the chemical and basic metals sub-sectors (Fallon and Pereira de Silva, 1994). Strategic intervention (for example Mossgas, SASOL) to reduce the dependence of South Africa on imports of products such as liquid fuels further shaped the composition of domestic production.

Import substitution as a source of growth declined as this shift took place (Fallon and Pereira de Silva, 1994). Protection had also raised the anti-export bias, which discouraged export growth and diversification. By the 1970s, South Africa was exceedingly dependent on gold as a source of foreign exchange (Jenkins et al., 1997). Indeed, gold was critical to holding the apartheid economy together.

Concerns over this dependency led to the Reynders Commission of Inquiry in 1972, which emphasized the need to diversify into non-gold exports through export promotion methods. Rapid growth through exports in some of the newly industrialized countries of South East Asia had helped diminish the export pessimism of the 1950s and 1960s (Jenkins et al., 1997). These forces, amongst others, initiated a shift in trade policy in the early 1970s towards a more open regime. A chronology of the trade policy changes that followed is shown in Table 8.2.[11]

Protection during the import substitution industrialization phase was largely achieved through a wide-ranging system of quantitative restrictions rather than tariff-based protection (Belli et al., 1993). The first shift away from import substitution industrialization in 1972 thus began with the relaxation of quantitative restrictions (QRs) and the introduction of an Export Development Assistance scheme. Although increases in tariffs compensated for the relaxation of QRs, Bell (1992, 1997) argues these were not fully compensatory, resulting in a net decline in protection. However, overall trade policy remained protectionist as the incentives introduced were an attempt to redress some of the anti-export bias rather than to shift the economy towards export-orientated growth (Jenkins et al., 1997: 7).

During the 1980s, the picture becomes more confusing. While the relaxation of QRs continued into the 1990s, import surcharges implemented in response to balance of payments pressures arising from a debt crisis in 1986 raised protection levels once more. Initially set at 10 per cent on imported goods not bound under the GATT in 1985, these surcharges rose in August 1988 to 60 per cent for luxury goods, 10 per cent for intermediate and capital goods and 20 per cent for motor vehicles. The net impact was a sizeable increase in average protection, as measured by collection rates over this period (Figure 8.1).

Furthermore, there was an increase in the number of applications for

Table 8.2 Chronology of trade policy changes from the early 1970s to 1994

1972–1976	Export Development Assistance scheme introduced.
	Substitution of tariffs for QRs resulting in net decline in protection (Bell, 1997).
1979–80	Rise in gold price resulting in the appreciation of rand.
1980	Reinforced system of export incentives.
1983–85	Proportion of value of imports subject to QRs fell from 77% to 23% over period.
	Relaxation of import permits by switching from a positive list to a negative list.
	Real depreciation of rand.
1985–1992	Proportion of tariff items subject to QRs fell from 28% in 1985 to less than 15% in 1992.
September 1985	Introduction of 10% import surcharge on all imported goods not bound by GATT.
August 1988	Differential surcharge rates applied to Luxury goods (60%), Capital goods (10%), Motor vehicles (20%) and Intermediate goods (10%).
	Increased applications for *ad valorem* and formula duties by businesses (Bell, 1992).
1989	"Structural adjustment programmes" involving a system of duty free imports for exports implemented for motor vehicles and textiles and clothing.
1990	General Export Incentive Scheme (GEIS) introduced. Provided a tax-free financial export subsidy to exporters based on the value of exports, degree of processing and local content of the exported product.
1990–91	Reduction of import surcharges to 40%, 5%, 15% and 5% for Luxury, Capital, Motor vehicles and Intermediate goods, respectively.
23/6/1994	Import surcharges abolished for Capital and Intermediate goods.

Source: Bell (1992, 1997), Belli et al. (1993), GATT (1993) and WTO (1998, 2003).

protection in the form of *ad valorem* and formula duties as businesses experienced the effects of the economic downturn (Bell, 1992). Evidence suggests that by 1988 the economy had become more protected than in 1984. Using effective protection rates, Holden (1992: 187) estimates a 30 per cent weighted average effective protection rate in 1984 with a range between 7 per cent and 143 per cent. By 1988 the average had risen to 70 per cent while the range had widened to between 9.9 per cent and 348 per cent.[12] Belli et al. (1993) also noted that by the end of the 1980s South Africa had the most tariff rates, the widest range of tariffs, and the second highest level

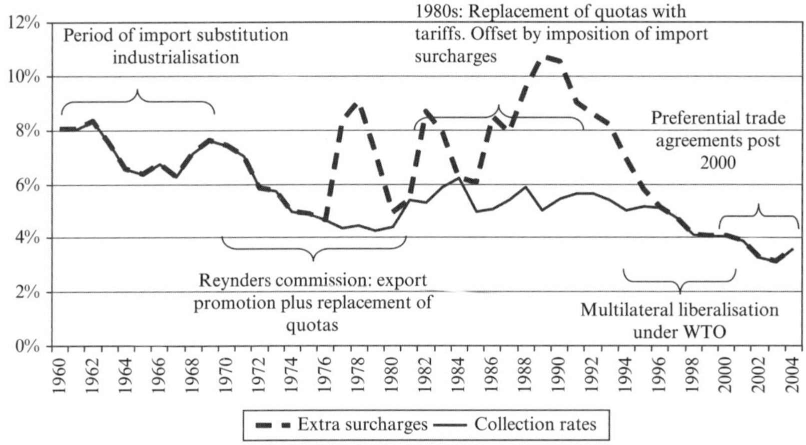

Note: Collection rates = ratio of duty collected to merchandise imports.

Source: Own calculations using South African Reserve Bank data.

Figure 8.1 Trade liberalization in SACU: collection rates, 1960–2004

of tariff dispersion compared to a range of similar developing countries. In addition, a wide variety of duties (*ad valorem*, specific, compound, mixed and formula duties) increased the complexity and opaqueness of the tariff regime (WTO, 1998).

During the following six years, the implementation of 'structural adjustment programmes' for motor vehicles, clothing and textiles; the introduction of the General Export Incentive Scheme (GEIS); and the reduction of import surcharges substantially reduced the overall level of protection and the anti-export bias. By 1994 the process of reducing QRs was largely complete and the focus of trade reform shifted to import liberalization through tariff reductions as reflected in South Africa's participation in the Uruguay Round.[13] Nevertheless, at the time of the transition South Africa remained highly protected, and non-resource export performance depended on direct subsidies (GEIS was phased out only by 1997). But, seen historically, sweeping changes to the trade regime had been made.

Besides the economic imperatives described above, what else had driven these, particularly leading up to 1994? Bell (1997) argues that in many instances trade liberalization episodes follow soon after regime changes, but that in South Africa's case it was the anticipation of regime change that generated support for trade reform. There was a widespread assumption that the incoming ANC government was going to be more protectionist and more interventionist than the apartheid state. A more liberal trade regime would reduce the amount of discretion that such an incoming government would have. Similarly, in his view, white business in South Africa saw trade liberalization as a means of curbing the political power of trade unions. This was seen as being especially important given the troubled state of business–labour relations in the 1980s, and because the labour movement was so closely aligned to the ANC.

Finally, South Africa was at the time participating fully in the Uruguay Round of the GATT. The apartheid government entered these negotiations at their start, and self-designated South Africa a developed country. The eventual concessions made were onerous, and it is likely that some of the trade policy changes in the late 1980s were undertaken by the apartheid state in anticipation of these new commitments.[14]

TRADE LIBERALIZATION IN THE POST-APARTHEID ERA

South Africa's 1994 offer to the GATT/WTO committed the government to comprehensive trade policy reform. The following specific commitments were made (Tsikata, 1999):

- Reduce industrial tariffs by one third from 1995–2000 with the exception of the clothing, textiles and motor vehicle industries where the phase-down was over the period 1995–2003.
- Rationalize over 12 000 tariff lines, and unilaterally reduce the number of tariff bands to six (0, 5, 10, 15, 20 and 30 per cent), with the exception of the sensitive products (the latter was not legally required).
- Increase the number of bindings for industrial products from 55 per cent to 98 per cent of all lines, and replace all quantitative restrictions and formula duties to bound *ad valorem* rates.[15]
- Convert all quantitative restrictions on agricultural products to *ad valorem* rates, lower agricultural tariffs by a minimum of 15 per cent individually and by 21 per cent on average, and reduce agricultural subsidies by an export weighted amount of 36 per cent.
- Phase out the export subsidy scheme (GEIS) by the end of 1997.

Table 8.3 documents the post-1994 liberalization through to 2006, the last significant year in South Africa's trade reform.

As shown in Table 8.4, the impact of these commitments on the tariff structure is clear: the number of tariff bands dropped from 723 in 1994 to 275 in 1998, the number of HS8 tariff lines from 11231 to 7773. These were

Table 8.3 Chronology of post-apartheid trade liberalisation, 1994–2004

1994	SA's GATT offer during Uruguay Round: (1) Bound about 98% of all tariff lines at the Harmonised System (HS) eight-digit level as against 18% before the round (2) Reduction in the number of tariff bands to six: 0, 5, 10, 15, 20 and 30% (3) Rationalization of the over 12000 tariff lines (4) Tariffication of QRs on agricultural products (5) Special provisions (extensions of the adjustment period and raised maximum tariff rates) for textile, clothing and motor vehicle industries granted. Decision taken to phase out GEIS. Adoption of anti-dumping and countervailing duties legislation.
1995	Payments under GEIS became taxable, range of eligible products reduced.
1/10/1995	Remaining import surcharges abolished.
From 1994–97	Deregulation of agricultural marketing and control boards established under the Agricultural Marketing Act of 1968. Import control on agricultural products removed.
1996	New Tariff Rationalisation Process (TRP) formulated: Tariff lines and peaks to be reduced, Formula and specific duties to be converted into *ad valorem* rates. Imports that have no 'suitable substitutes' to be duty free, *ad valorem* rates of 30% on final products, 20% on intermediate goods and 10% on primary goods are generally not to be exceeded. GEIS limited to fully manufacturing goods, although the local content requirement for the maximum subsidy was reduced from 75% to 65%.
Aug 1996	Signing of the SADC Free Trade Protocol (implemented in September 2000)
1 July 1997	Termination of export subsidies provided under GEIS.
1 Jan 2000	Implementation of SA-EU Trade, Development and Cooperation Agreement (TDCA)
2000	Preferential access to US for some products under African Growth and Opportunity Act (AGOA)
21 October 2002	2002 SACU Agreement introduces a new institutional structure; a dispute settlement mechanism; the requirement to have common policies on industrial development, agriculture, competition, and unfair trade practices; and a new system regarding the common revenue pool and sharing formula (WTO, 2003: viii)
December 2004	Preferential Trade Agreement signed between SACU and MERCOSUR (not yet implemented)
July 2006	Free Trade Agreement signed between SACU and EFTA (implemented 1 May 2008)

Source: Bell (1992, 1997), Belli et al. (1993), GATT (1993) and WTO (1998, 2003).

Table 8.4 *Structure of MFN tariffs of SACU,[a] 1990–2006*

	1990	1994	1998	2002 MFN	2002 EU	2002 SADC	2007 MFN	2007 EU	2007 SADC
Number of tariff lines	12475	11231	7773	7919	7919	7919	6,667	6,667	6,667
Share *ad valorem* (%)	69	69	75	75	96	99	97	98	99.9
Number of tariff bands	733	723	275				102	95	9
Ad valorem	38	37	45				39	38	6
Other	695	686	230				63	57	3
Duty-free tariff lines (% all lines)	24	26	42	44	45	65	55	66	99
Domestic tariff 'spikes' (% all lines)[b]	0.7	3.7	4.5	4.6	6.4	8.7	8	13	0.6
International tariff 'spikes' (% all lines)[c]	43.7	43.5	39.4	35.1	33.3	8.7	20	8	0.1
Coefficient of variation[d]	0.9	1.1	1.2	1.1	1.1	1.5	1.4	1.6	0.0
'Nuisance' applied rates (% all lines)[e]	2.2	1.5	1.9	1.5	1.4	0.1	0.0	0.0	0.0

Notes:
Calculations based on tariff schedules including *ad valorem* equivalents.
a South Africa is part of the five-country Southern African Customs Union. The other members are Botswana, Lesotho, Namibia, and Swaziland (the 'BLNS'). SACU trade policy has always reflected shifting South African priorities.
b Domestic tariff spikes are defined as those exceeding three times the overall simple average applied rate. For 2002 and 2006 these are presented separately for each trade agreement.
c International tariff spikes are defined as those exceeding 15%.
d Coefficient of variation is calculated as the standard deviation divided by the overall average.
e Nuisance rates are those greater than zero, but less than or equal to 2%.

Source: Edwards (2005) updated with the 2007 tariff schedule.

reduced further to 102 bands and 6667 HS8 lines by 2007. Formula, mixed or specific duties declined from 31 per cent of all lines in 1994 to 3 per cent in 2007. Tariff simplification is an essential part of trade policy reform, as it increases the transparency and strength of the price signals important to importers and exporters, and facilitates trade.

However, the simplification falls short of the goals set out in South Africa's Uruguay Round offer of six *ad valorem* tariff bands. In 2007 the number stood at 39, one more than in 1990. Indeed the reduction in the overall number of tariff bands has come from reduced use of non-*ad valorem* tariffs. The Trade, Development and Cooperation Agreement (TDCA) schedule, governing imports into South Africa from the EU, had 54 *ad valorem* bands in 2004 and 39 in 2007. Only the Southern African Development Community (SADC) Trade Protocol appears strongly committed to a simple tariff regime, showing only six *ad valorem* tariff bands in 2007, and almost no use of non-*ad valorem* rates.

Furthermore, there has been a proliferation in the number and types of rebates and drawbacks, which has increased the dispersion of the tariff structure, within and across sectors (the level and extent of rebates tend to be sector-specific), even at the HS6 level of disaggregation (Flatters and Stern, 2007). It also blunts or confuses price signals. Finally, the TDCA and the SADC Trade Protocol introduced two new tariff schedules (and rules of origin). The combined effect is a considerable increase in the complexity of the overall tariff regime and consequent demands on customs procedures.[16]

Nevertheless, the net result was substantial progress in simplifying the tariff structure and lowering protection during the 1990s (Table 8.4). Nominal and effective protection also dropped substantially (Figure 8.2). The economy-wide simple average tariff rate fell from 23 per cent in 1994 to 6.7 per cent by 2006, while effective protection in manufacturing declined from a high 48 per cent in 1993 to 11.5 per cent in 2006. The removal of surcharges accounts for a substantial share of the overall decline (see Figure 8.1), but lower tariff rates also played an important part. Protection fell in all sectors, but relatively large declines were experienced in beverages, textiles, footwear, wearing apparel and communication equipment. Lower reductions in tariffs were experienced in wood products, paper products, basic chemicals and basic iron & steel sectors (Edwards, 2005). Despite the decline in overall protection, nominal protection using scheduled rates remains high in wearing apparel, tobacco, footwear and vehicles where average tariffs exceed 20 per cent.[17]

South Africa has therefore closely followed other middle-income economies that liberalized during the 1990s (Edwards, 2005). Liberalization of MFN tariffs, however, stalled in 2000 as the government shifted towards tariff reform through regional trade agreements. The phase-down of tariffs

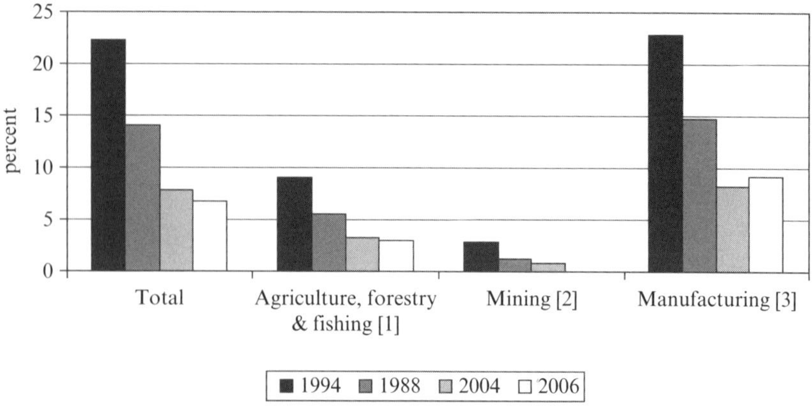

Source: Edwards (2005) and own calculations for 2006.

Figure 8.2 Measures of nominal protection

in accordance with TDCA and the SADC Trade Protocol commenced from January 2000, and have almost been eliminated in the case of SADC, although restrictive rules of origin remain (Flatters, 2005a).

The MFN tariff structure and associated imports today is roughly bi-modal (that is has only two peaks; see Figure 8.3). Interestingly, tariff dispersion, as measured by the coefficient of variation of the *ad valorem* rates, rose during the 2000s and has not begun to drop. This is explained by two things. First, the 'tariffication' of South Africa's quantitative restrictions introduced a large number of new tariff lines, many at very high rates. Second, as tariffs have been reduced, many to zero, the remaining tariff peaks tend to exert a greater influence on the distribution. Nevertheless, the number of international tariff peaks (commonly defined as tariffs greater than 15 per cent) remains substantial, at 20 per cent of all *ad valorem* rates, having stood at 43.7 per cent in 1994.

THE POLITICAL ECONOMY OF THE POST-APARTHEID REFORMS

Many countries have used multilateral commitments to 'lock-in' reforms they have already undertaken (for example China, New Zealand). South Africa is clearly not among these countries – when it made its Uruguay Round commitments the economy was only partially reformed.

However, one cannot therefore conclude that external pressure alone drove the process of liberalization in South Africa. Tariff protection in

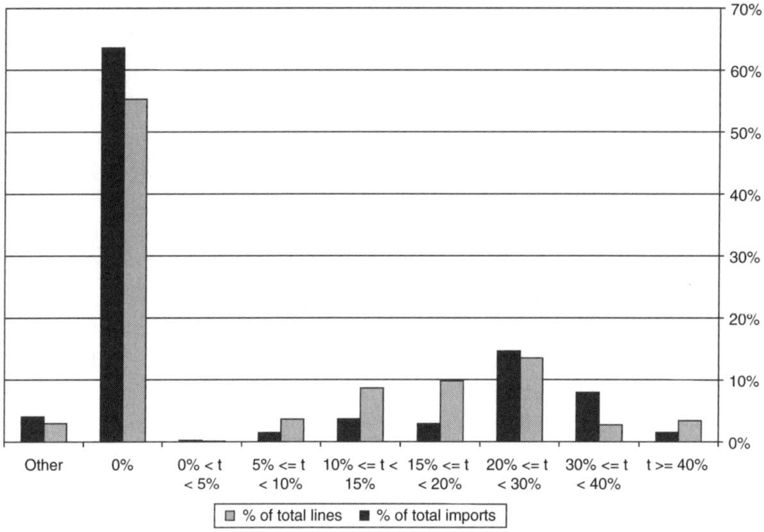

Source: SACU Secretariat and South African Customs and Excise, and own calculations.

Figure 8.3 Distribution of MFN SACU tariffs and South African imports, 2007

many sectors fell at a faster pace than was required under South Africa's offer to the WTO (Bell, 1997), indicating a strong unilateral thrust to the ANC government's trade policy reform effort. For example, South Africa unilaterally reduced the GATT agreed 12-year adjustment period and maximum tariff level of 45 per cent for textiles and clothing to an 8-year phase-down period and a 40 per cent terminal tariff. Similarly, tariffs on motor vehicles and automotive components fell faster than the phase-down specially negotiated in GATT (Edwards et al., forthcoming, 2009).

Why did the ANC government appear to embrace liberalization so emphatically during the second half of the 1990s? To be sure, during the late 1980s and early 1990s ANC and COSATU thinking on trade policy *was* broadly in favour of liberalization, specifically in the form of tariff reductions. Bell (1997) argues that this is most clearly evident in a 1993 COSATU conference paper, wherein the authors conclude that there were no good grounds to oppose reductions in protection. The ANC appeared to have accepted the neoclassical argument that liberalization improves growth and disciplines pricing behaviour. Liberalization was therefore both a way of enhancing economic growth, reducing consumer prices, and disciplining monopolies, as well as a means of signalling to the world that the new political order differed from the old.

Yet in 1994 there was no reason to expect trade liberalization to top the ANC government's list of priorities – the breadth and depth of the challenges facing it were significant, and much attention focused on appropriate fiscal and monetary policy stances. Indeed, trade liberalization as an explicit policy goal did not feature prominently in government documents until 1996, as we shall see. Hence the policy-making process after 1994 is important to understanding why the ANC government eventually came to pursue liberalization so aggressively. It emerged as the government's official view only after ideological battles within the tripartite alliance, fought against the backdrop of an unstable macro-economy, had been won.

The ANC had begun research on post-apartheid economic policy in the mid-1980s. The ANC's own Department of Economics and Planning (DEP, later renamed the Department of Economic Policy) was established in this period, and by 1992 was run by Trevor Manuel, supported by Tito Mboweni. Mboweni had earned a postgraduate degree in economics from the University of East Anglia, but Manuel had no relevant background when he joined in 1986. Manuel would nevertheless become Trade and Industry Minister in Mandela's first cabinet; Mboweni received the Labour portfolio. In 1996 Manuel became South Africa's first black, and arguably most successful finance minister, presiding over the economy's longest ever unbroken expansion. Mboweni became governor of the South African Reserve Bank (SARB) in 1999, and has managed a largely successful inflation targeting regime since 2000. However, in the early 1990s neither Manuel nor Mboweni were particularly experienced, nor did they agree with each other on the right approach to take (Gumede, 2005).

The DEP thus fell under the informal intellectual guidance of Thabo Mbeki, who had studied economics at the University of Sussex. Mbeki and Manuel developed a close relationship; Mbeki is said to have been Manuel's mentor (Gevisser, 2007). While Sussex in the 1960s was intentionally unorthodox and anti-Oxbridge in its approach, Mbeki still came away with a view on economic policy far removed from the radical left within the ANC and COSATU. This was reinforced by the aforementioned concerns over international perceptions of the ANC's ability to manage a complex economy.

> Mandela and Mbeki were desperate to dispel predictions that a black government in South Africa would go the same way as those in countries north of the Limpopo River. Mbeki, in particular, would have no truck with anything that could vaguely be construed as Eastern European socialism or its African equivalent (Gumede, 2005: 73).

In 1986 the DEP was joined by a COSATU-initiated group called Economic Trends (ET). COSATU had for some time considered itself 'better' at economics than the ANC (Gumede, 2005). The ET, especially after launching the Industrial Strategy Project (ISP) in 1990 worked closely with Alec Erwin, member of COSATU at the time, who would go on to become deputy finance minister in 1994 and Minister of Trade and Industry from 1996 (Padayachee, no date).

The ISP (see Joffe et al., 1995) focused primarily on microeconomics – productivity, competitiveness, technological capabilities, labour markets, and other 'supply side' issues. The ISP noted in particular the problems with productivity and competitiveness in South African manufacturing, and had advised the removal of some trade protection as one solution. It also noted that since the signing of the Uruguay Round agreement, there was little option. Nevertheless, it argued that tariff reductions would raise the rate of growth in manufacturing and the economy more widely, improve export performance, and encourage diversification. The work also suggested that import liberalization was in the interests of low-income consumers, who were, in the new political arrangement, the ANC's single largest constituency. This was especially pertinent to the liberalization of agricultural imports (Bell, 1997: 80–81).

However, the ISP project urged caution with tariff reforms. The potential dislocation caused by new import competition was significant precisely because much of South African manufacturing was uncompetitive. And, of course, if new import growth was not matched by new export growth, the current account would come under strain, worsening the macroeconomic outlook. Furthermore, the ISP argued in favour of a strategic rather than blanket approach to tariff reductions, with a view to retaining trade policy space to develop certain manufactured exports, such as automobiles.

In 1991 the ANC, with the help of the Canadian state-funded International Development Research Centre (IDRC), established another, independent policy research and advisory network called the Macroeconomic Research Group (MERG). This network involved local and international academics and policy experts, and was tasked with developing a coherent macroeconomic framework for a democratic South Africa. Their research complemented the ISP – indeed many of the South Africans in the MERG network were also working on the ISP. It also quickly expanded to cover a range of issues, such as housing, land reform, energy, transport, education, social security, and even mining (Hirsch, 2005).

MERG published its findings in 1993. According to one of its four editors:

> The theoretical foundations of the MERG policy framework lie, in what I would characterise as a Cambridge or Post-Keynesian approach (in the tradition of Keynes, Robinson, Kaldor and Kalecki) where effective demand failures

> and the possibility of under-full employment equilibrium, are recognised as key problems. MERG envisioned a two-phase, 'crowding-in' approach to South Africa's development, a state-led social and physical infrastructural investment programme as the growth driver in the first phase, followed by a more sustainable growth phase which would see private sector investment kick in more forcefully as growth picked up (Padayachee, no date: 9).

The MERG report was therefore grounded in demand-side concerns, whereas the ISP concentrated more on supply-side issues. The former paid less attention to trade and investment liberalization, prioritizing the domestic economy – specifically the stimulation of domestic demand – instead. MERG never had a direct mandate from the ANC; their recommendations would be considered in tandem with many others. According to Hirsch (2005), who was involved in the group's work, the research did not proceed smoothly, and failed to produce a unified view on the range of issues under study. As such the final MERG report, submitted to the ANC's DEP in 1993, was internally inconsistent, and in some cases ran counter to the commitments the ANC had already made in 'Ready to Govern'.[18] The DEP responded with little enthusiasm. Mandela at the last moment withdrew his offer to write the report's foreword, and Mbeki failed to attend the launch event, where he was supposed to be the keynote speaker (Gevisser, 2007).[19]

MERG's work is therefore less important for its content than for its impact on alliance politics. The ANC's rejection of MERG's findings, which were clearly in consonance with the 'growth through redistribution' idea, is seen as the beginnings of the fractures in ANC thinking on economic policy, which remain significant today. 'The MERG report is now commonly portrayed as a coherent left-wing alternative to the ANC mainstream' (Hirsch, 2005: 56). Left-wing critics felt that the ANC had already 'sold out' to white business by the time MERG was ready to make its recommendations, and that ultimately conservatives in the ANC had betrayed the MERG economists and the entire left-wing of the liberation movement. The reality was that the MERG report's ideas 'were *not ideologically* controversial in the ANC; their 'back-burner' status was more an outcome of a realistic (or pessimistic) assessment of the likely capacity of government administration after the first democratic elections' (Hirsch, 2005: 56, emphasis added).

As the transition neared, Mbeki was officially only in charge of the ANC's international relations work, but he would soon also become the ANC's top strategist on economic policy. Mbeki was one of a small group in the ANC who could follow technical economic debates properly. And, given his innate internationalism, he was well connected to multilateral and multinational financial organizations. These bankers and bureaucrats would come to Mbeki first for insight into the ANC's thinking on post-1994 policy. Mbeki also, from 1992, began to send DEP staffers on training at Goldman Sachs (Gevisser, 2007). Slowly but surely, with the belated support of Mandela, Mbeki would steer the ANC towards economic centrism and moderation.[20]

Because of this, the moderate stance the ANC was taking in negotiations with the National Party over the economy, and the moderate tone in 'Ready to Govern', COSATU responded. COSATU was increasingly of the view that the ANC did not take economic transformation seriously enough, and was in any event a political organization out of touch with the finer details of South Africa's economic problems (Hirsch, 2005; Gumede, 2005). So in 1993 it presented to the ANC a programme for South Africa's reconstruction and development, which would go on to become the ANC's election manifesto and central policy programme from 1994 (after some revision). The ANC was willing to listen closely, because COSATU had become an indispensable political ally, able to raise considerable support for the ANC at the poll, and by then South Africa's first democratic elections were only a few months away.

Five iterations of the COSATU document resulted in the official Reconstruction and Development Programme (RDP) of 1994. The document received input from the broadest possible range of stakeholders, reflecting Mandela's concern for stability and inclusivity. Its biggest surprise was the explicit reintroduction of the link between redistribution and growth that the MERG report (1993) advocated. Alec Erwin among others in COSATU felt strongly that growth could not and should not be pursued without explicit redistribution.

This reversion reflected two things. One, COSATU had successfully engineered a significant degree of influence over ANC economic policy-making, or at worst had used political circumstances cleverly to ensure conservative critics within the ANC would not raise their concerns. And two, once in office the ANC to some extent overcame its caution with respect to public sector capacity. Thus the RDP took the ANC back to its pre-'Ready to Govern' policy statements. Throughout the process, however, the ANC stressed that it would seek only to redirect public spending, not increase it as a percentage of GDP (Hirsch, 2005). It also ensured that no serious talk of nationalization resurfaced.

The RDP sought to combine publicly-driven investment, institutional reform and macroeconomic stability. It was believed that the public spending would provide a strong demand stimulus sorely lacking in the economy at the time, which would kick-start an upswing through self-reinforcing feedback processes. Since such spending would be on things like large-scale housing projects, it would also be strongly redistributive.

In practice the RDP was a list of targets for the budget, focused heavily on social needs. But, since the RDP also re-committed the government to fiscal prudence, it was not clear how these spending targets would be financed; the government saw foreign borrowing as being risky and unnecessarily expensive (Naidoo, 2006).[21] Also, perhaps taking the ANC by surprise, major public sector capacity constraints would soon reveal themselves and seriously hamper delivery (Hirsch, 2005).

Mandela established an RDP office in the Presidency, and placed COSATU leader and principal RDP author, Jay Naidoo, in charge. The RDP office struggled, however, to play the strong coordinating role required of it, partly because it was not afforded the explicit authority needed to do so.[22] The National Treasury was wary of the demands on the budget, wishing to avoid rapid over-spending so soon after the political transition. The government had also promised the IMF in 1993 that it would commit to fiscal austerity.

Since 1994 Mbeki, by now Deputy President of the ANC and the country, had been in charge of overseeing all economic policy. Mbeki had never liked the 'populist irresponsibility' of the RDP, but he understood and accepted the importance of RDP symbolism in the immediate post-transition environment (Gumede, 2005; Gevisser, 2007). According to Gevisser (2007: 670) 'the programme could hardly be abolished: it was the ANC's contract with its people, and had a powerful, romantic pull. And so Mbeki moved to ring-fence it, downscaling it from growth a development strategy to a service delivery mechanism.'

Mbeki had also been working hard behind the scenes to devise something that could build on the RDP. He had managed to convince Alec Erwin, then deputy minister of finance, that the government was paying far too little attention to macroeconomic concerns. Trevor Manuel, in charge of Trade and Industry at the time, was in no need of such persuasion. Collectively the three believed that although pursuing a more orthodox set of macroeconomic policies would probably not result in significant trickle-down benefits, there was little alternative. They felt the macroeconomy, in large part because of the RDP, was at risk of imminent derailment, rendering all other debates less important. Mbeki had taken it upon himself to put these ideas onto paper, and by the time Manuel became Finance Minister in 1996, a draft policy was already in place (Gumede, 2005; Gevisser, 2007).

Mbeki, Manuel and Erwin (who moved to Trade and Industry when Manuel moved to Finance) were proven correct sooner than they expected. Whatever the internal wrangling over the RDP, by 1996 debates were being overtaken by economic events. The envisioned output response to the government's demand stimulus had never materialized; instead the main short-term change was increased imports, placing further strain on the balance of payments. Also, the hoped-for influx of foreign capital hadn't been forthcoming. Indeed, much private capital was still trying to get out of the country. Finally, it was becoming obvious that more growth and much more macroeconomic stability would be required for any of the RDP targets to be met. Not prioritizing macroeconomic stability may have been the RDP's biggest error in practice, even if such concerns were evident in the policy itself.

A currency crisis in 1996 proved decisive in shifting policy. Markets reacted badly to rumours over Mandela's health and temporary finance minister Chris Liebenberg's departure, and the rand lost 30 per cent in nominal terms against the US dollar over the first half of 1996. The SARB lost huge amounts of foreign exchange trying to defend it. The crisis gave Mbeki and Manuel the space required to promote their ideas. By June 1996 a new macroeconomic policy package, called Growth, Employment, and Redistribution (GEAR), was in place. Its overarching goal was to solve once and for all the bedevilling macroeconomic instability seen as the main drag on the economy's performance, and on the government's ability to deliver on transformation.

Mbeki and Manuel were eager to stress the continuities with the RDP, but criticism, especially from COSATU and the SACP, was vociferous. There had apparently been little consultation with any constituencies outside government over GEAR's formulation; indeed ministries themselves were taken by surprise (Gumede, 2005). And once in place, implementation was quickly handed to well-insulated technocrats in the Treasury. GEAR was devised in semi-secretive conditions, rammed through cabinet and parliament in the midst of the first major macroeconomic crisis under the ANC's tenure, and implemented with remarkable speed. Gevisser (2007: 670) quotes Tito Mboweni in 1997 saying that,

> You have to remember the context. Extremely schizophrenic market conditions. Extreme pressure ... It looked like there was [a] macroeconomic policy vacuum. And a new minister of finance, hardly settled down, lots of criticism ... Day in and day out, as we weren't plugging the holes, reserves were going down. We were facing the IMF. You had to *do* something.

GEAR's implementation, combined with the closure of the RDP office in early 1996, made it clear that COSATU's influence over ANC economic policy was declining. Over time, GEAR would come to replace the 1993 MERG report as the lightning rod of the left, which wanted a return to the RDP (and still does) (Gevisser, 2007; Gumede, 2005). Because of the importance to the ANC of its alliance with COSATU, and because of COSATU's ability to destabilize the economy through mass labour action,

Mbeki had to ensure that COSATU leadership was dissuaded from taking drastic action.

This he managed to do. Through informal discussions away from bureaucrats and union hardliners, Mbeki placated the fears of the new COSATU leader at the time, Mbhazima Shilowa (who became Premier of South Africa's largest provincial economy, Gauteng), and two prominent union intellectuals, Kgalema Mothlante (now ANC deputy president) and Gwede Mantashe (now ANC secretary general), among others. These interactions created new, meaningful bonds between senior ANC and COSATU leaders, which would ensure COSATU's official 'buy-in' throughout the late 1990s, and especially after Mbeki became state president in 1999 (Gevisser, 2007).[23] The SACP, on the other hand, remained strongly opposed.[24]

GEAR's principal assumption was that 'Sustained growth on a higher plane requires a transformation towards a competitive outward oriented economy' (GEAR, 1996: 1). Just like the 1972 Reynder's Commission, GEAR argued that a rapid expansion in the tradables sector was crucial – non-gold exports had to grow. In the long run only a strong manufacturing sector would generate enough jobs and income growth to meet the country's crushing social needs. In other words, the meta-objectives were, as always, to widen inclusion in the formal economy, to increase investment and growth, and to reduce poverty, unemployment and inequality.

But the core operational-level question was how to improve the manufacturing sector, especially tradables. GEAR's preferred methods for generating better manufactured export performance were tariff liberalization and the maintenance of a competitive and stable real exchange rate. Therefore, as with most developing country trade liberalization episodes, South Africa's came as part of a broader macroeconomic reform package. The arguments in favour of trade liberalization were supported by GEAR's analysis of South Africa's external position, which argued that South Africa's persistent balance of payments deficit was a major constraint on economic growth. The GEAR strategy for reducing the deficit was threefold: to raise foreign direct investment inflows in the short term; to relax exchange controls in an effort to deepen capital markets; and to liberalize trade barriers to improve competitiveness and productivity, and to diversify exports (Naidoo, 2006). GEAR also sought to limit domestic consumption growth, thereby slowing import growth.

Of course, implementing South Africa's GATT/WTO commitments would have had to happen regardless of the ANC government's priorities, and indeed substantial liberalization had begun in 1995. But GEAR explicitly aligned the government's priorities with the WTO obligations, indeed created conditions under which liberalization could proceed more rapidly than required. More importantly, GEAR, its underlying philosophy, and the policy-makers responsible for it, signalled that liberalization would continue, and that the new government was committed to a market-oriented, export-led growth strategy combined with fiscal discipline. Trade liberalization was a necessary part of this package (that is increased protection would have been inconsistent with the other policies). Finally, there was also no obvious attempt to liberalize in a 'strategic' manner – protection came down across the board.

THE IMPACTS OF TRADE POLICY REFORM

Few disagree that South African manufacturing has performed poorly. According to Kaplan (2007), growth in manufacturing output per capita has been flat since 1985 and as a consequence South Africa's share of global manufacturing value-added has declined steadily. In addition, growth in manufactured exports has lagged global and especially developing country averages, and South Africa's export basket remains unsophisticated with few dynamic products.

The benefits of trade liberalization – significantly more rapid export, output and employment growth – have therefore not met expectations. But this does not mean there have been no benefits. The empirical evidence of trade reform in South Africa shows that it has had significant positive effects on trade performance, pricing behaviour and productivity, while the impacts on employment have been mixed.

Some indication of the relationship between exports and trade liberalization can be seen in Figure 8.4, taken from Edwards and Lawrence (2008). The figure presents an index of the volume of commodity and non-commodity manufacturing,[25] the inverse of the real effective exchange rate such that a rise reflects a real depreciation, and the inverse of the collection rates presented earlier in Figure 8.1. What is noticeable is that manufacturing exports remained stagnant for most of the 1970s and 1980s. There is some increase in export volumes from 1985 in response to the large depreciation, but it is really from the early 1990s that exports, particularly non-commodity exports, accelerate. The range of export destinations also expanded dramatically, although Europe and the US remain major trade partners.

Critical in the analysis of Edwards and Lawrence (2008) is that changes in the real effective exchange rate – often the most important single determinant of export performance – cannot explain the majority of the improved performance from the early 1990s, as it did not depreciate significantly prior to or during this period, and it remained relatively volatile throughout.

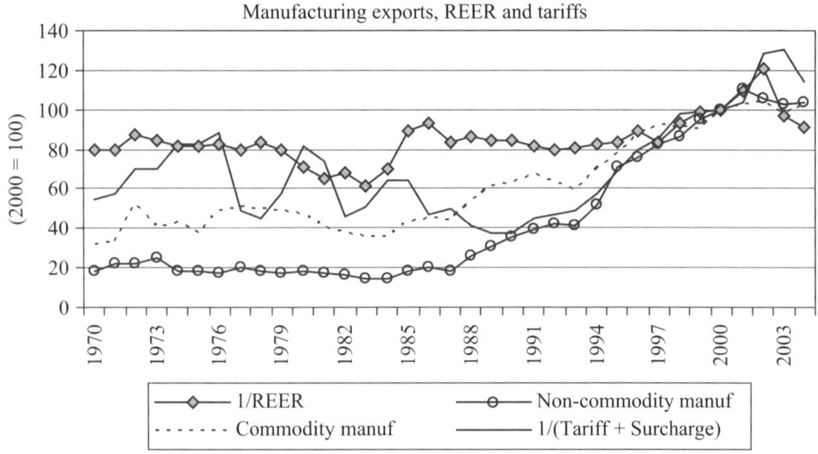

Source: Edwards and Lawrence (2008).

Figure 8.4 Exports, tariffs, and the exchange rate

The big policy shift after 1994 affecting the relative profitability of exporting was tariff liberalization, which was greatest in the non-commodity sectors.[26] Since most of South Africa's manufactured exports rely heavily on imported inputs, reducing the import prices of these inputs made exporting relatively more profitable, and stimulated an export response. The close association between lower tariffs on intermediate inputs *and* final goods on the one hand and manufacturing export growth on the other is also found to be statistically significant (Edwards and Lawrence, 2008); and remains so when controlling for the 'standard' determinants of trade performance (the real effective exchange rate, skills, the capital–labour ratio). Their conclusion is that South Africa thus developed a comparative advantage in capital-intensive primary and commodity-based manufactures in part because of its natural resource endowments, but also because of a pattern of protection that was particularly detrimental to exports of non-commodity manufactured goods.

Indeed, the overall manufacturing and especially export response would have been greater if the exchange rate had remained more stable, and if fewer supply-side problems (major bottlenecks and high input costs, especially in transport and telecommunications) had developed (Alves and Edwards, 2006). Also, liberalization was taking place at the same time that export subsidies under the General Export Incentive Scheme (GEIS) were phasing out.

Sector-specific trade and industrial policy has also influenced the export performance, particularly the motor vehicle industry. Under the Motor Industry Development Programme (MIDP), implemented in 1995, high nominal tariffs coupled with an extensive rebate scheme have been retained in order to protect some exporters (they also receive large effective subsidies under the programme – see Flatters, 2005b). Export orientation soared by 261 per cent between 1994 and 2004. This sector has also produced the best export performance (measured by growth in exports) of any manufacturing sub-sector since 1994. But both developments occurred despite a relatively modest decline (compared to other sectors) in effective protection of 61 per cent, and an even more modest decline in nominal protection.

Market power, excessive pricing and high inflation were all serious challenges after 1994. Liberalization has helped address all three, although the market power of certain domestic producers remains problematic. Empirical estimates at the industry level by Fedderke et al. (2006) and Edwards and van de Winkel (2005) suggest that import penetration and liberalization have been effective in disciplining the pricing behaviour (mark-ups) of South African firms. Interestingly, the effect of import penetration on pricing behaviour is greater from developed economies. Imports from China and India have grown rapidly, especially since 2002, and their contribution to containing inflation considerable. But they do not appear to discipline pricing behaviour greatly, probably because the bulk of these imports are low value-added products where price mark-ups are already minimal (Edwards and van de Winkel, 2005).

Liberalization has also been pro-poor – a likely outcome identified in 1995 by the ISP work of the ET group (Joffe et al., 1995). Poorer households spend a relatively large proportion of their income on tradable products, including food, beverages, clothing and textiles. As a consequence, they pay a disproportionate share of the tariff burden relative to their share of expenditure. Whereas the poorest 10 per cent of households spent 16 per cent of total expenditure on tariffs in 1995, the richest 10 per cent spent just 9 per cent (Daniels and Edwards, 2007). The removal of tariffs, in general, has reduced this regressive tax.

Improvements in productivity and output in response to openness are also evident (Belli et al. 1993; Fallon and Pereira de Silva, 1994; Jonsson and Subramanian, 2000; Arora and Bhundia, 2003; Fedderke, 2005; Harding and Ratts, 2005; Harmse and Abuka, 2005). Jonsson and Subramanian (2000), for example, estimate that increased foreign trade, as measured by exports plus imports as share of GDP, explain 90 per cent of total factor productivity growth during 1970–97. Similarly, Fedderke (2005) finds that output growth would improve by 0.5 per cent per annum through the TFP channel due to a 5 per cent improvement in the net export ratio. Consistent results using similar approaches are found by Belli et al. (1993) and Fallon and Pereira de Silva (1994). Harding and Rattso (2005) use collection rates as their measure of tariff protection and estimate that 70 per cent of productivity improvements in the post sanction period is explained by liberalization. Liberalization also enhanced the spillover of foreign technology to the domestic market.

However, these results are not conclusive. Most analysis is conducted at the aggregate or industry level. The evidence thus may merely reflect changes in the firm-level composition of production – less efficient firms close down in response to increased international competition and relatively efficient exporters grow (Melitz, 2003). Nevertheless, the empirical evidence suggests that liberalization during the 1990s has led to a substantial restructuring of production within sectors – and across sectors – and has therefore contributed to more efficient resource allocation and improvements in productivity growth.

Overall, however, as Cassim and van Seventer (2004) note, if one takes an economy-wide view, two things are clear. First, there has been structural shift of resources into non-commodity exports and away from mining. And second, almost every manufacturing sub-sector has become far more outward-oriented than it was prior to 1994, just as import penetration ratios have risen. 'This has implied that trade liberalization has not resulted in de-industrialisation effects' (Cassim and van Seventer, 2004: 12). But the process has induced an increase in capital, technology, and skills intensities in the growing, outward-oriented sectors, implying that impacts on employment are likely to have been different from those on output and productivity.

The literature surveying the impacts of trade liberalization on employment is less comprehensive that that reviewed above, primarily because employment data are weak in South Africa and there is a lack of panel data to evaluate firm-level adjustments to liberalization. As noted earlier in this chapter, the demand for labour in manufacturing has been falling consistently since the 1970s, but actually turned negative between 1990 and 2002. Demand for less-skilled workers in manufacturing fell most rapidly (Dunne and Edwards, 2007; Thurlow, 2006). Between 1990 and 2002 South Africa's tradable sectors shed 700 000 jobs; by 2002 employment in South African manufacturing was 11 per cent below 1994 levels (Flatters and Stern, 2007; Dunne and Edwards, 2007).

However, about 83 per cent of the 700 000 jobs lost were in agriculture, mining, and resource-based heavy industry. Only 17 per cent of the jobs lost were in non-commodity-based manufacturing activities – industries that have on average substantially liberalized. The period since 2002 probably follows a slightly different pattern, as exchange rate appreciation and the explosive emergence of China began to show impacts after 2003. Also, mining investment, output and employment rose sharply in 2005 and 2006. Hence jobs lost in non-commodity manufacturing have probably accounted for a larger share of the total in the period after 2002.

The relationship between these employment losses and trade liberalization is not directly evident and is contested. There is little correlation between sector-level employment changes and changes in protection or trade flows, although there is a bias in tariff reductions against labour-intensive sectors (Dunne and Edwards, 2007). This will have negatively affected labour demand, and is consistent with the argument by Rodrik (2006) that liberalization contributed towards the structural shift in employment away from manufacturing towards services.

Estimated employment changes based on changes in the volume of exports and imports are generally small, and have operated in opposite directions, leaving the net direct effect of trade flows on labour demand in manufacturing close to zero (Edwards, 2001; Dunne and Edwards, 2007; Jenkins, 2008). These studies suggest that technological change, in part induced by increased openness, in part due to a range of other factors, has been the single largest source of the decrease in demand for labour in manufacturing.

In contrast to employment growth in manufacturing, downstream sectors, such as retail and wholesale, have created jobs during the liberalization period. Trade liberalization will have contributed to this growth, but the size of the contribution is unknown. Further, some of these service jobs may reflect the outsourcing of services such as cleaning, catering and transport in the face of increased competition. Valid concerns over the quality of new jobs, and the tendency towards 'casualization', have been repeatedly raised. As low-skill service sector jobs tend to be less productive than comparable jobs in manufacturing, remuneration tends to be lower. These workers also tend to lack union representation, limiting their ability to stop employers flouting labour regulations. Thus while the unemployment rate in South Africa may be at worst stable (but high), this process of shifting jobs out of manufacturing and into services may have increased the number of the working poor. Clearly, further analysis on the trade–employment relationship is needed.

BEYOND GEAR: WHERE IS ECONOMIC POLICY GOING?

GEAR has largely achieved sustained macroeconomic stability. Since 1996 inflation and interest rates have been significantly lower and more stable;

the current account deficit averaged less than 1 per cent of GDP between 1994 and 2003; government debt and the associated interest burden has been significantly reduced; and, for the first time in decades the economy grew consistently for over ten years, albeit slowly compared to many other developing countries (Naidoo, 2006).

South Africa also navigated the 1997/98 Asian financial crisis and another currency crisis in 2001 without significant real economy disruptions. The policy response to each came with short-term costs to the economy, but government managed to stay the course on both occasions. This is thanks to GEAR's legitimacy, and the introduction of inflation-targeting in 2000. The latter was largely in response to the impacts of the Asian crisis, and has assisted the government in its battle to keep the ship steady.[27] Because of these successes, the government and the SARB have developed a good degree of credibility amongst all stakeholders. The institutions in charge of managing the economy have behaved in a consistent manner for an extended period of time, and the South African economy is now much more predictable than it was towards the end of apartheid.

However, certain macroeconomic indicators began to worsen again after 2003. These are largely because of the higher GDP growth, in turn driven by the lengthy period of benign global conditions from 2001/02–2007. Fiscal policy has remained prudent and government finances healthy as a result. But under relatively easy monetary conditions, credit extension and household consumption boomed, fuelling a surge in imports and in investment. Export growth and savings did not keep up, leading to a large current account deficit by the end of 2007 (over 7 per cent of GDP).[28] Inflation is also once again a serious concern, but seemingly part of a global trend. And, throughout the period since GEAR's implementation, exchange rate volatility has been high and persistent.

In 2005/6 the government introduced the Accelerated and Shared Growth Initiative for South Africa (AsgiSA). It does not replace GEAR, but is rather a programme for removing some of the 'binding constraints' to higher and more equitable growth. Several have been identified, most prominent among them the aforementioned exchange rate volatility. The 'cost of doing business' is another. AsgiSA will thus preside over a substantial increase in public investment, which collapsed in the late 1990s. Energy, transport, communications and broadcasting, ports, and other publicly provided infrastructure services will all be upgraded and extended to those parts of the population that still don't receive them. AsgiSA's overarching aim is to reduce South Africa's high cost structure.

However, AsgiSA's introduction also reflects a recent change in thinking in South Africa. Now that the world is firmly in the 'post-Washington Consensus' era, criticism of GEAR as a growth and employment-creation strategy has re-developed. And the critics are supported by the aggregate evidence: output and employment growth, although better than in the 1980s, remained too low to make significant inroads into South Africa's unemployment and poverty problems. There are also valid questions over South Africa's ability to generate enough jobs given its capital, skills and natural resource-intensive economic structure. Is this because the initial challenges were much bigger than anyone imagined, or because GEAR failed? Or is it because a range of microeconomic reforms that should have accompanied GEAR never materialized?

The government's answer appears to reflect all three views. Because GEAR's intellectual hegemony is waning, those in favour of a more interventionist industrial policy and a more 'developmental state' have gained prominence. Stabilization and liberalization are no longer the only priorities, and progress towards implementing a new National Industrial Policy Framework (NIPF), published in 2007, is moving ahead. The key difference between today's debate and that which took place pre-1994 is the context – South Africa is now a relatively open, liberal market-based economy.

This may be why AsgiSA does not identify improved trade performance as an important means of accelerating economic growth. The document expresses a desire to diversify further out of primary product exports, but the mechanism for achieving this is not clearly outlined. The current view is that South Africa cannot have a sensible or beneficial trade policy in the absence of clearly defined industrial policy objectives, citing Asian examples from the 1950s and 1960s.

The NIPF suggests that the threat of de-industrialization in South Africa is real, and that the state must intervene to deepen industrial capabilities. The most common analogy put forth by policy-makers is that of an underweight, untrained boxer being forced into the boxing ring with a seasoned heavyweight. Trade liberalization, according to this view, has forced many underweight South African manufacturers into the ring with Asian, European and North American manufacturers. South African manufacturers have not been able to cope, and therefore require assistance, including perhaps greater effective protection.[29] The NIPF argues that a structural shift away from reliance on natural resource-based exports is still lacking, and that without judicious, persistent intervention, this shift will never materialise.

Decisions regarding trade policy will therefore be 'dictated by the needs of imperatives of sector strategies' [*sic*] (DTI, 2007: 41). So far this has meant reducing further tariffs on inputs and eliminating 'nuisance' tariffs (below 2 per cent). This is in fact a reversal of previous liberalization efforts, as effective protection will be raised in downstream industries and may actually diminish the incentive to supply the export market relative to the domestic market.

There is thus no strategic direction on the future of trade policy. Trade negotiations may force deeper reform, but of those South Africa is currently party to, only a comprehensive Doha Round agreement would do so. But Doha looks unlikely to succeed at all, let alone deliver a meaningful deal. Besides, the South African government's negotiating objectives in the WTO are enhancing market access for products of export interest; eliminating industrial country subsidies and support to inefficient producers, particularly agriculture; and re-negotiating rules that perpetuate imbalances in the international trade regime (Department of Foreign Affairs, 2006). Tariffs are bargaining chips in the negotiating process and hence are not to be discarded without adequate reciprocal reductions.

Yet empirical research suggests there is considerable scope to improve the current tariff structure unilaterally, and that this would deliver further gains to the South African economy (Edwards and Lawrence, 2008). That is, AsgiSA's omission of trade policy as a tool for growing the South African economy and assisting in poverty reduction appears to be a mistake.

A major concern with South Africa's 1990s liberalization is the manner in which it was undertaken – there appears to have been no clear rationale underpinning decision-making. While it is commendable that South Africa moved well ahead of the pace of reform required under the WTO, the resulting discretion in tariff decisions has led to a considerable degree of incoherence and complexity. The complexity results from the multiple schedules, the numerous exceptions to the current MFN schedule, and the fact that the MFN schedule itself is needlessly complicated.

Regarding incoherence, Edwards and Lawrence (2008) find that the cost to the consumer per job protected in certain sectors is extremely high, especially compared to wages in those sectors (examples include autos, tobacco, clothing and footwear). They also find that the tariff structure protects many products South Africa produces competitively, and does not promote sectors that offer long-term dynamic competitiveness gains. That is, if there has been an attempt at protecting infant industries, those industries are the least likely to boost economy-wide competitiveness in future (for example clothing). In short, South Africa's tariffs still reflect the rent-seeking power of particular special interests.

A rule guiding the setting of tariffs would help. By rule, we mean a clear policy on desired tariff levels from which exceptions will occasionally be granted. Standard trade theory suggests the rule should be a uniform tariff, or a few tariff bands applied to most products. Such a tariff structure is simple to administer, is less susceptible to corruption and illicit trade, and is easier to defend against special interests and rent-seeking behaviour. It also does not run the risk of creating pockets of protection where they are not needed, or indeed undesirable. Without such a rule, the process of setting tariffs is likely to be captured by industry lobby groups. South Africa has a long history of effective lobbying by industries for tariff increases, as was evident by the numerous tariff changes implemented in the late 1980s by the Board of Trade and Tariffs (Bell, 1992).

Finally, neither AsgiSA nor the NIPF discuss microeconomic and regulatory reform in any detail. In many other countries that have liberalized border constraints to trade, pressure has grown to enact such reforms to improve firm-level productivity and competitiveness. South Africa is no different. AsgiSA does seek to reduce general business costs through physical infrastructure improvements, but does not advocate regulatory overhaul in key areas. These include rules governing a range of tradable service sectors in which South African providers are often inefficient (such as transport, energy and telecommunications); labour market regulations, specifically the non-wage labour costs associated with hiring and firing, and the rules governing wage-setting; and trade facilitation (especially customs procedures).

CONCLUSION

AsgiSA does not identify South Africa's relatively poor trade performance as a major constraint to growth. The NIPF document does not consider comprehensive trade policy as central to its vision for industrial restructuring. Trade policy, in general, is currently not considered instrumental in accelerating overall economic growth or directing industrial policy.

In many ways the country is returning to the debates of the early 1990s. Then parties agreed on only two things – that comprehensive macroeconomic and microeconomic reform was desperately needed, and that in the long run only a strong manufacturing sector would generate enough jobs and income growth to meet the country's crushing social needs. Now all parties seem to agree on only one thing – that more reform is needed, because many socio-economic goals are yet to be achieved. But in both cases – 1994 and now – there exists substantial disagreement over how best to address this.

South Africa's economic policy debates therefore continue to be conducted on two levels. The 'meta questions' are how to widen inclusion in the formal economy, how to increase investment and growth, and how to reduce poverty, unemployment and inequality. But the core operational-level question is how to improve the manufacturing sector, especially tradables. As convincingly argued by Rodrik (2006), the decline in the tradable sectors has adversely affected employment and the 'weakness in particular of export oriented manufacturing has deprived South Africa from growth opportunities as well as from job creation at the relatively low end of the skill distribution' (Rodrik, 2006: abstract).

South Africa is relatively abundant in natural resources, and that is where its comparative advantage lies. To trade successfully in the modern world, an economy must be relatively open, but opening in the context of significant resource wealth will create challenges to manufacturers that are not necessarily present in relatively labour-rich countries. Furthermore, the rise of East Asia, which has become a tightly integrated manufacturing hub truly global in scale, has limited the opportunities for late reformers like South Africa to use export-oriented manufacturing to greatly accelerate economic development. Seen in this light, the performance of non-commodity manufactured exports, much improved over earlier decades, is noteworthy. Trade policy reform's direct contribution to this achievement, as noted in this chapter, should not be disregarded.

Perhaps most interesting is that those in favour of liberalizing and stabilizing South Africa's economy after 1994, through orthodox macroeconomic policies, had no obvious intellectual home. These economic liberals also had no significant support base; there was no strong 'pro-trade' lobby in the private sector outside of mining.

To a great extent these are still features of the modern South African political economy. Much of import-competing manufacturing in South Africa is yet to convincingly press government for further trade liberalization, preferring instead to note the difficulties it faces. These include an unpredictable exchange rate, burdensome labour regulations, expensive and inefficient business infrastructure, and significant skills shortages. All bar labour regulation form part of the current focus under AsgiSA, and until the country sees results in these areas, South African manufacturing will remain wary of greater exposure to international competition. This view continues to receive strong support from South Africa's labour movement, which remains opposed to further liberalization and is highly critical of policies implemented since 1996. COSATU and the SACP frequently call for a return to the RDP. Taken together, these interest group dynamics are why debates over macroeconomic policy continue. And these debates will be likely to remain unresolved until South Africa's unemployment, poverty and inequalities challenges have been comprehensively met.

However, South Africa urgently needs to confront more fully its extensive microeconomic constraints. South Africa will realize its potential only when competition is strengthened and markets are deepened, when labour markets are more flexible, when the costs of doing business are lower, when the education and health systems are far stronger, when black economic empowerment and employment equity legislation is no longer needed, and when the efficiency of the public sector is greatly improved.

NOTES

1. Since the transition from apartheid in 1994 South Africa has had a 'ruling tripartite alliance', but it is not a classic governing coalition. Until now only the ANC contests elections; the SACP will contest for the first time in 2009. The SACP and COSATU influence the ANC and its policies informally, through alliance politics, which takes place outside of state structures. Because the ANC is so dominant at all levels of government, including a large majority in the legislature, most ANC policy choices translate into state policies. COSATU and the SACP therefore have a greater influence over South Africa's strategic economic policy decisions than do opposition parties, when they are influential within the alliance.
2. In truth the apartheid state was much more of a threat to its neighbours than vice versa.
3. By 1994 total public debt amounted to 56 per cent of GDP. Annual debt servicing costs were twice what was spent on health and roughly equivalent to that spent on education. See Pillay (1997).
4. The concentration in South Africa's manufacturing sector in the 1980s, the complexity of the tariff structure protecting it, and the power of some lobby groups were such that some tariff headings effectively applied to individual firms. See SDS (2000).
5. The public service under apartheid neglected the black majority of South Africa's population. This applied to everything from municipal services such as sanitation and policing, to provincial- and national-level issues such as housing, health and education.
6. These include the state-formed petro-chemicals giant SASOL, and MOSGAS, which were developed in response to concerns over the reliability of South Africa's access to crude oil supplies.
7. According to Van der Berg et al. (2007), 44 per cent of the population, the majority of whom are black, live in poverty. As South Africa has no official poverty line, this estimate is based on a benchmark well above US$2 per day.
8. Some argue that the ANC understood the Asian miracle in the same way as authors like Robert Wade and Alice Amsden understood it ('governed markets') who were writing at that time. However, many also argue that China's unequivocal embrace of free(r) markets was an equally important influence.
9. Such was their conviction that after entering government the ANC retained the previous regime's white central bank governor (Chris Stals) and white minister of finance (Derek Keys). Keys left in late 1994, and was replaced by another white minister, Chris Liebenberg, a private sector banker.
10. This section draws on Edwards (2005) and Edwards et al. (forthcoming 2009).
11. For a more detailed discussion on trade liberalization see Holden (1992), Bell (1992, 1997) and Jenkins et al. (1997).
12. These estimates do not include the protectionist impact of quantitative restrictions. It is not clear for example whether the changes in effective protection rates reflect the replacement of quantitative restrictions with tariff equivalents or increases in protection.
13. QRs on agricultural products were still prevalent.
14. ANC officials joined the government negotiating team towards the end of the round, but did not seek to disrupt matters.
15. Formula duties, which set a price floor for imports, were frequently used as an instrument to prevent dumping. Anti-dumping and countervailing duty legislation was adopted to replace the need for these types of duties.
16. A schedule for the PTA with Mercosur does not yet exist; the schedule for the FTA with EFTA is not yet available, but the agreement is in force.

17. The 2006 import weighted tariff for vehicles is 26 per cent which is significantly higher than the simple average rate of 13 per cent.
18. This view is contested. See Gumede (2005) and Padayachee (n.d.).
19. The astute reader will note the irony. The ANC rejected the work of the MERG network, which was established at its behest and produced policy recommendations very agreeable to Alec Erwin and COSATU's political leadership. In contrast, the ANC's DEP considered the COSATU-linked ISP's work useful and uncontroversial. The difference may have stemmed from the fact that the ISP was not directly interested in macroeconomic policy recommendations.
20. Mbeki was pushing a moderate line on most issues as early as 1986. He was of the view that if the ANC was to convince western governments of its governance credentials – if it really was to be taken seriously as a government-in-waiting – it would increasingly need to show a moderate face. This would also help the ANC take greater control of the transition process with the apartheid government, mitigating the risk of having an unbalanced settlement forced upon it at the eleventh hour, as happened to the liberation movements in Zimbabwe and Tanzania (Gumede, 2005).
21. And, by the end of the negotiations for a democratic South Africa in 1993, the ANC and National Party had already accepted a US$850 million facility from the IMF. This was for balance of payments support, as South Africa's external position by then was severe. It nevertheless added to already very high national debt levels, raising pressure to improve government saving.
22. Clashes with Mbeki specifically over the chain of command proved problematic.
23. This lasted only as long as these people remained influential in COSATU. COSATU's new leadership is less amenable to 'Mbeki-ite' economic policy.
24. See for example J. Cronin, 'Why the SACP rejects GEAR', Mail & Guardian, 10–16 July 1998.
25. Given South Africa's resource endowments, manufacturing exports are classified according to their dependence on primary commodities. Commodity manufactures include coke and refined petroleum, food, tobacco, iron and steel, other manufacturing, non-metallic minerals, wood and wood products, basic chemicals, and basic non-ferrous metals. Non-commodity manufactures include the remaining sectors.
26. The removal of sanctions also facilitated export growth post-1992. Evenett (2002) estimates that sanctions imposed by the European Community and the US reduced South African exports by 27 per cent and 34 per cent, respectively. In addition, he finds that the removal of sanctions did not lead to a full recovery of exports, particularly to the US, implying that the adverse consequences of sanctions are sustained long after their removal.
27. The target band for core inflation is 3–6 per cent. The SARB is independent, but has a constitutional responsibility to 'defend the value of the rand.' It is not clear what this means in practice. Besides, South Africa does not have the foreign currency means to do so effectively. Since the Asian crisis, when the SARB's attempted defence of the rand failed as it had done once before in 1996, there has been little interest in direct currency management.
28. Whether or not it will again act as an external constraint on growth is currently an important debate in South Africa.
29. Zalk, N (2006). Mr Zalk is Chief Director in charge of industrial policy in the DTI.

REFERENCES

African National Congress (1992), 'ANC Policy guidelines for a democratic South Africa', policy adopted at the ANC National Conference, 28–31 May.

Alleyne, Trevor S. and Arvind Subramanian (2001), 'What does South Africa's pattern of trade say about its labour markets?' IMF Working Paper 01/148, Washington, DC: International Monetary Fund.

Arora, V. and A. Bhundia (2003), 'Potential output and total factor productivity growth in post-apartheid South Africa', IMF Working Paper WP/03/178, Washington, DC: International Monetary Fund.

Alves, P. and L. Edwards (2006), 'South Africa's export performance: Determinants of export supply', *South African Journal of Economics*, **74**(3), 473–500.

Bell, T. (1992), 'Should South Africa further liberalise its foreign trade?', Working Paper no. 16, Cape Town: Economic Trends Research Group.

Bell, T. (1997), 'Trade policy', in J. Michie and V. Padayachee (eds), *The Political Economy of South Africa's Transition*, London: Dryden Press.

Bell, Trevor and Niki Cattaneo (1997), 'Foreign trade and employment in South African manufacturing industry', Occasional Report no.4, Employment and Training Department, Geneva: International Labour Office.

Belli, P., M. Finger and A. Ballivian (1993), 'South Africa: A review of trade policies', World Bank Informal Discussion Papers on Aspects of the South African Economy no. 4, Washington, DC: The World Bank Southern Africa Department.

Cassim, R. and D. van Seventer (2004), 'South African trade reform since democracy', Paper presented at the TIPS/DPRU Annual Forum, Somerset West, October.

Daniels, R. and L. Edwards (2007), 'The benefit-incidence of tariff liberalization in South Africa', *Studies in Economics and Econometrics*, **31**(2), August, 69–88.

Department of Finance, Growth, Employment, and Redistribution (1996), *A Macroeconomic Strategy*, Pretoria: Department of Finance.

Department of Foreign Affairs (2006), 'A broad South African approach to new multilateral trade negotiations in the World Trade Organisation', (online), http://www.dfa.gov.za, accessed November 2006.

DTI (Department of Trade and Industry) (2007), *A National Industrial Policy Framework*, Pretoria: DTI.

Dunne, P. and L. Edwards (2007), 'Trade and poverty in South Africa: exploring the trade–labour linkages', *Studies in Economics and Econometrics*, **31**(2), August, 49–68.

Edwards, Lawrence (2001), 'Globalisation and the skill bias of occupational employment in South Africa', *South African Journal of Economics*, **69**(1), 40–71.

Edwards, L. (2005), 'Has South Africa liberalised its trade?', *South African Journal of Economics*, **73**(4), 754–75.

Edwards, L. and R.Z. Lawrence (2008), 'SACU tariff policies: where should they go from here?', CID Working Paper 169, Harvard University's Centre for International Development, May, See http://www.cid.harvard.edu/cidwp/169.html.

Edwards, L. and R.Z. Lawrence (2008, forthcoming), 'South African trade policy matters: trade performance and trade policy', forthcoming in *Economics of Transition*.

Edwards, L. and M. Stern (2006), 'Trade and poverty research project in South Africa: lessons and policy conclusions', *Studies in Economics and Econometrics*, **31**(2), August, 1–22.

Edwards, L. and T. van de Winkel (2005), 'The market disciplining effects of trade liberalization and regional import penetration on manufacturing in South Africa', Trade and Industrial Policy Strategies Working Paper.

Edwards, L., D. van Seventer and R. Cassim (2009, forthcoming), 'Trade policy in South Africa', mimeo.

Evenett, S. (2002), 'The impact of economic sanctions in South African exports', *Scottish Journal of Political Economy*, **49**(5), 557–73.
Fallon, P. and L. Pereira de Silva (1994), 'South Africa: economic performance and policies', World Bank Informal Discussion Papers on Aspects of the South African Economy no. 7, Washington DC: The World Bank Southern Africa Department.
Fedderke, J. (2005), 'Technology, human capital and growth' mimeo.
Fedderke, J., C. Kularatne and M. Mariotti (2006), 'Mark-up pricing in South African industry', *Journal of African Economies*, **16**(1), 28–69.
Fedderke, Johannes, Yongcheol Shin and Prabhat Vaze (2003), 'Trade and labour usage: an examination of the South African manufacturing industry', Econometric Research Southern Africa Working Paper, No. 15.
Flatters, F. (2005a), 'Rules of origin and SADC: the case for change in the mid term review of the trade protocol', Africa Region Working Paper Series No. 83 June.
Flatters, F. (2005b), 'The economics of the MIDP and the South African motor industry.' prepared for the TIPS/NEDLAC South Africa Trade and Poverty Programme (SATPP) Policy Dialogue Workshop, Johannesburg, 2 November.
Flatters, F. and M. Stem (2007), 'Trade and trade policy in South Africa: Recent trends and future prospects', Development Network Africa, June.
GATT (1993), *Trade Policy Review: South Africa*, Geneva: General Agreement on Tariffs and Trade.
Gelb, S. (1991), *South Africa's Economic Crisis*, London: Zed Books.
Gevisser, M. (2007), *Thabo Mbeki: The Dream Deferred*, Jeppestown: Jonathan Ball Publishers.
Gumede, W.M. (2005), *Thabo Mbeki and the Battle for the Soul of the ANC*, Cape Town: Zebra Press.
Harding, Torfinn and Jørn Rattsø (2005), 'The barrier model of productivity growth: South Africa', Trade and Industry Policy Strategies Working Paper no. 5.
Harmse, C. and C.A. Abuka (2005), 'The links between trade policy and total factor productivity in South Africa's manufacturing sector', *South African Journal of Economics*, **73**(3), 389–405.
Herbst, J. (1994), 'South Africa: economic crisis and distributional imperative', in S. Stedman (ed.), *South Africa: The Political Economy of Transformation*, London: Lynne Rienner Publishers, pp. 29–46.
Hirsch, A. (2005), *Season of Hope: Economic Reform under Mandela and Mbeki*, Scottsville: University of KwaZulu-Natal Press.
Holden, M. (1992), 'The structure and incidence of protection in South Africa', in P. Black and B. Dollery (eds), *Leading Issues in South African Microeconomics*, Johannesburg: Southern Book Publishers.
Jenkins, C., M. Bleaney, M. Holden and N. Siwisa (1997), 'A review of South Africa's trade policy', paper presented at the Trade and Industrial Policy Annual Forum, Muldersdrift, September.
Jenkins, R. (2008), 'Trade, technology and employment in South Africa', *Journal of Development Studies*, **44**(1), 60–79.
Joffe, A., D. Kaplan, R. Kaplinsky and D. Lewis (1993), 'Meeting the global challenge: a framework for industrial revival in South Africa', in P. Baker, A. Boraine and W. Krafchik (eds), *South Africa and the World Economy in the 1990s*, Cape Town: David Philip Publishers, pp. 91–126.
Joffe, A., D. Kaplan, R. Kaplinsky and D. Lewis (1995), 'Improving manufacturing

performance in South Africa: report of the industrial strategy project', Cape Town: University of Cape Town Press.
Jonsson, Gunnar and Arvind Subramanian (2000), 'Dynamic gains from trade: Evidence from South Africa', International Monetary Fund Working Paper no. 00/45.
Kaplan, D. (2007), 'The constraints and institutional challenges facing industrial policy in South Africa: a way forward', *Transformation*, **64**, UKZN Press, May.
Macroeconomic Research Group (MERG) (1993), 'Making democracy work: a framework for macroeconomic policy in South Africa', Cape Town: Centre for Development Studies, University of the Western Cape.
Melitz, Marc J. (2003), 'The impact of trade on intra-industry reallocations and aggregate industry productivity', *Econometrica*, **71**(6), 1695–725.
Michie, J. and V. Padayachee (1997), 'South Africa's transition: the policy agenda', in J. Michie and V. Padayachee (eds), *The Political Economy of South Africa's Transition*, London: The Dryden Press, pp. 9–26.
Naidoo, K. (2006), 'Operationalising South Africa's move from macroeconomic stability to microeconomic reform', in V. Padaychee (ed.) *The Development Decade? Economic and Social Change in South Africa, 1994–2004*, Pretoria: HSRC Press, chapter 6: pp. 108–25.
Padayachee, V. (no date), 'Progressive academic economists and the challenge of development in South Africa's decade of liberation', CSDS, University of Natal, Durban, available online at: http://www.ukzn.ac.za/CCS/files/Padayachee per cent20background per cent20on per cent20SA per cent20poli per cent20econ.pdf, Accessed 12 July 2008.
Pillay, V. (1997), 'South Africa's monetary and exchange rate policy', in J. Michie and V. Padayachee (eds), *The Political Economy of South Africa's Transition*, London: The Dryden Press, pp. 101–23.
Price, R. (1994), 'South Africa: the political economy of growth and democracy.' in S. Stedman (ed.), *South Africa: The Political Economy of Transformation*, London: Lynne Rienner Publishers, pp. 181–98.
Rodrik, D. (2006), 'Understanding South Africa's economic puzzles', Centre for International Development Working Paper no. 130, August, Centre for International Development South Africa Growth Initiative, Harvard University, see http://www.cid.harvard.edu/cidwp/130.htm.
SDS (2000), 'Benchmarking: a tool for attaining global competitiveness', School of Development Studies Policy Brief no. 5, University of Kwa-Zulu Natal, available at http://www.ukzn.ac.za/csds/Publications/sodspb5.pdf.
Seboni, V. (2005), 'Non-agricultural market access', speech delivered by Deputy President of the Congress of South African Trade Unions to SANGOCO workshop on non-agricultural market access on 24 June.
South African Department of Finance (1996), 'Growth, employment, and redistribution: a macroeconomic strategy', Pretoria: Department of Finance.
South African Department of Trade and Industry (2007), 'A National industrial policy framework', Pretoria: Department of Trade and Industry.
Thurlow, J. (2006), 'Trade liberalization and pro-poor growth in South Africa', *Studies in Economics and Econometrics*, **31**(2), August, 161–79.
Tsikata, Y. (1999), 'Liberalization and trade performance in South Africa', World Bank Informal Discussion Papers on Aspects of the South African Economy no. 13, The Southern Africa Department, The World Bank.

Van der Berg, S., M. Louw and L. Du Toit (2007), 'Poverty trends since the transition: what we know', University of Stellenbosch Department of Economics.
WTO (1998), *Trade Policy Review: Southern African Customs Union*, Geneva: World Trade Organisation Secretariat.
WTO (2003), *Trade Policy Review: Southern African Customs Union*, Geneva: World Trade Organisation Secretariat.
Zalk, N. (2006), 'Untold story of global industrialization', *Business Day*, 13 March.

9. Conclusion: what lessons for the twenty-first century?

Razeen Sally and Philip Alves

All seven country studies show that the liberalization of trade and FDI has worked. It has reduced discrimination against tradable sectors, enabled specialization according to comparative advantage, boosted both imports and exports, increased inward investment and triggered major productivity gains. This has raised economic growth. Trade and FDI have increased in absolute terms and as a proportion of national economic activity. All these countries have integrated rapidly into the global economy.

The supporting evidence is strongest for the small countries in the sample, Australia, New Zealand, Chile and Malaysia. Opening to trade and FDI has been critical to their successful transformation into more prosperous, globalized economies. But the supporting evidence is also strong for the large and medium-sized economies in the sample, India, Brazil and South Africa. Imports and inward investment have been a boon to consumers, and spurred competition, restructuring and innovation in domestic business. Brazil has become an exporting powerhouse in agricultural commodities, agro-food products and other commodities. It is even doing well in some parts of manufacturing. Both Brazil and to a lesser extent South Africa have reaped the benefits of the global commodities boom. India, unlike China, has not exploited comparative advantage in labour-intensive products, but it has emerged as a leading exporter of IT services. And it is breaking into niche manufacturing exports.

All the above would not have been possible without external liberalization. But the latter has not happened in isolation. Rather it is embedded in bigger packages of macro- and microeconomic reforms; a combination of ensuring macroeconomic stability and rolling out widespread – internal, not just external – liberalization.

These country stories run counter to old–new arguments against liberalization and in favour of protectionism and industrial-policy interventionism. Better economic performance has not resulted from retaining high levels of protection, relying on Northern (developed-country) liberalization and using 'hard' industrial policies (of the import-substituting, infant-industry variety). On the contrary, there was egregious import-substitution and industrial-policy failure in all these countries before decisive external opening. When the latter occurred, it did so overwhelmingly through unilateral liberalization, not trade negotiations. (South Africa is the one exception, having done the first phase of major trade liberalization through its Uruguay Round commitments. Although as noted in that chapter, South Africa liberalized far more quickly and by more than its commitments required.)

That still leaves unanswered questions, more for Brazil, India and South Africa than the others. Why has external opening not delivered higher growth, employment generation and poverty reduction? Why does growth seem to be 'jobless'? Populist opinion goes further, asserting that liberalization has been excessive, and that it has led to a diminished national economic base and unemployment.

Such views are misleading, indeed downright false. Opening to imports has led to the downsizing of inefficient industries, especially in previously protected, import-substituting manufacturing sectors. But capital and jobs have flowed to more efficient sectors, including factor-abundant sectors engaged in international trade. True, this shift has not been fast or widespread enough in Brazil, India and South Africa. It has been widespread in the other four countries, with shorter or longer lags before beneficial effects have been felt (longer for Chile than the other three). Liberalization, however, is not to blame for not delivering the goods quickly and bountifully. Quite the reverse: it is the lack of liberalization, and the maintenance of highly regulated and distorted domestic markets, that is to blame.

Brazil, India and South Africa all do badly or very badly in the World Bank's ease-of-doing-business indicators. Rigid labour markets – the product of repressive employment legislation – figure prominently. So do 'trading across borders' indicators on customs clearance, documentation and the cost of importing and exporting. The high costs of doing business that result, cramp external and internal trade, and domestic as well as foreign investment. Australia, New Zealand, Chile and, to a lesser extent, Malaysia, do much better on the same indicators; they have lower-cost, trade-and-investment-friendly business climates. Core obstacles to growth and employment lie here in these second-generation, domestic regulatory – though still highly trade-related – issues. 'Excessive' liberalization is not the problem.

UNFINISHED BUSINESS: THE CASE FOR FURTHER LIBERALIZATION AND REGULATORY REFORM

The country studies also show that there is much unfinished business – more so for Brazil, India, South Africa and, to a lesser extent, Malaysia than for Australia, New Zealand and Chile.

Australia, New Zealand and Chile are strong reformers. Tariffs have come down to low levels; tariff regimes have been simplified (especially in Chile with its uniform tariff); few border NTBs remain; the door to FDI is largely open on a non-discriminatory basis; and services sectors have been liberalized extensively. The challenge for these countries is to remove small pockets of protection (for example, automobiles, textiles, clothing and footwear in Australia and New Zealand, and parts of agriculture in Chile), and, especially, go deeper into second-generation reforms (for example in infrastructure, education, skills, tax, labour markets, pensions and social security).

Malaysia sits in between. Its relatively open trade and FDI regime (by developing-country standards) has created an electronics niche powered by inward investment and plugged into regional production networks and global supply chains. It is also a leading exporter of plantation products, and has an expanding oil and gas sector. But Malaysia is a dual economy: globally competitive industries coexist with highly protected, uncompetitive sectors in services, parts of manufacturing and agriculture. Structural reforms have hardly begun. Reform blockage is intimately bound up with race-based politics and a hitherto sacrosanct *Bumiputera* policy that confers cradle-to-grave advantages to the Malay majority. In particular, it has entrenched tight and corrupt links between politicians, officials and the business elite. Malaysia needs to remove trade and FDI barriers in several sectors and undertake serious second-generation reforms (for example in education, skills and government procurement). That also means tackling the *Bumiputera* policy head on. These are the requirements to improve the international competitiveness of manufacturing and enable diversification into tradable services.

Brazil, South Africa and India have liberalized extensively by their own standards, but much remains to be done. Tariffs should be reduced and simplified, NTBs removed, and FDI and services further opened up. At least as important, governments need to get serious about second-generation reforms to tackle high-cost domestic business climates. That includes improving infrastructure, customs administration and assorted trade-facilitation measures. It also includes public-sector and labour-market reforms. The latter are the hardest nuts to crack politically. But they are necessary to maintain growth rates (especially when global economic conditions are less benign than they have been in the last five years), diversify economic activity (especially into services), and translate growth into better employment generation and poverty reduction.

THE POLITICAL ECONOMY OF TRADE-POLICY REFORM

Now we turn to the political economy of trade-policy reform in the countries concerned. We group our observations under the following headings: a) crises; b) country size; c) interests; d) ideas; e) institutions; f) foreign policy and international politics. This more-or-less follows the classification in the introductory chapter.

Crises

An economic crisis has been the catalyst for major economic-policy reforms in nearly all the countries covered. In some cases it has occurred alongside a political turning point. In Brazil, pro-market reforms, including big tariff liberalization, got going alongside the transition to full democracy in the late 1980s. The last big instalment was part of the *Plano Real* for macroeconomic stabilization in 1994. South Africa's big opening in the mid-1990s took place following the collapse of the apartheid economic and political systems, and alongside the transition to multi-party democracy. The rand crisis of 1996 induced a further bout of trade liberalization. Chile's external opening followed hard on the heels of the military coup in 1973.

India's big burst of external liberalization, in 1991–93, was linked to macroeconomic stabilization, both set against the backdrop of an extreme balance-of-payments crisis in 1991. But political continuity was ensured, as it was in Malaysia, Australia and New Zealand. The latter had a severe economic crisis in 1983. In Australia it was much less dramatic. Malaysian reforms have been gradual over an extended period, though a mini-crisis in the mid-1980s triggered a bout of external liberalization.

However, 'post-crisis' experience points to the limits of crises as an explanation of continuing reforms, beyond short-term shifts. Above all, it shows how difficult it is to take reforms farther, especially into domestic regulatory territory, after a crisis has been overcome and in a relatively benign macroeconomic environment. Brazil has not seen external opening since the mid-1990s. South Africa's external liberalization has been stuck since 2000. India has seen stop–go reforms since 1993; and they have been more 'stop' than 'go' since 2004. Malaysian reforms have been sluggish since the Asian crisis in 1997/8.

It may not seem urgent to pursue liberalizing reforms in 'normal' conditions, especially after so much reform heavy-lifting has been done. But complacency is dangerous. It means the economy is continuing to live off reforms accomplished some time ago. Reforms needed to make the economy flexible and adaptable to changing global conditions, and resilient to unanticipated shocks, are being neglected. Meanwhile, distortions and rigidities are building up. A future crisis is then the trigger for long overdue reforms. These come at a much higher political, economic and social cost than would otherwise be the case.

Depending on a crisis for reform is myopic, and ultimately crazy, policy. It is far better to nurture a culture of permanent, incremental and mutually reinforcing reforms. But that is terribly difficult in practice. Still, star reformers such as Chile, Australia and New Zealand show that it can be done. All three have followed up crisis-induced first-generation reforms with deeper second-generation reforms rolled out over almost two decades. These, however, are small open economies where the reform imperative is stronger than in medium-sized and large economies.

Country Size

Generally, small countries reliant on the world economy have liberalized farther and faster than bigger countries. This is the case in the OECD and the developing world. Ireland, Chile, Australia, New Zealand and Estonia (among other east-central European and Baltic countries) stand out as very strong reformers. So do Hong Kong and Singapore, with long traditions as free-port city-states. Malaysia has relatively good reform credentials. Sri Lanka pioneered liberalizing reforms in south Asia, before ethnic conflict compromised economic prospects from 1983. Mauritius and Botswana stand out in Africa.

It is generally believed that the economics and politics of reform in small countries are easier. Larger countries have more differentiated economies. They are less reliant on the world economy and have more inward-looking, protectionist-inclined interests. That translates into more complicated politics. But big countries are not pre-programmed to avoid reforms or do them sluggishly. China is the most populous country on Earth, but it has been a strong reformer. Other large and medium-sized developing countries have more mixed records, but some have reformed substantially compared with their pre-reform starting positions. That applies to Brazil, India and South Africa.

Interests

Organized interests have become more active in trade negotiations since the end of the Uruguay Round and with the advent of new FTAs. The picture is variegated, especially in larger, populous, complex countries such as Brazil, India and South Africa.

In Brazil, protectionist interests, especially in manufacturing, coexist with expanding export-oriented interests. Most strikingly, Brazil's agricultural sectors (such as sugar, corn, beef, poultry, soya and cotton) have become strongly export-oriented as a result of trade liberalization, and are correspondingly much better organized and mobilized. Brazil's services sectors, in contrast, are weakly organized and have no national representation. In South Africa, the powerful national union federation, COSATU, an ally of the governing ANC, is generally sceptical about trade liberalization and especially protectionist in manufacturing. Business is divided. Protectionist interests are bunched in manufacturing and the public sector, but the big mining houses are export-oriented with multinational production platforms. Export-oriented agriculture is also well organized. There are private-sector services providers expanding across Africa, but they are weakly organized. Overall, South Africa's open-economy business interests are not particularly active in promoting their trade-policy preferences. They are overshadowed by COSATU and more defensive business interests.

In India, trade unions remain very protectionist. Their fortress is extremely restrictive employment laws that make it unviable for firms to take on new workers beyond a certain size. Unions represent a tiny minority of workers in industrial sectors that were long protected under the licence raj. State-owned enterprises, for example in power, energy, infrastructure, agriculture and financial services, are also bastions of protection. India's private sector, in contrast, has changed since the opening of the economy from 1991. It was dominated by long-established conglomerates that benefited from the licence raj. But India's leading business houses have restructured, expanded exports and are investing in production abroad. Many still lobby for protection, but in more muted form given their wider international interests. This is reflected in the changing positions of their industry associations. Finally, India's stellar IT-services firms, notably in software and business-process outsourcing, are very open-economy oriented. They operate in a far less regulated policy environment compared with other sectors, have myriad links with foreign multinationals, and have fast-expanding exports and foreign investments.

The other countries in the sample are all small, open and globalized. They have less differentiated interest-group constellations. Open-economy interests generally prevail over protectionist interests, with perhaps the exception of South Africa. Australia, New Zealand and Chile, like Brazil, have well-organized and influential agricultural exporters. Mining interests are also powerful in Australia and Chile. Protectionist interests exist in pockets of these economies, but they have shrunk considerably over the past two decades.

In South Africa the protectionist lobby, led by COSATU and manufacturers' organizations in import-competing sectors, was simply marginalized during the 1990s, and is now reasserting its central role in economic policy decision-making. During this hiatus no obvious pro-trade lobby emerged in the private sector (outside mining and agriculture); liberalization was led by enlightened politicians and WTO pressure, and these forces are now much less influential. There is, however, no reason to expect a sweeping re-embrace of protection. The economy-wide benefits are clear, and nowhere are they valued more than in the National Treasury, Presidency and Central Bank. Hence the new battles will be fought over the details, not the thrust, of economic policy.

Malaysia, though the most globalized economy in the sample, has more powerful and entrenched protectionist interests compared with the other three small open economies. Manufacturing exporting interests are prominent, especially multinational enterprises with export platforms. But significant parts of the economy are highly protected. They are bound up with the *Bumiputera* policy and 'crony-capitalist' links uniting businesspeople, politicians and officials. Government-linked companies and those in the private sector benefiting from government largesse, especially in public procurement, have little interest in liberalization.

What concluding generalizations can be made about organized interests in trade policy? Interest-group landscapes have clearly changed with external opening. The balance has shifted towards open-economy interests. They form countervailing coalitions against protectionist interests, and decrease the risk of liberalization reversal.

Now the biggest challenge is to harness open-economy interests to the wagon of further liberalization, and especially to domestic regulatory reforms. Their stakes in structural, microeconomic reforms are becoming ever clearer. Previous liberalization has spurred firm-level restructuring, export-orientation and overseas expansion. But firms remain hamstrung by high-cost domestic business environments (especially in Brazil, India and South Africa; much less so in the small open economies in the sample). This they feel puts them at a disadvantage to foreign competitors with more salubrious business climates in their home markets. That also translates into defensiveness in trade negotiations. Structural reforms at home would lower business costs, boost the international competitiveness of local firms, make them less resistant to opening domestic markets to foreign competition, and translate into less defensive positions in trade negotiations.

Starting this virtuous cycle begins with reforms at home, not in the WTO or FTAs. For interest-group activity it implies a new and different political economy to that of hitching exporting interests to tariff concessions in trade negotiations.

Ideas

Much is made of technocrat-economists (dubbed 'technopols' by John Williamson) as carriers of Washington Consensus ideas. They are often Western (especially US)-trained economists, many with IMF or World Bank experience. The most famous example is that of the 'Chicago Boys', Chicago-trained economists at the Catholic University in Santiago who controlled economic policy in Chile from the mid-1970s to the early 1980s. Technopols have continued to hold the levers of economic policy in successive Chilean governments, though they have been more pragmatic and less doctrinaire than the Chicago Boys.

Undoubtedly, technopols have been pivotal in specific circumstances. But, as a general explanation, their role in policy reform should not be exaggerated – a trap economists fall into when writing about fellow economists in policy-making positions. Economists are not Platonic Guardians; they are not immune to political pressures and the temptations of power; and this has often led to bad or indifferent decisions. India, for example, has an economic-policy 'dream team' with excellent academic and research credentials, led by Prime Minister Manmohan Singh. But it has a reputation as a do-nothing team incapable of making basic policy decisions. The lesson to draw is that economists, and indeed other academic experts, should be on tap but not necessarily on top: they do not always make good high-level decision-makers.

At least as important as technopols are two other factors. First, 'the vision thing' (to borrow a phrase coined by the first President Bush). Strong-reforming countries often have leaders and leadership teams who have a powerful vision of the future, with ambitious goals for growth, poverty reduction, job creation and global integration. East Asia stands out. The region has had national policy elites with a relentless focus on growth and prosperity, and with the will to mobilize resources and implement policies to achieve set goals. The Hawke and Keating governments in Australia, and economic-policy teams led by Roger Douglas and Ruth Richardson in New Zealand, also stand out in this regard.

Second, policy pragmatism that issues from past experience and a 'demonstration effect'. More important than ideology, perhaps, is the perception that past policies (for example macroeconomic profligacy and import-substitution) have failed, and that alternative policies have succeeded elsewhere. The experience of the east-Asian Tigers, of Chile in Latin America, and more recently of China, has exerted a powerful influence on policy-makers elsewhere, setting in train a process of copycatting reforms.

The transmission of Washington Consensus ideas to policy reforms has a mixed record. Technopols have had most influence in macroeconomic policy by occupying key positions in ministries of finance, central banks and presidential/prime-ministerial offices. This has translated into influence on liberalization and microeconomic reform in crisis situations, but much less so post-crises. Liberal economists are less in evidence and less influential in line ministries and regulatory agencies, which control microeconomic policies in normal conditions.

In Brazil, South Africa and India, Washington Consensus macroeconomic orthodoxy has been more influential than ideas on liberalization and microeconomic reform. South Africa has seen the pendulum swing towards selective industrial policies and away from trade liberalization. This is reflected in the government's overarching economic-policy programme, AsgiSA (Accelerated and Shared Growth Initiative), and the Department of Trade and Industry's NIPF (National Industrial Policy Framework). Meanwhile, the Ministry of Finance and the Reserve Bank have held the line on macroeconomic stability. In contrast, Australia, New Zealand and Chile – all stronger reformers – have seen market-liberal ideas spread more widely and exercise more influence over microeconomic policy and external liberalization.

Institutions

Making generalizations about institutional constraints on policy choice, and how this might explain differences in national and regional economic performance over time, is notoriously difficult. What follow are some observations on institutions and trade policy in the countries studied.

First, to what extent must 'good' institutions be in place before 'good' policies can take hold and work their magic? Conversely, to what extent are institutions the result, rather than the cause, of policy choices? These are chicken-and-egg questions.

Writing from the 1990s rightly stresses institutional capacity, within the state and beyond it (World Bank, 1997; Rodrik, 2003). This fills in the institutional vacuum in studies on market-based policy reforms in the 1970s and 1980s. But the later literature sometimes goes too far in setting high institutional preconditions for reformist policies to work. The extreme is 'institutions come first'. The reality is a complex interplay between market-based policies, including trade and FDI liberalization, and improving domestic institutions. Often policy reforms provide the stimulus for institutional change. As Adam Smith realized over two centuries ago, opening to international trade and investment triggers powerful incentives to improve infrastructure, public administration and the rule of law. Then producers and consumers can reap more gains from international commerce (Myint, 1977).

Australia and New Zealand, both long-established developed countries, had sophisticated institutions in place when market reforms got going in the 1980s. Of course that was less the case with the developing countries in the sample. But Chile, Malaysia and (to some extent) South Africa have had relatively strong institutions by developing-country standards (going by World Bank governance and business-climate indicators, in addition to other institutional indicators). Brazil and India have relatively weak institutions.

Second, what about the link between political systems and economic-policy reforms? Strong generalizations are difficult and misleading. Across the developing world, liberalization has taken place under authoritarian and democratic systems. All the countries covered here are functioning democracies. All except Malaysia would be categorized as liberal democracies. Malaysia's democracy is the least constitutionally liberal in the sample: it has fewer guarantees of individual rights and defences against executive power. In Chile, the first decade-and-a-half of reforms took place under a dictatorship, but since 1989 ongoing reforms have occurred under stable democratic conditions. South Africa and Brazil saw economic-policy reforms proceed in tandem with the switch to democracy. India, Australia and New Zealand have been 'liberal democracies' throughout.

The complications of liberal-democratic politics – constitutional 'checks and balances' to executive decision-making, freewheeling interest-group activity, media scrutiny, public discussion, multiple 'veto points' – may slow down reforms. It becomes necessary to build reform-supporting coalitions among organized interests and the wider public, and forge consensus wherever possible. It increases the urgency to deliver results quickly for broad sections of the population, while compensating potential losers from reforms (for example through social safety nets, education and training programmes). Democracy also makes it difficult to pursue comprehensive reform, especially politically sensitive domestic regulatory reforms. Public-sector and labour-market reforms are perhaps the hardest nuts to crack, as reform experiences from India, Brazil and South Africa show. Affirmative-action policies in favour of ethnic majorities have clearly compromised market-based reforms in Malaysia and South Africa. This includes trade-related reforms, for example in services deregulation and government procurement. One last complication: Brazil and India are large, decentralized federal polities with much policy competence residing with state or provincial administrations (that is also true for Australia, though it has a small population).

Third, take a look at institutions in the narrower sense of how trade-policy decision-making is organized. To start with general observations:

- The capacity to formulate and implement trade policy has had to increase in line with the external opening of economies, the greater role of trade and FDI in GDP, and more complex and demanding international trade agreements. Greater demands on trade-negotiating capacity were felt from the late 1980s with the Uruguay Round negotiations and 'new-generation' bilateral and regional FTAs.
- Strong and sustained trade-policy and wider economic-policy reforms were driven, more often than not, by powerful presidential or prime-ministerial offices, ministries of finance and central banks, insulated from blocking pressures in other parts of government and outside government. Ministries of finance were particularly important in driving trade liberalization during crises, often overriding protectionist-inclined ministries of trade and industry. But, post-crises, the former have retreated to their core macroeconomic functions, leaving line ministries and regulatory agencies to handle trade policy with much less oversight.
- As national economies have become more globally integrated, some regions within nations have risen to prominence. States in the south and west of India, and the São Paolo region in Brazil, come to mind. Sub-national policies to attract international trade and FDI have had more impact, not just in the regions concerned, but also in setting examples to be emulated in other sub-national regions.

Now turn to country detail. In Brazil, the Ministry of Finance spurred trade liberalization in the early- to mid-1990s, but not thereafter. The Ministry of External Affairs (MEA) rose to prominence and subsequently acquired control of trade negotiations, though regulatory and operational functions remain with the Ministry of Development, Industry and Foreign Trade. Organized business has become active in trade policy, but many business organizations have several complaints, directed particularly at the MEA. They say that it does not consult business seriously, gives too much weight to some NGOs and lacks transparency. Above all, they complain that, especially under President Lula da Silva, trade policy has too much of a 'geopolitical' focus and does not focus enough on Brazilian commercial priorities.

In India, trade policy is controlled by the Ministry of Commerce and Industry (MOCI). The Ministry of Finance was influential in liberalization in 1991–93, but less so thereafter. Organized business and NGOs have become more active since the Uruguay Round. Inter-agency coordination on trade policy functions badly, and state governments are largely left out of the loop. Business input is still insufficient. The MOCI remains defensive in trade negotiations and ambivalent about unilateral liberalization – rather at odds with the global integration of the Indian economy since 1991.

In South Africa, trade policy-making reflects institutional flux in the transition from apartheid to democracy. Policy-making is controlled by a strong, centralized executive, with a weak role for the parliament. The National Treasury, the cockpit of economic-policy reform overall and the guardian of macroeconomic stability, has remained on the sidelines of trade policy. The latter is run by the Department of Trade and Industry (DTI), which has become more sceptical of trade liberalization and inclined to industrial-policy intervention in recent years. The DTI's trade-policy capacity is shallow; it often seems dysfunctional; it is not transparent; and it is excessively sensitive to criticism.

Australia has little left to do beyond reducing some pockets of protection in manufacturing and services. The Treasury under Paul Keating led the reform process, which made good use of the independent Tariff Board's research, and annual budget announcements. Critically, the government ensured 'buy-in' from unions, who have acted responsibly since. Nowadays the Department of Foreign Affairs and Trade (DFAT) leads in the trade policy domain; this reflects the relative unimportance of unilateral border liberalization measures in the modern evolution of Australia's trade policy regime.

New Zealand reformed in more emergency-like circumstances. Technopols in the finance ministry were able to push through and implement with remarkable speed an extensive liberalization and stabilization package. Electoral reform soon followed to ensure greater checks on executive power in future. Nowadays, as in Australia, the ministries of finance and of foreign affairs and trade take the lead roles in economic management. Competitive export-oriented industries in the primary sector lobby to ensure that market access in Europe is maintained in the face of growing 'green' protectionism, and for new markets in Asia to be pried open.

Chile's reforms were enacted under a military dictatorship, which has given way to successive responsible, prudent administrations that have deepened and broadened Chile's liberalization. This has been relatively easy in the absence of any strong protectionist lobby. The finance ministry takes the lead in economic management. What may reasonably be called trade policy in Chile is left to negotiators and diplomats in the foreign ministry; the investment promotion agency ProChile; and those responsible for ensuring that Chile's private sector understands its export opportunities and the agreements that govern them.

Malaysia is another steady liberalizer, and has used a combination of unilateral and external initiatives to open the economy. The lead institution is the Ministry of International Trade and Industry, modelled on its now near-mythical Japanese counterpart. But overall strategy and coordination takes place in the Economic Planning Unit, which resides in the Prime Minister's office, and even oversees the finance ministry. Malaysia's biggest challenge lies in insulating these bureaucrats from political and business pressure, and rebuilding emasculated democratic institutions. Only then can politically sensitive microeconomic reform, such as public sector restructuring, or the *Bumiputera* policies, occur.

Foreign policy and International Politics

Trade policy links down to national economic policies and institutions. But it also links up to foreign policy and international politics. A reasonably stable international political order is the categorical imperative for economic development. Without the global Pax – an orderly framework for international relations – there can be no security for international commerce.

The end of the Cold War and the collapse of the Soviet Union reshaped international politics. It was the catalyst for twin political and economic transitions in eastern Europe and the former Soviet Union. But it also reverberated elsewhere – nowhere more so than in India. India's foreign policy was gutted: it lost its 'first friend', the Soviet Union; and its leadership of the Non-Aligned Movement was meaningless. This brought on a foreign-policy transformation. India looked west to a rapprochement and closer relations with the USA, and in the second instance with Europe. It also looked east, first to southeast Asia and then to China. Closer engagement, looking east and west, started in the early 1990s, paused in the mid-to late 1990s, and has been renewed and strengthened ever since. It corresponds with the timing of external liberalization. Stronger security relations with the USA and other countries have proceeded in tandem with stronger commercial relations with the same countries. Arguably, India's foreign-policy shift is an important factor influencing its belated embrace of the world economy.

Of all the countries in the sample, Brazil has perhaps the tightest link between foreign policy and trade policy. The MEA leads and coordinates trade negotiations. These, in both the WTO and FTAs, are geared to achieving foreign-policy goals, such as Brazilian leadership in South America, and alliances with other 'southern' powers, notably India, China and South Africa, to counterbalance US power. South African foreign policy came out of its long apartheid isolation to prioritize closer relations with the West and a leadership role in Africa. Like Brazil, South Africa now has a stronger accent on South–South alliances, which strongly influences its WTO and FTA activities.

Like Brazil, Chile, Australia and New Zealand have foreign ministries that take the lead on and coordinate trade negotiations. Chile's foreign policy priorities are arguably in its own region, and with the USA. Chile has shied away from regional integration initiatives in Latin America, but actively supported the now defunct Free Trade Area of the Americas process. New Zealand and Australia are increasingly defining themselves as 'Asian', to ensure the closest possible exposure to the world's most dynamic region. This is epitomized in both countries' pursuits of FTAs with China. New Zealand is now the first OECD country to grant market economy status to, and sign a comprehensive FTA with, China. Australia's involvements in the recent US foreign policy initiatives, and its FTA with the USA, have also cemented its ties with that country. New Zealand's ties with the US are more complicated due to its refusal to allow nuclear-powered US warships into New Zealand's harbours. However, apart from WTO interactions, these foreign policy considerations are arguably less important for Chile, Australia and New Zealand than they are for Brazil or South Africa.

Historically, Malaysian trade policy has the reputation for being pragmatic and broadly in line with domestic commercial interests. But, occasionally, foreign-policy priorities have compromised such pragmatism. This was the case in the aftermath of the Asian crisis when Dr Mahathir Mohamed was prime minister. His anti-globalization rhetoric and emphasis on Malaysia's Third World credentials translated into defensive positions in the WTO.

Summary

In most of the countries covered, an economic crisis, sometimes combined with a political crisis, has led to a big opening of the economy. New open-economy interest-group constellations have emerged to counter traditional protectionist interests. Washington Consensus ideas have spread through technopols (though more influential in macroeconomic than microeconomic policy), leadership focus on growth (more so in Australia, New Zealand, Chile and Malaysia, less so in Brazil, India and South Africa), and pragmatic emulation of successful policies elsewhere. A party-political and wider public consensus, however partial and patchy, has gradually formed around reforms. Gradually improving institutions are better able to support and manage open-market policies, though they remain relatively weak in some of the countries covered (notably Brazil and India). Shifts in foreign policy have also encouraged external opening and closer relations with major trading partners.

MULTI-TRACK TRADE POLICY

All countries in this sample have pursued liberalization in a combination of ways – unilaterally, multilaterally and through bilateral/regional agreements.

Unilateral liberalization

The countries covered have relied overwhelmingly on unilateral trade and FDI liberalization, and much less on trade negotiations.

Chile deserves special mention because it, more than any other developing country, was the first to experiment with radical unilateral trade and FDI liberalization. Massive external opening of the economy took place between 1974 and 1979, at a time when other developing countries were committed to import-substitution regimes, and when there was no pressure from donors and international organisations to liberalize. There had of course been prior unilateral liberalization in northeast Asia, but it was much more partial and gradual. Continuing incremental liberalization since the late 1980s has left Chile with one of the most open, simple and transparent trade and FDI regimes in the developing world: the uniform tariff is very low; there are hardly any border NTBs; and there are few inward-investment restrictions.

Next consider Malaysia, because unilateral liberalization has been stronger in east Asia than in any other developing-country region. The bulk of trade-and-investment liberalization by the first and second-generation Tigers of northeast and southeast Asia was done unilaterally. In the 1980s, the old ASEAN countries – including Malaysia – reduced import and inward-investment barriers simultaneously in order to attract Japanese manufacturing multinational enterprises (which relied on imports of capital goods and components for labour-intensive local processing and assembly of goods for export). This is how they inserted themselves into regional and global manufacturing supply chains, first in electronics and then spreading to other industries (for example sport footwear, televisions and radio receivers, office equipment, electrical machinery, power and machine tools, cameras and watches, and printing and publishing). In the 1990s, China also undertook unilateral and simultaneous trade and inward investment liberalization, and thereby inserted itself as the cheap-labour, final-assembly stage in these expanding supply chains. This in turn triggered additional unilateral liberalization by the southeast Asian countries. More openness to trade and FDI allowed the more advanced ASEAN countries (Singapore, Malaysia and Thailand) to move up to higher-value production of parts and components in 'Factory Asia', while more labour-intensive production migrated to China, and more recently to Vietnam. To repeat: these measures were not brought about by GATT/WTO, the ASEAN-FTA (AFTA) or other FTA agreements; rather they were unilateral responses to market conditions, resulting in market-led regional and global integration (Baldwin, 2006a and 2006b; Athukorala, 2006).

The three other developing countries in the sample liberalized later, and they remain more protectionist than Chile and Malaysia. In Brazil, trade and FDI liberalization from the late 1980s has been primarily unilateral. In India, the IMF and World Bank packages in 1991 induced some trade opening, but liberalization thereafter was genuinely unilateral: it was not the result of donor pressure or international trade negotiations. South Africa relied more on external forces than the others for its trade opening, but progress on FDI liberalization has been unilaterally driven. There was a burst of unilateral trade liberalization in 1996 in response to the rand crisis, which helped align government priorities with Uruguay Round obligations. These, however, were much more the lever used by the transitional government to open up the economy than the result of haggling over reciprocal concessions – otherwise South Africa wouldn't have gone faster or deeper than its commitments required.

Finally, Australia and New Zealand had very strong unilateral trade and FDI liberalization from the early 1980s to the early 1990s, with incremental liberalization thereafter. This has historically transformed the most protected countries in the OECD into very open small economies. Trade protection has been reduced to a few rump sectors (automobiles, textiles, clothing and footwear), and the door is almost wholly open to FDI.

Unilateral liberalization has been exceptionally strong and comprehensive, and buttressed by domestic structural reforms, in Chile, Australia and New Zealand. The others in the sample, in contrast, reflect the general developing-country pattern. Unilateral liberalization has been more successful in manufacturing than in services and agriculture (although Brazil and South Africa have very open farm sectors); and it has tackled border barriers much better than non-border regulatory barriers. For instance, unilateral liberalization in Malaysia, as elsewhere in east Asia, has been strong in 'fragmentation-based' manufacturing products that feature in global supply chains, as well as in labour-intensive consumer goods such as garments and toys. But it has been weaker in other areas of manufacturing, very uneven in services, weak in agriculture, and still has a long way to go with trade-related structural reforms in goods, services and investment.

Finally, unilateral liberalization has slowed down across the developing world. In Brazil and South Africa, trade policy has forsaken unilateral liberalization and become totally reliant on trade negotiations. India continues incremental unilateral liberalization, though at a slower pace than before. That is also true of Malaysia after the Asian crisis.

Multilateral liberalization

Unilateral measures do not lock in liberalization against future backtracking. They do not provide fair, stable and predictable rules for international commerce. Arguably, the best the WTO can hope for post-Doha Round is to lock in pre-existing unilateral liberalization through binding commitments, and gradually improve the functioning of non-discriminatory multilateral rules. That implies scaling back ambitions and expectations. Market-access negotiations (to deliver extra liberalization) should be more modest and incremental; and maybe trade rounds should become a thing of the past. There should be a shift of focus to safeguarding and improving trade rules. This is more important for most WTO members than extra multilateral liberalization. Finally, to get business done, WTO decision-making should fall in line with political and economic realities outside Geneva. About 30 countries (counting the EU as one) account for almost 90 per cent of international trade and FDI. That includes 20–25 developing countries. They should gather in plurilateral 'coalitions of the willing' to make key market-access and rule-making decisions, and correspondingly take on stronger commitments than the rest of the WTO membership. In other words, the WTO needs 'variable geometry' in order to function effectively.

All the countries covered should be active in a broad, informal WTO 'first division' of 30 or so countries. South Africa, Chile and Malaysia are developing-country 'middle powers' who can make a stronger contribution than the bulk of developing countries. But India and Brazil, along with China, are the three developing-country 'big beasts' in the WTO. They should exercise co-leadership alongside the USA, EU and perhaps Japan (if the latter can get its act together). Without that, nothing will move.

Along with India, Brazil remains the most active developing-country member in the WTO. It is active on all fronts. In dispute settlement, it launched and won landmark cases against the USA on cotton and the EU on sugar. In the Doha Round, it launched and has since led the G20 in agriculture. Inevitably, Brazil has a combination of offensive and defensive positions on specific negotiating issues. But many voices from organized business in Brazil complain that these positions are not congruent with Brazil's commercial interests, and have been hijacked by extraneous foreign-policy goals (such as a permanent seat on the UN Security Council and leadership credentials in the South). Notably, Brazil's accommodation of India in the G20 means that it cannot promote its agricultural exporting interests as strongly as it could otherwise. Also, its defensive position in the NAMA (non-agricultural market-access) negotiations does not reflect Brazil's export strength in industrial goods.

India's defensiveness in the Uruguay Round has continued in the Doha Round. It is rigidly defensive in agriculture and rather defensive in NAMA. It was strongly opposed to the inclusion of most of the Singapore issues, and remains in favour of strong Special and Differential Treatment for developing countries. That said, India is not as militantly obstructive as it was in the GATT. Its main negotiating shift has been in services, where it has discovered offensive interests in the wake of the IT-services take-off at home.

Still, Indian trade policy appears somewhat schizophrenic: domestic economic considerations have driven unilateral liberalization, but this has not translated into greater flexibility in the WTO (except to some extent in services). The domestic backlash against India's Uruguay Round commitments (negotiated by the MOCI largely without wider consultation or discussion) and messy coalition politics have combined to restrict the government's room for manoeuvre in the WTO. Hence unilateral and multilateral trade-policy tracks seem disconnected.

South Africa appears active in the WTO, and was especially so when Alec Erwin was the minister of trade and industry. But its trade-policy capacity, in its Geneva mission and back in Pretoria, is shallow. It lacks depth compared with China, India and Brazil. It is a member of the Cairns Group, but its negotiating activity in agriculture has been focused on the G20 since the Cancun Ministerial Conference. It is defensive in NAMA and inactive in services. These positions do not seem consonant with South Africa's export interests. These are not only in agriculture, which has a relatively small share in total exports, but also in intermediate manufactures and especially services, mainly to other African countries.

Chile is a small country that punches above its weight in the WTO. It was one of the first developing countries to become active in the GATT, and was also one of the first to make serious commitments in a GATT negotiating round (at the end of the Tokyo Round in 1979). This followed on the back of its unilateral opening from 1974. It was active in the run-up to and during the Uruguay Round, and its participation has deepened in the WTO. Chile has been very active with FTAs for almost twenty years, but this has not crowded out its commitment to the WTO. Its negotiating positions favour strong market access (liberalization, that is, especially in agriculture) and stronger, more transparent WTO rules. Again, this follows logically from unilateral opening and strong integration with the global economy.

Malaysia has more mixed positions in the WTO. It has been generally pragmatic, combining offensive positions in industrial goods and tropical products with more defensive positions in services and agriculture. It was active in the Uruguay Round as part of the ASEAN caucus. Then followed a phase when it was generally defensive and critical across the board, which spilled over into its Doha Round participation. This coincided with the Asian crisis and its aftermath, which slowed down unilateral liberalization and triggered Dr Mahathir's anti-globalisation rhetoric. Since his exit the rhetoric has been toned down, but Malaysia has largely neglected the Doha Round in favour of bilateral FTAs.

Australia and New Zealand both became more active in the GATT after they started liberalizing unilaterally: it was definitely the latter that led to the former, not the other way around. They were active in the Uruguay Round, particularly in the Cairns Group, which Australia effectively led. Like Chile, Australia and New Zealand have a strong market-access and rules focus in the WTO, reflecting their unilateral opening and strong integration with the global economy. But their Doha Round activity pales in comparison with their activity in the Uruguay Round. As 'middle powers' they have been squeezed by the North–South polarization in the WTO – a symptom of which is the eclipse of the Cairns Group and the rise of the G20. Also, both have been distracted by FTAs. This has been more visible in Australia's case: its FTA negotiations with the USA in particular took priority over the Doha Round, and correspondingly diminished its independent middle-power bona fides in the WTO.

Overall, the countries in the sample have some way to go before they make a positive contribution to setting the WTO on its legs again. Brazil, India, South Africa and Malaysia need to be less defensive and more flexible across negotiating issues. India and Brazil need to move from reactive positioning to proactive co-leadership. All are distracted by FTAs. All these factors assume more importance in the 'post-Doha' future of the WTO.

Bilateral and regional liberalization

The countries covered tend to have 'trade-light' PTAs, with some exceptions. These are driven by foreign-policy aspirations, but with justifications that are all too often vague, muddled and trivial, having little relevance to commercial realities and the economic nuts and bolts of trade agreements. This can amount to little more than symbolic copycatting of other countries' PTA activity and otherwise empty gesture politics. In such cases economic strategy is conspicuous by its absence. The predictable results are bitty, quick-fix sectoral deals. Politically sensitive sectors in goods and services are carved out, as are crucial areas where progress in the WTO is elusive (especially disciplines on anti-dumping duties and agricultural subsidies). Little progress is usually made in tackling domestic regulatory barriers (for example relating to investment, competition, government procurement, trade facilitation, cross-border labour movement, and food-safety and technical standards). These PTAs hardly go beyond WTO commitments, deliver little, if any, net liberalization and pro-competitive regulatory reform, and get tied up in knots of restrictive, overlapping rules of origin (ROOs). Especially for developing countries with limited negotiating capacity, resource-intensive PTA negotiations risk diverting political and bureaucratic attention from the WTO and from necessary domestic reforms. Finally, the sway of power politics can result in highly asymmetrical deals, especially when one of the negotiating parties is a major player.

Brazil's main PTA is Mercosur, its customs union with Argentina, Paraguay and Uruguay, which has a common external tariff (CET). Mercosur is weak: the CET has several loopholes; little progress has been made on NTBs, services and investment; and Brazil has undermined the customs union by pursuing separate FTAs with third countries. Brazil has prioritized the latter (such as a triangular PTA with South Africa and India) alongside Mercosur FTAs with third countries. These are mostly very trade-light, amounting to fixed preferences on a limited range of tariff lines.

Business representatives complain that these FTAs are foreign-policy driven and do not make commercial sense. They are mostly with countries with which Brazil does little trade, while the Brazilian government has neglected FTA initiatives with its two most important trading partners, the EU and USA. EU–Mercosur FTA negotiations have been stuck for several years; and Brazil has put the FTAA negotiations on the backburner. The author of the chapter on Brazil characterized his country's approach to the latter two FTA negotiations as 'aimless wandering'.

South Africa's PTA picture looks similar. It is the lead player in SACU, which, since 2002, is supposed to decide on tariffs and trade remedies jointly, and have a common tariff revenue-sharing arrangement. But SACU has hardly any supranational capacity to implement joint powers. Moreover, it is undermined by South Africa's FTAs with the EU, and threatens to be undermined further by the Economic Partnership Agreements (EPAs) between ACP countries and the EU, and SADC's own customs union plans. SADC hopes to have a customs union in place by 2010, followed later by a common market and then a monetary union. Indeed the African Union failed to recognize SACU as an official Regional Economic Community on expectation that the SADC customs union would subsume it. Yet SADC's joint capacity is extremely weak; there will be significant difficulties devising a SADC-wide common external tariff; many SADC members belong to two other PTAs, COMESA (Community of Southern and Eastern African States) and the EAC (East African Community); and the SADC EPA with the EU will now, at best, include only half of the SADC membership.

The result is a comical mess of overlapping PTAs in southern Africa, with a plethora of different and restrictive ROOs. Not least, it adds to the complexity of South Africa's trade regime. Finally, like Brazil, South Africa is prioritizing FTAs with countries with which it does relatively little trade – more for foreign-policy than commercial reasons. Its most commercially serious FTA negotiation – with the USA – stalled precisely because South Africa and other SACU members were not interested in the kind of strong WTO-plus FTA the USA insists on.

Malaysia's main FTA is AFTA, which has an accelerated timetable for intra-ASEAN tariff elimination with relatively simple rules of origin (40 per cent local content across the board). There are plans for an ASEAN Economic Community – a single market for goods, services, capital and skilled labour – by 2015. This looks good on paper, but ASEAN has made very little progress beyond tariff elimination, for example on NTBs, services, investment and mutual recognition of standards. These 'AFTA-plus' items – all concerning regulatory barriers to trade – are far bigger obstacles than tariffs to regional economic integration.

Malaysia's FTA activity outside ASEAN followed in the footsteps of Singapore and Thailand. It has a bilateral FTA with Japan, and is considering or negotiating several others. It is also part of ASEAN FTAs with several third countries. Some of these negotiations, for example with China and South Korea, have made headway with tariff elimination, but so far they have done little to tackle far more important regulatory barriers to trade and investment. A 'noodle bowl' of different ROOs within and across ASEAN FTAs is also problematic.

India is very active with FTAs, in its south-Asian backyard and in other developing-country regions. Hitherto loose regional cooperation is supposed to be transformed into the South Asian FTA (SAFTA) by 2010, leading to a customs union by 2015 and economic union (whatever that means) by 2020. This looks unachievable in practice. For starters, SAFTA excludes Indo-Pakistani trade. Planned negotiations are only on goods; they do not cover services, investment and other non-border market-access issues. There are bound to be plenty of exemptions, given similar trade structures with competing products (especially in agriculture).

India's approach to FTAs outside south Asia is mostly about foreign policy and is trade light. An FTA with ASEAN is planned for completion by 2011; and bilateral FTAs are also in place with Thailand and Singapore. ASEAN–India and India–Thailand negotiations have been bedevilled by India's insistence on exempting swathes of products and on very restrictive rules of origin for products covered. Fear of Chinese competition is probably the main factor driving product exemptions and restrictive ROOs. In addition, India is part of the BIMSTEC group (the other members being Bangladesh, Sri Lanka, Nepal, Bhutan, Thailand and Myanmar) which plans an FTA by 2017. It has mini-FTAs – basically limited tariff-concession schemes – in force or planned with several countries and regions, for example Chile, SACU, Mercosur and IBSA. FTA negotiations with South Korea and Japan are ongoing.

India's most serious FTA negotiation is with the EU. Both sides have committed to an ambitious agreement, with tariff elimination on more than 90 per cent of goods trade and a strong GATS-plus agreement in services. Most of agriculture will be exempted by mutual agreement. Whatever the rhetoric, the EU will find it extremely difficult to tackle India's high trade-related regulatory barriers through an FTA, and, specifically, to open up government procurement and some services sectors (for example professional services, financial services, retail and distribution). Given stalled policy reforms in Delhi, snail-like unilateral liberalization, WTO defensiveness and other trade-light FTAs, a 'deep-integration' FTA with India is next to impossible (Sally, 2007b).

In Latin America and indeed among developing countries generally, Chile is a trailblazer regarding regional and bilateral trade agreements. After its emergence from military rule in 1990, Chile chose not to rejoin the dysfunctional Andean Community or the newly-formed Mercosur. Chile did not want to be held back by its region, or overly exposed to regional instability. Chile negotiated an FTA on goods with Mexico in 1991 covering almost all products, at Chile's request, and followed this with similar deals with Colombia and Venezuela.

Chile then went on to negotiate comprehensive FTAs with all its major trading partners – the USA, the EU, EFTA, Canada, Mercosur, Ecuador, Peru, Korea, and China. It was an active participant in the FTAA talks, is part of an FTA including New Zealand, Singapore and Brunei, and is an active member of the Asia Pacific Economic Cooperation forum (APEC). Chile is committed to serious FTAs only – in its deals with EFTA and Canada, for example, parties managed to agree to eliminate anti-dumping duties, something unimaginable in a WTO context.

Australia and New Zealand, like Chile, avoid trade-light endeavours, but do also pay attention to foreign policy concerns. Relations with the US after 2001 explain both Australia's FTA with that country, and New Zealand's lack thereof. The APEC process is also an important set of foreign policy considerations for both countries.

New Zealand and Australia have in place FTAs with Thailand, Singapore, Chile and each other. New Zealand has recently concluded one with China, which will serve to remove any remaining border protection in the New Zealand economy. Australia's negotiations with China are ongoing. Both countries are, in line with their efforts to become 'more Asian', attempting to negotiate deals with ASEAN collectively and Malaysia separately, and with the Gulf Cooperation Council. Australia is also pursuing a deal with Japan, and investigating the feasibility of deals with India, Korea and Indonesia. New Zealand is negotiating a Closer Economic Relations agreement (CER) with Hong Kong, which, like Singapore, is a free trade zone already.

For both countries, however, the bilateral FTA between them has been the most significant and commercially meaningful to date. This Closer Economic Relations (CER) agreement, enacted in 1983 and updated to include investment and services in 1988, helped both countries with their own liberalization efforts. Thus of all the FTAs either New Zealand or Australia has since signed, the CER has had the largest impact on protection levels.

In addition to bilateral FTAs, Asia – east Asia in particular – is awash in regional economic integration initiatives. An APEC FTA initiative (FTAAP – Free Trade Area of the Asia Pacific) was launched at the APEC Hanoi Summit in 2006. It will go nowhere: political and economic divisions in such a large, heterogeneous grouping are manifold and intractable. An 'ASEAN Plus Three' FTA (the 'three' being Japan, South Korea and China) has been touted, as has an east Asian FTA that might include Australia and New Zealand. There is talk of a pan-Asian FTA that would include India or SAFTA. Visions of an East Asian Economic Community and even an Asian Economic Community have appeared on the horizon.

So far this talk is loose and empty – nothing more. Regional players are speeding ahead with quick and dirty bilateral FTAs, while little progress is being made with the larger ASEAN FTAs (beyond tariff elimination in goods trade). The emerging pattern is of a patchwork of bilateral 'hub-and-spoke' FTAs, in a noodle bowl of trade-restricting rules of origin. This threatens to slow down and distort the advance of regional and global production networks. In particular, it could undermine the dense networks of east Asian production-sharing and trade in manufacturing parts and components, which are in turn linked to final export markets in Europe and North America. More generally, bitter nationalist rivalries (especially in Northeast Asia and between India and Pakistan), and vast inter-country differences in economic structure, development, policies and institutions, will continue to stymie Asian regional-integration efforts for a long time to come. This applies to east Asia; it applies even more to south Asia.

Regional integration initiatives in Southern Africa and Latin America present an even larger set of problems and disappointments. Few of the numerous regional organizations, most of which have long histories, are formulated on economic logic. They are political entities, historically and practically, and are driven by political processes. They are thus generally weak vehicles for serious liberalization, and in any event offer no obvious economic benefits from doing so. With perhaps the exception of Mercosur, which contains Brazil, no regional integration initiative in southern Africa or Latin America contains a large, rapidly growing, diversified economy. Hence the powers of agglomeration are likely to trump those of convergence as these groups integrate. Put differently, the relatively stronger economies will reap all of the meagre benefits from integration, leaving the weaker ones at best no better off (Collier, 2007). Given this lack of clear incentive it is unsurprising that so many countries, especially in Africa, are members of more than one regional organization.

Nevertheless many are still planning different forms of 'deep' integration in the near future. SADC wants a customs union by 2010 and a common market by 2012. COMESA's customs union project is close to completion. This should force a 'shaking out' of some of the problems, such as overlapping membership. But as long as supra-national capabilities remain weak or non-existent, and as long as member government refuse to cede sovereignty over some aspects of economic policy, these plans will bear very little fruit. In the meantime bureaucratic costs to governments and businesses will mount, and ultimately be passed on to consumers.

CONCLUSION

The countries in this book have relied overwhelmingly on unilateral liberalization to open their economies to the world. They are 'first-division' reformers. Brazil, Chile, India, Malaysia and South Africa belong to a group of 20–25 developing countries – the 'new globalizers' – that have already gone far with macroeconomic stabilization, and internal and external liberalization. They have plugged themselves into globalization, with varying degrees of success, and have reaped, accordingly, different types and degrees of benefit so far. Australia and New Zealand, though developed countries, have had a similar trajectory: dramatic market-based reforms ended long-established protection and embraced global integration.

But unilateral liberalization has stalled or slowed down. All countries face reform complacency and fatigue. In some countries trade negotiations have gained the upper hand over unilateral measures, but have led to little or no additional liberalization. The WTO has been of second-line assistance by providing a framework of multilateral trade rules for unilateral reforms. But GATT/WTO commitments have contributed little to liberalization itself, except in South Africa. Even in South Africa the primary thrust of reforms was domestic, coming from national leaderships rather than external pressure in trade negotiations.

In Brazil, South Africa, India and Malaysia, PTAs are trade-light: they are driven more by foreign policy than commercial strategy; their noodle-bowl discriminatory patchwork causes complications for business and multilateral rules; and they are unlikely to spur regional or global integration. Some bilateral FTAs of Australia, New Zealand and Chile are stronger than those of the other countries in the sample, but for the most part they are not especially trade or investment-creating. The main exception to this norm is the Australia–New Zealand CER, which is a comprehensive deep-integration agreement.

Hence further substantial liberalization through trade negotiations, whether in the WTO or PTAs, is unlikely. Trade negotiations and resulting agreements are subject to diminishing returns as a vehicle for extra liberalization, especially on non-border regulatory issues.

Foreign aid has been important in some crisis situations, for example in India in 1991. But it has played a marginal role in the medium to long-term trade-policy reforms of these countries. Generally, aid-induced liberalization has not really worked: its political economy is dubious. Hence it would be a mistake to rely on aid for further market-based reforms.

Unilateral measures and competitive emulation are likely to be the main vehicle for future trade and FDI liberalization. Much depends on a Chinese engine. Further unilateral liberalization in China will probably set imitative reforms in train, elsewhere in Asia and beyond. A workable post-Doha WTO can help to lock in reforms, but more by strengthening multilateral rules than through market-access negotiations. Much more caution needs to be exercised with PTAs; and serious attempts should be made to minimize the damage from their discriminatory provisions.

Given this, the task for all these countries is not just to go further with dismantling border barriers to trade and FDI. More important to their future prosperity is progress on the myriad trade-related domestic reforms – of the 'microeconomic', 'structural' and 'institutional' sort. The advanced countries in this book have gone much further than the others in this regard.

Governments in India, Brazil and South Africa, for example, have barely touched highly restrictive labour markets and the bloated, malfunctioning domain of the state. That affects external as well as internal trade, and foreign as well as domestic investment. In essence, such policies continue to restrict economic freedom for individuals and enterprises, consumers and producers. They act as structural, long-term deterrents to productive investment, entrepreneurship and wealth creation (Greenspan, 2007). That leaves a vast pro-market reform agenda yet to be tackled. But how?

Firstly, there needs to be a clearer link between trade policy, on the one hand, and domestic economic-policy and institutional reforms, on the other. Trade policy should be coupled strongly with competition-friendly measures to improve the domestic business climate. It should be better hitched to domestic reforms, most of which are these days of the microeconomic variety. For example, there should be ways of linking trade and FDI liberalization, and trade-related regulatory reform, to measures to reduce and simplify regulations that hinder business at home. Such red tape includes procedural hurdles to overcome before starting a business, dealing with various licensing procedures, registering property, getting access to credit, employing workers, bankruptcy procedures, and time taken to clear goods through customs. These regulations are documented, classified and ranked in the World Bank's annual *Doing Business* Report (World Bank, 2006). Second-generation trade-policy reforms also depend on the quality of public administration and the rule of law (that is the quality of the legal framework governing property rights and contracts, and their enforcement by the judicial system). These relate to some of the World Bank's governance indicators and cross-country rankings.

Secondly, and following directly from the previous point, trade policy should be seen less through the prism of trade negotiations and international organizations, and (as argued above) more through the prism of the domestic economy. Second-generation reforms in particular are bundled up with domestic politics and economics; initiating and implementing them is overwhelmingly a domestic affair; and the scope for productive international negotiations and solutions is restricted. That is already becoming evident with the regulation of services trade and trade-related product standards, and of policies towards inward investment. It will become even more evident as global production networks and the movement of people across borders bite ever deeper into domestic institutions. Unilateral reforms should then be locked in through stronger WTO commitments. This should be the foundation for advancing national market-access and rule-making interests in the WTO. It should also make clear that the only PTAs worth considering are those that are comprehensive, WTO-plus, and clearly linked to competition-enhancing domestic reforms.

Thirdly, there should be much more policy transparency. Trade policy-making is usually opaque. Too little is known and understood about the effects of this or that set of trade policies. Consequently, public discussion of policy choices is usually uninformed and misguided. One should add that this applies almost as much to developed countries as to developing countries. For example, anti-dumping and rules-of-origin procedures in the EU are shrouded in secretive, discretionary and ultimately arbitrary behaviour, with restricted external access to information. The situation is not much better elsewhere.

What is lacking is what Patrick Messerlin calls a 'culture of evaluation' (Messerlin, 2005). Independent think tanks and even government bodies should do much more detailed research and analysis on the costs and benefits of trade policies in different sectors of the economy, and then disseminate findings to the public. This would facilitate more informed, intelligent public discussion of policy choices. As discussed at length in Bill Bowen's chapter in this volume, the Australian Productivity Commission (formerly called the Tariff Board, and then the Industries Assistance Commission) has played a central role in bringing transparency to a critical area of Australian economic policy. This is a governmental body, but it is independent and has statutory powers. It provides research and analysis on trade-related issues in Australia; and its conclusions do make their way into the public debate. The Tariff Board's ground-breaking work did much to reveal the costs of protection to the Australian public back in the 1970s, at a time when Australia was a highly-protected economy. This generated much public discussion at the time, and in many ways prepared the ground for the radical opening of the Australian economy in the 1980s. Such 'transparency boards' could be set up at relatively low cost in developing countries.

But even once this has been achieved, these countries still face several other policy challenges, all directly or indirectly related to trade policy. How should trade-policy reforms be sequenced with other reforms, such as those relating to macroeconomic policy? Should reforms be fast or gradual? There are no general answers to these questions. They depend on circumstances, and expediency will dictate different answers in different places at different times. What matters more is the general thrust: a medium- to long-term commitment to liberalize in the direction of a market-based, globally-integrated economy.

What is the link with political systems? Is democracy or authoritarianism better suited to market-based policy reform? Do such reforms have a better chance under right-wing or left-wing governments? Again, there are no general answers. For every example to support one thesis, there is a counter-example to support the opposite thesis. Reforms have succeeded in widely differing political systems, and under governments of different political hues, just as they have failed across the spectrum of political systems and partisan politics. What is clear is that political stability is the *sine qua non* for progress in any form.

What role is there for industrial policy? There is leeway for experimentation, adapted to different local conditions. Economy-wide measures, such as improving transport and communications infrastructure, as well as education and skills, can dovetail with trade and wider economic-policy reforms; so can other 'soft' measures such as trade and investment promotion through information dissemination, organizing trade fairs and the like. But selective promotion and protection of this or that industry has a questionable record; and 'hard' industrial policy of the picking-winners variety has an abysmal record. It should be avoided.

What about social policies? Are social safety nets needed alongside liberalizing reforms? How generous should they be? Should 'losers' be compensated? These questions of distribution and equity elicit quite different responses. The classical-liberal response is to keep government limited, focused on its role to provide and enforce a framework of rules for an open, competitive market economy. Basic social safety nets should be provided where affordable. Beyond that, the classical liberal has little interest in redistribution. In contrast, the social-democratic response is to give high priority to redistribution, with government playing an active role.

These debates have taken place mostly in developed countries, but they are of course relevant to developing countries. On the one hand, developing countries have less financial scope for redistribution compared with developed countries. They also have bigger institutional constraints. Ambitious social policies risk scattering scarce resources that should be focused on liberalizing reforms. On the other hand, big and widening differences between income groups and regions could undermine popular acceptance of core reforms.

Here also there are no general blueprints. There is room for experimentation and trial-and-error learning. But one thing is needed: better delivery of existing public services, including the provision of social safety nets. These are the last bastions of the command economy. Administrative mechanisms squander public funds and fail to serve those most in need. More market mechanisms are needed, including competition from private-sector suppliers of services. That also opens up possibilities for trade, FDI and cross-border labour movement in traditional public services such as health care, education and the utilities, and even beyond to cover housing, social security and pensions. These 'third-generation' reforms are the next frontier.

REFERENCES

Athukorala, T. (2006), 'Singapore and ASEAN in the New Regional Division of Labour', Departmental working paper 2006–11, Australian National University, Research School of Pacific and Asian Studies, Division of Economics.

Baldwin, R.E. (2006a), 'Managing the Noodle Bowl: The Fragility of East Asian Regionalism', Centre for Economic Policy Research Discussion Paper 5561, available at www.cepr.org/puts/dps/DP5561.asp.

Baldwin, R.E. (2006b), 'Multi lateralising regionalism: Spaghetti bowls as building blocks on the path to global free trade', *World Economy*, **29**(11), 1451–1518.

Collier, P. (2007), *The Bottom Billion: Why the Poorest Countries are Failing and what can be done about it*, New York: Oxford University Press.

Greenspan, A. (2007), *The Age of Turbulence: Adventures in a New World*, New York: Penguin Group.

Messerlin, P. (2005), 'A European Economic Agenda After the No Votes', London, 35th Wincott lecture, 3 October.

Myint, M. (1977), 'Adam Smith's Theory of International Trade in the Perspective of Economic Development', *Economica*, **44**(3), 231–48.

Rodrik, D. (ed.) (2003), 'In Search of Prosperity: Analytical Country Studies on Growth', Princeton, NJ: Princeton University Press.

Sally, R. (2007), 'Looking East: The European Union's New Trade Negotiations in Asia', Jan Tumlir Public Essay No. 3, Brussels: European Centre for International Political Economy.

World Bank (1997), *World Development Report 1997: The State in Economic Development*, Washington DC: World Bank Group.

World Bank (2006), *Doing Business 2006: Creating Jobs*, Washington DC: The World Bank and the International Finance Corporation.

Index